Better Homes and Gardens®

Easy Everyday
Cooking

Better Homes and Gardens® Books
Des Moines, Iowa

Pictured on front cover: Sausage and Bean Rigatoni, page 137

Better Homes and Gardens® Books
An imprint of Meredith® Books

Easy Everyday Cooking
Editor: Alrica Goldstein
Contributing Editor: Cathy Long
Contributing Designers: Seif Visual Communications, Diana Van Winkle
Copy Chief: Doug Kouma
Copy Editor: Kevin Cox
Publishing Operations Manager: Karen Schirm
Edit and Design Production Coordinator: Mary Lee Gavin
Editorial Assistant: Kellie Kramer
Book Production Managers: Marjorie J. Schenkelberg, Mark Weaver
Contributing Proofreaders: Sarah Enticknap
Contributing Indexer: Elizabeth Parson
Test Kitchen Director: Lynn Blanchard
Test Kitchen Product Supervisor: Marilyn Cornelius
Test Kitchen Culinary Specialists: Marilyn Cornelius, Juliana Hale, Maryellyn Krantz, Jill Moberly, Colleen Weeden, Lori Wilson
Test Kitchen Nutrition Specialists: Elizabeth Burt, R.D.,L.D.; Laura Marzen, R.D., L.D.

Meredith® Books
Editorial Director: John Riha
Managing Editor: Kathleen Armentrout
Deputy Editor: Jennifer Darling
Brand Manager: Janell Pittman
Group Editor: Jan Miller
Senior Associate Design Director: Mick Schnepf

Director, Marketing and Publicity: Amy Nichols
Executive Director, Sales: Ken Zagor
Director, Operations: George A. Susral
Director, Production: Douglas M. Johnston
Business Director: Janice Croat

Vice President and General Manager, SIM: Jeff Myers

Better Homes and Gardens® Magazine
Editor in Chief: Gayle Goodson Butler
Deputy Editor, Food and Entertaining: Nancy Hopkins

Meredith Publishing Group
President: Jack Griffin
Executive Vice President: Doug Olson

Meredith Corporation
Chairman of the Board: William T. Kerr
President and Chief Executive Officer: Stephen M. Lacy

In Memoriam: E. T. Meredith III (1933–2003)

DELICIOUS IDEAS FOR NO-FUSS MEALS!

Easy Everyday Cooking offers satisfying solutions for everyday meal preparation. Filled with more than 190 family-pleasing recipes, this appealing collection includes innovative ways to prepare meats, poultry, and seafood as well as ideas for appetizers, soups, salads, vegetarian dishes, and desserts. Choose from temptations such as Herb-Pepper Sirloin Steak, Ruby-Glazed Chicken Breasts, Four-Bean Enchiladas, Apple-Blueberry Pastries, Chocolate Cream Cake, and more.

Don't waste a minute. Try some of these exceptional everyday dishes. They're perfect any time and every time.

Contents

Appetizers
& SNACKS

Contents

LAYERED SOUTHWESTERN DIP
(recipe, page 10)

5

Summer Fruit Salsa

The refreshing ingredients in this summer salsa pair well with grilled chicken breasts and fish steaks.

1 tablespoon lime juice 1 tablespoon plum or peach jam ½ cup finely chopped peach ½ cup chopped strawberries ½ cup finely chopped fresh pineapple ½ cup finely chopped plums 2 tablespoons finely chopped red onion 1 jalapeño pepper, seeded and finely chopped Dash ground cloves Jalapeño peppers, cut into thin strips (optional) Baked tortilla chips	In a medium bowl stir together lime juice and plum or peach jam until smooth. Stir in peach, strawberries, pineapple, plums, red onion, finely chopped jalapeño pepper, and cloves. Cover and chill up to 2 hours to blend flavors. If desired, garnish with jalapeño pepper strips. Serve with baked tortilla chips. Makes 8 servings. *Nutrition information per serving: 114 cal., 2 g total fat (0 g sat. fat), 0 mg chol., 120 mg sodium, 21 g carbo., 2 g pro.*

Apples with Cinnamon-Cider Dip

Once cut, the apple slices brown quickly. Sprinkle with lemon or orange juice mixed with a little water, or treat them with an ascorbic acid color keeper.

2 tablespoons cornstarch 1 tablespoon brown sugar 1¼ cups apple cider 3 tablespoons honey 2 teaspoons lemon juice ½ teaspoon ground cinnamon ⅛ teaspoon salt (optional) Dash ground cloves Dash ground allspice 1 tablespoon butter or margarine 4 apples, cored and sliced	For dip, in a medium saucepan combine cornstarch and brown sugar. Stir in apple cider, honey, lemon juice, cinnamon, salt (if desired), cloves, and allspice. Cook and stir until thickened and bubbly. Cook and stir for 2 minutes more. Remove from heat. Add butter or margarine, stirring until melted. Serve dip warm with sliced apples. Makes 4 to 6 servings. *Nutrition information per serving: 221 cal., 3 g total fat (2 g sat. fat), 8 mg chol., 34 mg sodium, 51 g carbo., 0 g pro.*

Apples with Cinnamon-Cider Dip

Potted Pepper Dip

For an eye-catching presentation, use an assortment of colorful sweet peppers. If you want to make a lower-fat dip, use fat-free cream cheese and fat-free mayonnaise or salad dressing in place of the regular products.

2 tablespoons lemon juice
2 teaspoons olive oil or cooking oil
1 teaspoon sugar
¼ teaspoon salt
Dash black pepper
1 small onion, cut up
4 large red, green, yellow, or orange
   sweet peppers, seeded and cut up*
1 8-ounce package cream cheese,
   softened
¼ cup mayonnaise or salad dressing
1 teaspoon prepared horseradish
   Few dashes bottled hot pepper sauce
2 or 3 red, yellow, and/or orange
   sweet peppers, tops removed and
   seeded
   Assorted vegetable dippers and/or
   breadsticks
   Fresh herbs (optional)

In a blender container or food processor bowl combine the lemon juice, oil, sugar, salt, and black pepper. Add the onion and about one-third of the cut-up sweet peppers.

Cover and blend or process until smooth. Add the remaining cut-up sweet peppers. Cover and blend or process until smooth. Transfer the mixture to a medium bowl. Cover and let stand at room temperature at least 2 hours.

Place pureed vegetable mixture in a sieve and press gently to drain off excess liquid. In a medium bowl combine cream cheese, mayonnaise or salad dressing, horseradish, and hot pepper sauce. Stir in the pureed vegetable mixture. Cover and chill for 2 to 3 hours.

Spoon into the whole sweet pepper shells. Place filled peppers in the center of a serving platter; surround with vegetable dippers and/or breadsticks. If desired, garnish with fresh herbs. Makes about 2 cups.

*Note: To avoid getting tough pepper skins in the dip, cook seeded, quartered sweet peppers in boiling water for a few seconds. When cool enough to handle, peel off skins with a small knife and cut peppers into pieces.

Nutrition information per tablespoon dip: 46 cal., 4 g total fat (2 g sat. fat), 9 mg chol., 50 mg sodium, 2 g carbo., 1 g pro.

Creamy Onion Dip

We pepped up this version of a popular dip with a little crumbled blue cheese.

1½ cups dairy sour cream
2 tablespoons dry onion soup mix
½ cup crumbled blue cheese (2 ounces)
   Snipped parsley (optional)
   Assorted vegetable dippers (such
      as carrot, zucchini, jicama, or
      red sweet pepper strips, and/or
      broccoli or cauliflower florets)

In a medium mixing bowl stir together the sour cream and dry onion soup mix. Stir in blue cheese. Cover and chill up to 48 hours.

If desired, sprinkle with snipped parsley. Serve with vegetable dippers. Makes about 1¾ cups.

Nutrition information per tablespoon dip: 37 cal., 3 g total fat (2 g sat. fat), 7 mg chol., 103 mg sodium, 1 g carbo., 1 g pro.

Monterey Jack Fondue

Monterey Jack cheese could be called the American mozzarella. Long known in California, it became available across the nation in the late '60s. It's great shredded over Mexican foods, such as enchiladas, or used in a grilled cheese sandwich.

3 tablespoons margarine or butter
3 tablespoons all-purpose flour
1 teaspoon dried minced onion
⅛ teaspoon garlic powder
⅛ teaspoon ground red pepper
1 5-ounce can (⅔ cup) evaporated
   milk
½ cup chicken broth
1¼ cups shredded Monterey Jack cheese
   (5 ounces)
   French bread cubes

In a small saucepan melt margarine or butter. Stir in flour, dried minced onion, garlic powder, and red pepper. Stir in milk and chicken broth all at once.

Cook and stir until thickened and bubbly. Gradually add Monterey Jack cheese, stirring until cheese is melted. Transfer to a fondue pot; place over fondue burner.

Serve the fondue with bread cubes. (Add additional chicken broth, as necessary, for desired consistency.) Makes 6 servings.

Nutrition information per serving: 249 cal., 16 g total fat (7 g sat. fat), 28 mg chol., 418 mg sodium, 18 g carbo., 9 g pro.

Brie en Croûte

Jalapeño pepper jelly adds zing to this rich, buttery appetizer.

½ of a 17.3-ounce package (1 sheet) frozen puff pastry sheets, thawed
2 tablespoons jalapeño pepper jelly
2 4½-ounce rounds Brie or Camembert cheese
2 tablespoons chopped nuts, toasted
1 slightly beaten egg
1 tablespoon water
Apple and/or pear slices

Grease a baking sheet; set aside. Unfold pastry on a lightly floured surface; roll pastry into a 16×10-inch rectangle. Using an 8-inch round cake pan as a pattern, cut pastry into two 8-inch circles; reserve pastry trimmings.

Spread jelly over top of cheese rounds. Sprinkle with nuts; lightly press nuts into jelly. In a small bowl combine egg and water; set aside.

Place pastry circles on top of cheese rounds. Invert cheese and pastry together. Brush edges of pastry with egg mixture; pleat and pinch edges to cover and seal. Trim excess pastry. Place rounds, smooth sides up, on the prepared baking sheet. Brush egg mixture over tops and sides. Cut small slits for steam to escape. Using hors d'oeuvre cutters, cut shapes from reserved pastry. Brush shapes with egg mixture; place on top of rounds.

Bake in a 400° oven for 20 to 25 minutes or until pastry is deep golden brown. Let stand for 10 to 20 minutes before serving. Serve with apple and/or pear slices. Makes 12 servings.

Nutrition information per serving: 193 cal., 14 g total fat (4 g sat. fat), 38 mg chol., 216 mg sodium, 13 g carbo., 6 g pro.

TOASTING NUTS

Toasting heightens the flavor of nuts. To toast, spread the nuts in a single layer in a shallow baking pan. Bake in a 350° oven for 5 to 10 minutes or until light golden brown, watching carefully and stirring once or twice so nuts don't burn.

Popcorn 'n' Cranberry Snack Mix

The goodies tend to sink to the bottom, so stir occasionally while serving.

1 package unpopped microwave popcorn Nonstick cooking spray 2 to 3 tablespoons grated Parmesan cheese 2 cups potato sticks 1½ cups soy nuts 1 cup dried cranberries or mixed dried fruit	Pop popcorn according to package directions. Pour popcorn into a very large bowl; coat lightly with cooking spray. Sprinkle popcorn with Parmesan cheese; toss gently to coat. Stir in potato sticks, soy nuts, and dried cranberries or mixed dried fruit. Makes 12 servings. *Nutrition information per serving: 169 cal., 7 g total fat (2 g sat. fat), 1 mg chol., 159 mg sodium, 21 g carbo., 7 g pro.*

Cinnamon Bagel Chips

These crisp and crunchy snacks make great treats for kids as well as grown-ups.

3 unsplit plain, cinnamon-raisin, egg, sesame, or poppy seed bagels 2 teaspoons cooking oil 2 tablespoons sugar 1 teaspoon ground cinnamon ¼ teaspoon ground nutmeg	Slice bagels from top to bottom into ⅛-inch slices. Arrange bagel slices on an ungreased baking sheet. Brush very lightly with oil. Bake in a 325° oven for 20 to 25 minutes or until toasted. In a plastic bag combine the sugar, cinnamon, and nutmeg. Add hot bagel slices; seal bag. Toss chips until coated with spice mixture. Shake off excess coating. Cool chips before serving. Makes about 36 chips. *Nutrition information per chip: 21 cal., 0 g total fat (0 g sat. fat), 0 mg chol., 32 mg sodium, 4 g carbo., 1 g pro.*

Steamed Beef Dumplings

Steaming, a timeless Oriental cooking method, keeps the fat in these tasty bite-size morsels to a minimum.

2 cups all-purpose flour
½ teaspoon salt
⅔ cup boiling water
¼ cup cold water
2 tablespoons bottled hoisin sauce or
    reduced-sodium soy sauce
1 teaspoon cornstarch
1 cup finely chopped bok choy
1 medium carrot, shredded (½ cup)
2 tablespoons thinly sliced green
    onion
2 tablespoons snipped fresh cilantro
¼ teaspoon salt
12 ounces lean ground beef
    Soy Dipping Sauce
    Fresh cilantro (optional)

In a medium bowl stir together flour and the ½ teaspoon salt. Using a fork, stir in the boiling water. Add the cold water; mix with your hands until the dough forms a ball. (The dough will be sticky.) Cover and set aside.

For filling, in another medium bowl stir together hoisin or soy sauce and cornstarch. Stir in bok choy, carrot, green onion, the 2 tablespoons cilantro, and the ¼ teaspoon salt. Add ground beef; mix well. Using about 1 tablespoon filling for each, shape into 30 balls.

Divide dough in half. Return one portion to the bowl; cover and set aside. Divide the other portion into 15 balls. On a well-floured surface, roll each ball into a 3-inch circle. Place a ball of filling in the center of each dough circle. Fold each dough circle up and around filling, allowing the filling to show at the top. Press dough firmly around filling, pleating to fit. Gently flatten the bottom of each dumpling. Repeat with the remaining dough and filling.

In a steamer or Dutch oven bring water to boiling. Place dumplings, open sides up, on a greased steamer rack, making sure the edges don't touch. (If all the dumplings won't fit on a steamer rack, chill remainder until ready to steam.) Place rack over, but not touching, boiling water. Cover and steam dumplings for 16 to 18 minutes or until meat is done (160°). Serve warm with Soy Dipping Sauce. If desired, garnish with additional cilantro. Makes 30 appetizers.

Soy Dipping Sauce: In a small bowl combine ¼ cup *rice vinegar* or *white vinegar* and ¼ cup *reduced-sodium soy sauce.* Sprinkle with 1 teaspoon thinly sliced *green onion.*

Nutrition information per appetizer: 54 cal., 1 g total fat (1 g sat. fat), 7 mg chol., 201 mg sodium, 7 g carbo., 3 g pro.

Tuscan-Style Stuffed Chicken Breasts

If you wish, serve each pinwheel on a thin slice of crusty bread with mustard.

4 medium skinless, boneless chicken breast halves (about 1 pound total)
4 ounces fontina cheese, crumbled or sliced
1 cup bottled roasted red sweet peppers
12 fresh sage leaves or 1 teaspoon dried sage, crushed
¼ cup all-purpose flour
2 tablespoons olive oil
1 cup dry white wine or chicken broth

Place each chicken piece between two pieces of plastic wrap. Pound lightly with the flat side of a meat mallet until about ¼ inch thick. Remove plastic wrap. Sprinkle chicken with black pepper. For each roll, place one-fourth of the cheese, roasted peppers, and sage on a chicken piece. Fold in sides; roll up chicken. Roll in flour to coat.

In a large skillet cook chicken rolls in hot oil over medium heat about 5 minutes or until brown on all sides. Remove from skillet. Add wine or broth to skillet. Bring to boiling; reduce heat. Simmer, uncovered, about 2 minutes or until liquid is reduced to about ½ cup. Return chicken to skillet. Cover and simmer for 7 to 8 minutes or until chicken is no longer pink. To serve, trim ends of chicken rolls. Cut rolls into ¾-inch slices. Makes 16 appetizers.

Nutrition information per appetizer: 86 cal., 4 g total fat (2 g sat. fat), 25 mg chol., 72 mg sodium, 2 g carbo., 9 g pro.

Coffee Candied Nuts

These candy-coated nuts, with just a hint of coffee flavor, make a tasteful hostess gift.

1 egg white
1 tablespoon water
2 teaspoons instant espresso coffee powder or 4 teaspoons instant coffee crystals
½ cup sugar
3 cups salted mixed nuts (no peanuts)

Line a 15×10×1-inch baking pan with foil; grease foil. Set pan aside. In a large bowl beat together the egg white, water, and espresso powder or coffee crystals with a fork until powder is dissolved. Stir in sugar. Add nuts; stir to coat. Spread mixture in the prepared pan.

Bake in a 300° oven for 25 to 30 minutes or until coating becomes stiff and mixture is somewhat difficult to stir, stirring occasionally. Spread on a piece of lightly greased foil to cool. Break into pieces. Store, tightly covered, at room temperature. Makes 14 servings.

Nutrition information per serving: 218 cal., 17 g total fat (3 g sat. fat), 0 mg chol., 220 mg sodium, 14 g carbo., 5 g pro.

Tuscan-Style Stuffed Chicken Breasts

Mounds-of-Mushrooms Pizza

Mushrooms, especially shiitakes, are being studied for their ability to boost the immune system. Tossed with garlic and herbs, the mushrooms make a tasty, low-cal topper for a no-fuss pizza.

1 16-ounce loaf frozen bread dough, thawed
   Milk
6 cups sliced fresh mushrooms (such as shiitake, crimini, and/or oyster) (about 1 pound)
¼ cup snipped fresh herbs (such as oregano, basil, and/or parsley)
3 cloves garlic, minced
¼ cup olive oil
½ cup shredded provolone cheese (2 ounces)
¼ teaspoon coarse salt or salt

Grease a 15×10×1-inch baking pan; set aside. On a lightly floured surface, roll bread dough into a 15×10-inch rectangle. Transfer dough to the prepared pan. Prick dough generously with a fork. Let stand for 5 minutes. Brush with milk. Bake in a 425° oven about 10 minutes or until light brown. Cool on a wire rack about 5 minutes.

In a large bowl combine mushrooms, herbs, and garlic. Drizzle with olive oil; toss gently to coat. Sprinkle the cheese over baked crust. Top with mushroom mixture; sprinkle with salt.

Bake for 10 to 12 minutes more or until edges are golden brown and pizza is heated through. Makes 16 servings.

Nutrition information per serving: 121 cal., 5 g total fat (1 g sat. fat), 2 mg chol., 69 mg sodium, 13 g carbo., 4 g pro.

Mushroom Know-How

When shopping for fresh mushrooms, look for those that are firm, fresh, and plump with no bruising or moistness. If they're spotted or slimy, don't buy them.

Store mushrooms, unwashed, in the refrigerator up to 2 days. If they are prepackaged, store them in their original packaging. Don't store mushrooms in a closed plastic bag; mushrooms need to breathe. Store loose, unpackaged mushrooms in a paper bag or damp cloth bag in the refrigerator.

Quesadillas

American-made Mexican cheeses are now available in supermarkets. Look for asadero, Chihuahua, or queso quesadilla for their superior melting qualities.

1   medium Anaheim chile pepper or one 4-ounce can diced green chile peppers, drained
1½   cups shredded asadero, Chihuahua, queso quesadilla, or Monterey Jack cheese (6 ounces)
6   8-inch flour tortillas
1   cup shredded cooked chicken
½   cup chopped seeded tomato (1 small)
3   tablespoons finely chopped green onions
1   tablespoon snipped cilantro, fresh oregano, or basil
   Guacamole (optional)
   Salsa (optional)
   Cilantro leaves (optional)

If using the Anaheim chile pepper, halve pepper lengthwise; remove seeds and membrane. Cut pepper halves into thin slivers.

Sprinkle ¼ cup of the shredded cheese over half of each tortilla. Sprinkle pepper slivers or canned green chile peppers, chicken, tomato, green onions, and snipped cilantro, oregano, or basil over cheese. Fold tortillas in half, pressing gently.

In a large skillet or on a griddle cook quesadillas, 2 at a time, over medium heat for 3 to 4 minutes or until lightly browned, turning once. Remove quesadillas from skillet and place on a baking sheet. Keep warm in a 300° oven. Repeat with remaining quesadillas.

To serve, cut quesadillas in half. If desired, serve with Guacamole and salsa and garnish with cilantro leaves. Makes 12 servings.

Guacamole: In a medium bowl mash 2 medium ripe *avocados,* seeded and peeled, with 1 tablespoon *lemon juice* (mixture will be lumpy). In a food processor bowl or blender container combine 1 small chopped seeded *tomato;* ½ cup chopped *onion;* 2 tablespoons snipped *cilantro;* and 1 or 2 *serrano* or *jalapeño peppers,* seeded and finely chopped. Cover and process or blend until finely chopped. Stir tomato mixture and ¼ teaspoon *salt* into mashed avocado. Transfer to a serving bowl. Makes about 2½ cups.

Nutrition information per serving: 124 cal., 5 g total fat (2 g sat. fat), 11 mg chol., 238 mg sodium, 11 g carbo., 9 g pro.

Stuffed Jalapeños

This recipe works equally well with fresh Anaheim peppers. For best results, choose Anaheims that are long and skinny.

½   of an 8-ounce tub cream cheese
2   tablespoons finely chopped green onion
2   tablespoons chopped pimiento, drained
1   clove garlic, minced
12 fresh jalapeño peppers or 2 to 3 fresh Anaheim peppers, halved lengthwise and seeded

In a small bowl stir together cream cheese, green onion, pimiento, and garlic. Spoon the cheese mixture into the jalapeño or Anaheim pepper halves. Cover and chill until serving time.

Before serving, cut the stuffed Anaheim peppers into 2-inch bite-size pieces. Makes 12 appetizers.

Nutrition information per appetizer: 42 cal., 3 g total fat (2 g sat. fat), 10 mg chol., 35 mg sodium, 2 g carbo., 1 g pro.

Zesty Italian Peasant Bread

When you need a super-simple snack, it's hard to beat this bread, which also works well as an accompaniment to soup or as a side dish with grilled or broiled steaks and chops.

1   12-inch Italian bread shell (Boboli)
1   tablespoon olive oil or cooking oil
1   clove garlic, minced
⅛   teaspoon pepper
1   medium tomato, peeled, seeded, and chopped
⅓   cup crumbled Gorgonzola, blue, or feta cheese
1   tablespoon snipped fresh rosemary, oregano, or basil or 1 teaspoon dried rosemary, oregano, or basil, crushed
    Fresh rosemary, oregano, or basil sprigs (optional)

Lightly grease a baking sheet. Place bread shell on the prepared baking sheet. In a small bowl stir together oil, garlic, and pepper. Brush over bread shell. Sprinkle with tomato, crumbled cheese, and snipped fresh or dried herb.

Bake in a 400° oven for 10 to 15 minutes or until bread is heated through and cheese is slightly softened. Cut bread into 12 wedges. If desired, garnish with fresh herb sprigs. Serve hot. Makes 12 servings.

Nutrition information per serving: 126 cal., 5 g total fat (1 g sat. fat), 4 mg chol., 260 mg sodium, 17 g carbo., 5 g pro.

Spinach-Cheese Tart

The use of oil rather than shortening or butter in the pastry dough keeps saturated fat low. Try a fruity olive oil for added flavor.

Oil Pastry
2 eggs
1 cup light ricotta cheese
½ cup crumbled semisoft goat cheese (chèvre)
¼ cup fat-free milk
½ cup chopped spinach
¼ cup chopped, well drained, bottled roasted red sweet peppers
2 teaspoons snipped fresh oregano or ¾ teaspoon dried oregano, crushed
   Red and/or yellow sweet pepper strips (optional)
   Fresh oregano sprigs (optional)

Prepare Oil Pastry. On a lightly floured surface, roll pastry into a 12-inch circle. Ease into a 9½- or 10-inch tart pan with a removable bottom, being careful not to stretch the pastry. Trim pastry even with rim of pan. Do not prick.

Line pastry with a double thickness of foil. Bake in a 450° oven for 10 to 12 minutes or until edge is golden brown. Remove from oven. Remove foil. Reduce oven temperature to 325°.

Meanwhile, in a medium mixing bowl beat eggs slightly with an electric mixer. Add ricotta cheese, goat cheese, and milk; beat until smooth. Stir in spinach, roasted red peppers, and the snipped fresh or dried oregano. Pour egg mixture into tart shell.

Bake in the 325° oven about 20 minutes or until a knife inserted near the center comes out clean.

Let stand about 5 minutes before serving. If desired, top with sweet pepper strips and fresh oregano sprigs. Makes 12 servings.

Oil Pastry: In a medium bowl stir together 1¼ cups *all-purpose flour* and ¼ teaspoon *salt*. In a 1-cup measure combine ¼ cup *fat-free milk* and 3 tablespoons *cooking oil*. Add all at once to the flour mixture. Stir with a fork until dough forms a ball.

Nutrition information per serving: 142 cal., 7 g total fat (3 g sat. fat), 46 mg chol., 112 mg sodium, 12 g carbo., 6 g pro.

Fruited Cheese Spirals

Finger food gets a fresh new look! Dried fruit adds jewel tones to these clever spirals filled with prosciutto, cream cheese, and the cinnamon-pepper flavor of fresh basil.

½ cup orange juice or apple juice
1 cup dried fruit (such as cranberries, snipped tart or sweet cherries, and/or snipped apricots)
1 8-ounce tub cream cheese
½ cup dairy sour cream or plain yogurt
¼ cup fresh basil leaves, finely snipped
2 14- to 15-inch soft cracker bread rounds or four 7- to 8-inch flour tortillas
4 very thin slices prosciutto or fully cooked ham
Fresh basil leaves (optional)
Orange slices (optional)

In a small saucepan bring the orange juice or apple juice to boiling. Stir in dried fruit; remove from heat. Cover and let stand about 15 minutes or until fruit is softened. Drain. Meanwhile, in a medium mixing bowl stir together cream cheese, sour cream or yogurt, and the ¼ cup finely snipped basil.

Spread cream cheese mixture evenly over one side of each cracker bread or tortilla. Sprinkle each with the softened fruit. Place some of the prosciutto or ham near an edge of each round. Starting from the edge closest to meat, tightly roll up. Wrap each roll in plastic wrap and chill for 4 to 24 hours.

To serve, cut each roll into 1-inch slices. If desired, garnish with additional basil leaves and orange slices. Makes about 24 servings.

Nutrition information per serving: 115 cal., 6 g total fat (2 g sat. fat), 12 mg chol., 142 mg sodium, 14 g carbo., 3 g pro.

APPETIZER PARTY HINTS

When you plan an appetizer party, imagine how foods will look and taste together. Balance rich, highly flavored foods with simple, fresh ones. Plan one or two hot appetizers that can be made ahead and heated just before serving. Also select several chilled appetizers that can be prepared early and served without last-minute attention. If you serve buffet style, choose foods that guests can pick up easily. Too many choices that must be spooned out, sliced, or spread may cause people to bunch around the buffet table.

Iced Espresso

Orange Yogurt Drink

Yogurt, fat-free milk, and fat-free sour cream make this beverage taste positively dreamy.

2½ cups fat-free milk
2 8-ounce cartons vanilla, lemon, or
   orange low-fat yogurt
½ cup fat-free or light dairy sour cream
¼ cup frozen orange or apple juice
   concentrate, thawed

In a pitcher combine milk, yogurt, sour cream, and orange or apple juice concentrate. Beat with a wire whisk or rotary beater until smooth.

Serve immediately or chill. Store leftovers in the refrigerator. Makes 8 (5-ounce) servings.

Nutrition information per serving: 116 cal., 1 g total fat (1 g sat. fat), 5 mg chol., 90 mg sodium, 19 g carbo., 7 g pro.

Iced Espresso

Besides being a refreshing between-meal pick-me-up, this frosty coffee drink is wonderful after a light lunch or dinner in place of dessert.

½ cup ground espresso coffee or
   French roast coffee
1 teaspoon finely shredded orange
   peel
4 cups water
1½ cups fat-free milk
3 tablespoons sugar
   Ice cubes
   Orange peel strips (optional)
1 teaspoon grated semisweet chocolate
   (optional)

Prepare coffee with shredded orange peel and water in a drip coffeemaker or percolator according to the manufacturer's directions. Pour into a heatproof pitcher; stir in milk and sugar. Chill until serving time.

To serve, fill 6 glasses with ice cubes. Pour the coffee mixture over the ice. If desired, garnish each serving with an orange peel strip and grated chocolate. Makes 6 (6-ounce) servings.

Nutrition information per serving: 54 cal., 0 g total fat (0 g sat. fat), 1 mg chol., 35 mg sodium, 11 g carbo., 2 g pro.

Fizzy Mint-Chocolate Soda

Sipping one of these ice cream quenchers in your backyard is one of summer's simple pleasures. These old-fashioned favorites are bound to lure the neighbors.

¼ cup chocolate-flavored syrup
1 pint (2 cups) mint-chocolate chip
   ice cream
2 cups carbonated water or cream
   soda, chilled

Pour 1 teaspoon of the chocolate syrup into the bottom of each of 4 tall glasses. Add 1 scoop (¼ cup) of the ice cream to each glass.

Add 2 more teaspoons of chocolate syrup to each glass. Top with another scoop of ice cream. Slowly pour carbonated water or cream soda into glasses. Makes 4 servings.

Nutrition information per serving: 245 cal., 11 g total fat (6 g sat. fat), 26 mg chol., 84 mg sodium, 33 g carbo., 4 g pro.

Spiced Fruit Punch

To serve this punch without alcohol, substitute two 1-liter bottles of chilled club soda or carbonated water for the wine.

½ cup water
⅓ cup sugar
12 inches stick cinnamon, broken
½ teaspoon whole cloves
4 cups apple juice or apple cider,
   chilled
1 12-ounce can apricot nectar, chilled
¼ cup lemon juice
2 750-milliliter bottles dry white
   wine, chilled

In a small saucepan combine water, sugar, stick cinnamon, and whole cloves. Bring to boiling; reduce heat. Cover and simmer for 10 minutes. Cover and chill for 2 to 24 hours.

Pour the sugar mixture through a fine-mesh sieve; discard spices. In a punch bowl combine the sugar mixture, apple juice or cider, apricot nectar, and lemon juice. Pour in wine. Makes 24 (4-ounce) servings.

Nutrition information per serving: 81 cal., 0 g total fat (0 g sat. fat), 0 mg chol., 5 mg sodium, 10 g carbo., 0 g pro.

Pick-Your-Fruit Smoothie

For the best flavor and texture, chill the juice well before preparing the smoothie.

2   cups strawberry juice blend or
      strawberry drink, chilled
2   cups fresh or frozen unsweetened
      strawberries
1   8-ounce carton plain yogurt
2   to 4 tablespoons sugar or honey
½   teaspoon vanilla
      Toasted wheat germ with brown sugar
      and honey (optional)

In a blender container combine strawberry juice blend or strawberry drink, strawberries, yogurt, sugar or honey, and vanilla. Cover and blend until nearly smooth, with small chunks of strawberry visible.

Divide the strawberry mixture among 4 glasses. If desired, sprinkle with wheat germ. Makes 4 servings.

Nutrition information per serving: 142 cal., 1 g total fat (1 g sat. fat), 3 mg chol., 53 mg sodium, 30 g carbo., 3 g pro.

Kiwi Smoothie: Prepare as above, except substitute kiwifruit juice blend for the strawberry juice blend and 1 cup peeled and cut-up kiwifruit for the strawberries.

Melon Smoothie: Prepare as above, except substitute orange or orange-tangerine juice for the strawberry juice blend and 1 cup cubed cantaloupe for the strawberries.

Salads,
SOUPS & STEWS

Contents

Taco Salad

Although a tomatillo (tohm ah TEE oh) looks like a small green tomato, its flavor is a combination of lemon, apple, and herbs. Look for canned tomatillos in the Mexican foods section of your supermarket.

Tortilla Cups
Tomatillo Guacamole
8 ounces lean ground beef
3 cloves garlic, minced
1 15-ounce can dark red kidney beans, rinsed and drained
1 8-ounce jar taco sauce
¾ cup frozen whole kernel corn
1 tablespoon chili powder
8 cups torn leaf lettuce or iceberg lettuce
2 medium tomatoes, chopped
1 large green sweet pepper, chopped
¾ cup shredded sharp cheddar cheese (3 ounces)
4 green onions, thinly sliced

Prepare Tortilla Cups; set aside. Prepare Tomatillo Guacamole; chill.

In a medium skillet cook ground beef and garlic until beef is brown. Drain off fat. Stir in beans, taco sauce, corn, and chili powder. Bring to boiling; reduce heat. Cover and simmer for 10 minutes.

In large bowl combine lettuce, tomatoes, green pepper, cheese, and green onions. Divide the lettuce mixture among the Tortilla Cups. Top each with some of the beef mixture and the Tomatillo Guacamole. Makes 6 servings.

Tortilla Cups: Lightly brush six 9- or 10-inch *flour tortillas* with a small amount of *water* or spray *nonstick spray coating* onto 1 side of each tortilla. Spray nonstick coating into 6 small oven-safe bowls or 16-ounce individual casseroles. Press tortillas, coated sides up, into bowls or casseroles. Place a ball of foil into each tortilla cup. Bake in a 350° oven for 15 to 20 minutes or until light brown. Remove foil; cool. Remove Tortilla Cups from bowls. Serve immediately or store in an airtight container for up to 5 days.

Tomatillo Guacamole: Rinse, drain, and finely chop 4 canned *tomatillos* (about ⅓ cup). In a small mixing bowl combine tomatillos; ½ of a small seeded, peeled, and chopped *avocado* (about ½ cup); 2 tablespoons chopped canned *green chile peppers,* drained; and ⅛ teaspoon *garlic salt.* Cover and chill for up to 24 hours. Makes about ¾ cup.

Nutrition information per serving: 398 cal., 17 g total fat (6 g sat. fat), 38 mg chol., 801 mg sodium, 49 g carbo., 22 g pro.

Beef and Three-Cheese Tortellini Salad

Cheese-filled pasta, cubes of Colby or cheddar, and grated Parmesan make up the trio of cheeses in this make-ahead salad.

2   cups frozen or refrigerated cheese-
      filled tortellini (about 7 ounces)
8   ounces cooked lean beef or cooked
      lean ham, cut into thin strips
      (1½ cups)
1   cup cubed Colby or cheddar cheese
      (4 ounces)
1   cup broccoli florets
1   small yellow summer squash or
      zucchini, halved lengthwise
      and sliced (1 cup)
      Creamy Parmesan Dressing
      Curly endive or leaf lettuce
1   cup cherry tomatoes, halved

Cook tortellini according to package directions. Drain tortellini. Rinse with cold water; drain again.

In a large bowl combine tortellini, beef or ham strips, Colby or cheddar cheese, broccoli florets, and sliced yellow summer squash or zucchini. Pour Creamy Parmesan Dressing over beef mixture; toss gently to coat. Cover and chill for 4 to 24 hours.

To serve, line dinner plates with curly endive or leaf lettuce. Divide the beef mixture among plates. Top the salads with cherry tomatoes. Makes 4 servings.

Creamy Parmesan Dressing: In a small bowl combine ½ cup *mayonnaise* or *salad dressing*; 2 tablespoons grated *Parmesan cheese*; 1 tablespoon snipped *fresh marjoram* or 1 teaspoon *dried marjoram*, crushed; 1 tablespoon *red wine vinegar*; and ¼ teaspoon *pepper*.

Nutrition information per serving: 593 cal., 39 g total fat (11 g sat. fat), 111 mg chol., 641 mg sodium, 32 g carbo., 31 g pro.

Hearty Beef Salad with Horseradish Dressing

If the weather's right, you can grill the sirloin steak for this tasty salad. Place the meat on the rack of an uncovered grill directly over medium coals. Grill for 14 to 18 minutes for medium rare (145°) or 18 to 22 minutes for medium (160°).

  8   ounces green beans
1½   cups packaged, peeled baby carrots
 12   ounces boneless beef top sirloin
       steak, cut 1 inch thick
  4   cups torn Boston or Bibb lettuce
  1   16-ounce can julienne beets, rinsed
       and drained
       Horseradish Dressing
       Cracked pepper (optional)

Wash green beans; remove ends and strings. Cut beans in half crosswise. In a covered medium saucepan cook the green beans in boiling water for 5 minutes. Add the baby carrots and cook for 10 to 15 minutes more or until vegetables are tender; drain. Cover and chill for 4 to 24 hours.

Trim fat from meat. Place meat on the unheated rack of a broiler pan. Broil 3 to 4 inches from the heat to desired doneness, turning once. [Allow 15 to 17 minutes for medium rare (145°) or 20 to 22 minutes for medium (160°).] Thinly slice across grain into bite-size strips.

Divide torn lettuce among dinner plates. Arrange green beans, baby carrots, meat slices, and beets on lettuce. Spoon the Horseradish Dressing over salads. If desired, sprinkle each salad with pepper. Makes 4 servings.

Horseradish Dressing: In a small bowl beat together one-half of a 3-ounce package *cream cheese*, softened, and 2 tablespoons *horseradish sauce*. Stir in enough milk (3 to 4 tablespoons) to make a dressing of drizzling consistency. Cover and chill until serving time. (Dressing will thicken slightly if made ahead and chilled.)

Nutrition information per serving: 360 cal., 15 g total fat (6 g sat. fat), 94 mg chol., 497 mg sodium, 24 g carbo., 32 g pro.

Flank Steak Salad with Pineapple Salsa

The fresh fruit salsa that enlivens this warm steak salad starts with green picante sauce. Just add pineapple, sweet pepper, and mandarin oranges and serve.

2 cups peeled, cored, and chopped fresh pineapple
1 11-ounce can mandarin orange sections, drained
½ cup chopped red and/or green sweet pepper
⅓ cup mild green picante sauce or green taco sauce
12 ounces beef flank steak or boneless beef sirloin steak, cut ½ to ¾ inch thick
½ teaspoon purchased Mexican seasoning or Homemade Mexican Seasoning (see recipe, page 211)
1 tablespoon olive oil
4 to 6 cups torn mixed salad greens

For pineapple salsa, in a medium bowl gently stir together pineapple, mandarin oranges, sweet pepper, and green picante sauce or taco sauce. Set aside.

Trim fat from meat. Thinly slice meat across the grain into bite-size strips. Sprinkle with Mexican seasoning or chili powder; toss to coat.

In a large skillet cook and stir half of the seasoned meat in hot oil over medium-high heat for 2 to 3 minutes or until meat is slightly pink in center. Remove from skillet. Repeat with the remaining meat.

Divide mixed greens among dinner plates. Top with meat strips and pineapple salsa. Makes 4 servings.

Nutrition information per serving: 245 cal., 10 g total fat (3 g sat. fat), 40 mg chol., 224 mg sodium, 23 g carbo., 18 g pro.

PREPARING PINEAPPLE

To peel and core a pineapple, first slice off the bottom stem end and the green top. Stand the pineapple on one cut end and slice off the skin in wide strips from top to bottom. Remove the eyes by cutting diagonally around the fruit, following the pattern of the eyes and making narrow wedge-shaped grooves. Cut away as little of the fruit as possible. Then slice or chop the fruit away from the core. Discard core.

Spicy Steak & Ranch Salad

Steak and onions as you've never seen them before! Sirloin is perked up by Cajun seasoning before slicing, then arranged on tossed greens and topped with a scattering of crispy French-fried onions. This new version of the classic combo has the makings of an instant favorite.

½ cup French-fried onions
1 tablespoon Cajun seasoning
1 tablespoon lime juice
1 clove garlic, minced
1 pound boneless beef top sirloin steak, cut 1 inch thick
   Salt (optional)
1 10-ounce package European-style salad greens (iceberg lettuce, romaine, radicchio, escarole, and endive)
2 carrots, peeled into thin strips or cut into thin bite-size strips
½ cup thinly sliced radishes
½ cup bottled fat-free ranch salad dressing

In a large nonstick skillet cook French-fried onions over medium-high heat about 2 minutes or until browned, stirring occasionally. Set aside.

Meanwhile, combine Cajun seasoning, lime juice, and garlic; rub over both sides of steak. In the same skillet cook steak over medium heat to desired doneness, turning once. (Allow 6 to 8 minutes for medium rare or 9 to 12 minutes for medium.) Remove skillet from heat; let stand for 10 minutes. Cut steak into thin bite-size slices. If desired, season with salt.

In a large bowl toss together the salad greens, carrots, and radishes. Divide among 4 salad bowls or plates. Arrange steak strips over greens mixture. Drizzle dressing over salads. Sprinkle with onions. Makes 4 servings.

Nutrition information per serving: 310 cal., 13 g total fat (4 g sat. fat), 76 mg chol., 557 mg sodium, 16 g carbo., 28 g pro.

Pacific Rim Grilled Pork Salad

This dazzling salad blends grilled pork with ingredients from the cuisines of the eastern rim of the Pacific Ocean—soy sauce, ginger, hoisin sauce, rice wine vinegar, sesame oil, and enoki mushrooms.

⅓ cup water
¼ cup dry sherry
¼ cup soy sauce
4 teaspoons grated gingerroot
3 cloves garlic, minced
1 1½-pound boneless pork loin roast, cut into ½-inch-thick slices
¼ cup hoisin sauce
2 tablespoons brown sugar
2 tablespoons salad oil
2 tablespoons rice wine vinegar or white wine vinegar
1 tablespoon toasted sesame oil
12 cups torn spinach
6 thin red onion slices, separated into rings
1 tablespoon sesame seed, toasted (optional)
1 pound plums, pitted and sliced (3 cups)
   Enoki mushrooms (optional)

For marinade, in a small mixing bowl combine water, sherry, soy sauce, gingerroot, and garlic. Reserve 2 tablespoons of the marinade for the dressing. Place meat in a plastic bag set in a large bowl. Pour remaining marinade over meat. Close bag. Marinate in the refrigerator for 1 hour.

Drain meat; discard marinade. Grill meat on uncovered grill directly over medium-hot coals for 10 to 12 minutes or until slightly pink in center, turning once.

Meanwhile, for dressing, in a saucepan combine the reserved marinade, hoisin sauce, brown sugar, salad oil, and rice wine vinegar or white wine vinegar. Bring to boiling. Stir in sesame oil. Remove from heat.

Thinly slice meat into bite-size strips. In a large salad bowl combine meat, spinach, onion slices, and, if desired, sesame seed. Pour hot dressing over meat mixture. Toss gently to coat.

Serve on salad plates with plum slices. If desired, top with enoki mushrooms. Makes 6 servings.

Nutrition information per serving: *310 cal., 16 g total fat (4 g sat. fat), 51 mg chol., 1159 mg sodium, 22 g carbo., 21 g pro.*

Asian Pork-Cabbage Salad

Rice vinegars, known for their subtle tang and slightly sweet flavor, are used frequently in Oriental cooking. Made from rice wine or sake, they are usually clear to pale gold in color.

1 3-ounce package pork-flavored ramen noodles
¼ cup rice vinegar or white wine vinegar
2 tablespoons salad oil
1 tablespoon sugar
½ teaspoon toasted sesame oil
¼ teaspoon pepper
1 8¾-ounce can whole baby corn, drained
1 cup fresh pea pods or ½ of a 6-ounce package frozen pea pods, thawed
2 cups shredded cabbage
8 ounces cooked lean pork, cut into bite-size strips (1½ cups)
½ of a 14-ounce can straw mushrooms (1 cup) or one 6-ounce can whole mushrooms, drained
¼ cup sliced green onions
¼ cup sliced radishes
   Bok choy leaves
2 teaspoons sesame seeds, toasted

Cook ramen noodles according to package directions, omitting the seasoning package. Drain and set aside.

Meanwhile, for dressing, in a screw-top jar combine the seasoning package from the ramen noodles, the vinegar, salad oil, sugar, sesame oil, and pepper. Cover and shake well to dissolve seasonings.

Cut each ear of baby corn in half crosswise. If using fresh pea pods, trim ends and remove strings. In a large bowl combine cooked noodles, baby corn, pea pods, cabbage, pork, mushrooms, green onions, and radishes. Shake dressing well. Pour over cabbage mixture; toss gently to coat. Cover and chill for 4 to 24 hours.

Line dinner plates with bok choy leaves. Divide pork mixture among plates. Sprinkle each salad with sesame seeds. Makes 4 servings.

Nutrition information per serving: 386 cal., 20 g total fat (4 g sat. fat), 52 mg chol., 830 mg sodium, 31 g carbo., 23 g pro.

Greek Salad with Herb Vinaigrette

No leftover lamb around? Broil some lamb chops to medium-rare. Then, chill the chops completely before slicing them into thin strips.

3 cups torn curly endive or romaine
1½ cups torn spinach or iceberg lettuce
6 ounces cooked lean lamb or beef, cut into bite-size strips
1 medium tomato, chopped
½ small cucumber, thinly sliced
6 radishes, sliced
2 tablespoons sliced pitted ripe olives
½ cup crumbled feta cheese (2 ounces)
2 green onions, thinly sliced
½ cup Herb Vinaigrette
3 anchovy fillets, drained, rinsed, and patted dry (optional)

Toss together curly endive or romaine and spinach or lettuce. Divide greens among 3 salad plates.

Arrange meat strips, chopped tomato, sliced cucumber, sliced radishes, and olives on greens. Sprinkle with feta cheese and green onions. Shake Herb Vinaigrette well. Drizzle over salads. If desired, top with anchovy fillets. Makes 3 servings.

Herb Vinaigrette: In a screw-top jar combine ½ cup *salad oil;* ⅓ cup *white wine vinegar* or *vinegar;* 1 tablespoon *sugar;* 2 teaspoons snipped *fresh* or ½ teaspoon crushed *dried thyme, oregano,* or *basil;* ½ teaspoon *paprika;* ¼ teaspoon *dry mustard;* and ⅛ teaspoon *pepper.* Cover and shake well. Store dressing in the refrigerator for up to 2 weeks. Shake well before using. Makes about ¾ cup.

Nutrition information per serving: 431 cal., 35 g total fat (8 g sat. fat), 69 mg chol., 325 mg sodium, 11 g carbo., 20 g pro.

Curly Endive Cues

Also known as chicory, curly endive has crisp, frilly, narrow dark green leaves and a prickly texture. Look for heads with crisp, fresh leaves and no discoloration. Store the endive tightly wrapped in the refrigerator for up to 3 days. To use, rinse well in cold water and pat dry with paper towels.

Garlic-Ginger Chicken Strip Salad

If you're watching your sodium, switch to reduced-sodium soy sauce.

4 small skinless, boneless chicken breast halves (about 12 ounces total)
¼ cup soy sauce
¼ cup dry sherry
1 tablespoon snipped fresh basil or 1 teaspoon dried basil, crushed
1 tablespoon honey
2 teaspoons grated gingerroot
½ teaspoon crushed red pepper
½ teaspoon black pepper
¼ teaspoon five-spice powder
4 cloves garlic, minced
2 cups broccoli florets
5 cups torn mixed greens
1 cup enoki mushrooms or sliced fresh mushrooms
1 medium red sweet pepper, cut into ¾-inch pieces (1 cup)
1 cup coarsely chopped red cabbage
   Oriental Salad Dressing
   Leaf lettuce

Rinse chicken; pat dry. Cut breast halves into bite-size strips. For marinade, in a medium mixing bowl combine soy sauce, sherry, basil, honey, gingerroot, crushed red pepper, black pepper, five-spice powder, and garlic. Add chicken strips; stir to coat. Cover and marinate in the refrigerator for 4 to 24 hours.

Drain chicken strips, reserving marinade. Place chicken on unheated rack of a broiler pan. Broil 4 to 5 inches from heat about 5 minutes or until light brown, brushing once with reserved marinade. Turn and brush again. Broil 3 to 5 minutes more or until chicken is tender and no longer pink. Discard remaining marinade.

Meanwhile, in a covered medium saucepan cook the broccoli in a small amount of boiling water for 1 minute. Drain well and chill.

In a large mixing bowl toss together torn mixed greens, mushrooms, red sweet pepper, red cabbage, and cooked broccoli. Shake Oriental Salad Dressing well. Pour about ½ cup of the dressing over greens mixture; toss lightly to coat. Line 4 salad plates with leaf lettuce. Divide greens mixture among salad plates. Top with chicken strips. Drizzle remaining dressing over chicken. Makes 4 servings.

Oriental Salad Dressing: In a screw-top jar combine ⅓ cup unsweetened *pineapple juice*, ¼ cup *rice vinegar* or *white vinegar*, 1 tablespoon *soy sauce*, 2 teaspoons *sugar*, 1½ teaspoons toasted *sesame oil*, and ¼ teaspoon *black pepper*. Cover and shake well. Makes ⅔ cup.

Nutrition information per serving: 235 cal., 5 g total fat (1 g sat. fat), 45 mg chol., 1,368 mg sodium, 26 g carbo., 21 g pro.

Chicken Salad with Raspberry Vinaigrette

If you like, arrange all the ingredients on a large glass salad plate and pass the dressing in a small cruet.

2 cups torn leaf lettuce
2 cups torn radicchio
2 cups torn arugula
1 medium Belgian endive, cut up
1 tablespoon Dijon-style mustard
1 tablespoon honey
¼ teaspoon salt
⅛ teaspoon pepper
4 medium skinless, boneless
   chicken breast halves (about
   1 pound total)
2 medium oranges, peeled and sliced
1 pink grapefruit, peeled and
   sectioned
1 avocado, halved, seeded, peeled,
   and sliced
2 green onions, thinly bias-sliced
   Raspberry Vinaigrette
   Fresh red raspberries (optional)

In a large bowl combine the leaf lettuce, radicchio, arugula, and Belgian endive; toss gently to mix. Cover and chill up to 2 hours. For sauce, in a small bowl combine the Dijon mustard, honey, salt, and pepper; set aside.

Place chicken on the rack of an uncovered grill directly over medium coals. Grill for 12 to 15 minutes or until no longer pink (170°), turning once and brushing with sauce the last 2 minutes of grilling. Cool chicken slightly; cut into thin strips.

Arrange the lettuce mixture on dinner plates. Arrange chicken strips, oranges, grapefruit sections, avocado slices, and green onions on lettuce mixture. Drizzle some of the Raspberry Vinaigrette over salads. If desired, garnish with fresh raspberries. Makes 4 servings.

Raspberry Vinaigrette: In a blender container combine one 10-ounce package frozen *red raspberries*, thawed; 2 tablespoons *olive oil* or *salad oil*; 2 tablespoons *lemon juice*; and 1 clove *garlic*, minced. Cover and blend until smooth. Press the berry mixture through a fine-mesh sieve; discard seeds. Cover and chill until serving time. Reserve any remaining dressing for another use.

Nutrition information per serving: 331 cal., 15 g total fat (1 g sat. fat), 59 mg chol., 295 mg sodium, 26 g carbo., 25 g pro.

Chicken Fajita Salad

You can make the Tortilla Cups up to five days ahead. Simply store them in an airtight container at room temperature.

4 small skinless, boneless chicken breast halves (about 12 ounces total)
½ cup bottled Italian salad dressing
½ cup bottled salsa
1 tablespoon salad oil
1 small yellow summer squash or zucchini, cut into thin bite-size strips (1 cup)
1 medium red sweet pepper, cut into thin bite-size strips (1 cup)
3 green onions, bias-sliced into 1-inch pieces (⅓ cup)
4 Tortilla Cups
  Dairy sour cream (optional)
  Frozen avocado dip, thawed (optional)
  Bottled salsa (optional)
½ cup shredded cheddar cheese (2 ounces)
4 cups shredded iceberg lettuce
1 cup chopped tomato

Cut chicken into thin bite-size strips; set aside. For marinade, in a large bowl combine Italian salad dressing and the ½ cup salsa. Add chicken strips; stir to coat. Cover and marinate in the refrigerator for 4 to 24 hours. Drain chicken, discarding marinade.

Add salad oil to a wok or large skillet. Preheat over medium-high heat (add more oil if necessary during cooking). Stir-fry yellow squash or zucchini in hot oil about 2 minutes or until crisp-tender. Remove squash from wok.

Add the sweet pepper and green onions to wok. Stir-fry for 2 to 3 minutes or until crisp-tender. Remove from wok. Add chicken to wok. Stir-fry for 2 to 3 minutes or until chicken is no longer pink. Remove from heat.

To serve, place Tortilla Cups on dinner plates. Divide chicken strips and vegetables among cups. If desired, top with sour cream, avocado dip, and/or additional salsa. Sprinkle with cheese. Arrange lettuce and tomato on plates alongside the cups. Makes 4 servings.

Tortilla Cups: Lightly brush one side of six 9- or 10-inch *flour tortillas* with a small amount of *water* or coat with *nonstick cooking spray.* Coat 6 small oven-proof bowls or 16-ounce individual casseroles with cooking spray. Press tortillas, coated sides up, into bowls. Place a ball of foil into each tortilla cup. Bake in a 350° oven for 15 to 20 minutes or until cups are light brown. Remove foil; cool cups on wire racks. Remove from bowls.

Nutrition information per serving: 389 cal., 23 g total fat (5 g sat. fat), 69 mg chol., 488 mg sodium, 23 g carbo., 24 g pro.

Tarragon Turkey Salad with Wild Rice

Often teamed with turkey or chicken, aromatic tarragon has an aniselike flavor with undertones of sage.

⅓ cup uncooked wild rice
1 14-ounce can chicken broth
⅓ cup uncooked long grain rice
2½ cups chopped cooked turkey or
   chicken (12 ounces)
½ cup bias-sliced celery
¼ cup sliced green onions
¼ cup olive oil or salad oil
2 tablespoons snipped fresh tarragon
   or 1 teaspoon dried tarragon,
   crushed
2 tablespoons white wine tarragon
   vinegar
2 tablespoons water
1 teaspoon Dijon-style mustard
¼ teaspoon salt
¼ teaspoon cracked black pepper
1 cup chopped apple
   Red-tipped leaf lettuce
1 large apple, sliced (optional)

Rinse wild rice in a strainer under cold running water about 1 minute. In a medium saucepan combine wild rice and chicken broth. Bring to boiling; reduce heat. Cover and simmer for 20 minutes.

Stir in the long grain rice. Return to boiling; reduce heat. Cover and simmer about 20 minutes more or until wild rice and long grain rice are tender and liquid is absorbed. Cool about 10 minutes.

In a large bowl combine the warm rice, turkey or chicken, celery, and green onions.

For dressing, in a screw-top jar combine olive oil or salad oil, tarragon, vinegar, water, mustard, salt, and pepper. Cover and shake well. Pour dressing over rice mixture; toss gently to coat. Cover and chill for 2 to 24 hours.

To serve, stir chopped apple into the rice mixture. Line dinner plates with leaf lettuce. Divide the rice mixture among lettuce-lined plates. If desired, garnish with apple slices. Makes 4 servings.

Nutrition information per serving: 443 cal., 22 g total fat (4 g sat. fat), 85 mg chol., 599 mg sodium, 29 g carbo., 33 g pro.

Turkey and Fruit Pasta Salad

Savor this refreshing honey-dressed salad in the summertime when nectarines are at their peak.

1 cup packaged dried rope macaroni (gemelli) or 1⅓ cups corkscrew macaroni (4 ounces)
1½ cups chopped cooked turkey or chicken or fully cooked turkey ham (8 ounces)
2 green onions, sliced (¼ cup)
⅓ cup lime or lemon juice
¼ cup salad oil
1 tablespoon honey
2 teaspoons snipped fresh thyme or ½ teaspoon dried thyme, crushed
2 medium nectarines or plums, sliced
1 cup halved fresh strawberries

Cook pasta according to package directions. Drain pasta; rinse with cold water. Drain again.

In a large mixing bowl combine pasta; turkey, chicken, or turkey ham; and green onions. Toss to mix.

For dressing, in a screw-top jar combine lime or lemon juice, oil, honey, and thyme. Cover and shake well. Pour dressing over pasta mixture; toss to coat. Cover and chill for 4 to 24 hours.

Just before serving, add the nectarines or plums and strawberries. Toss to mix. Makes 4 servings.

Nutrition information per serving: 393 cal., 17 g total fat (3 g sat. fat), 43 mg chol., 42 mg sodium, 39 g carbo., 21 g pro.

PASTA FOR SALADS

The secret to fresh-tasting pasta salads is to avoid overcooking. Pasta cooked to just the right stage is called *al dente,* which means "to the tooth" in Italian. At this point, the pasta has a firm texture and is slightly chewy.

Salmon-Pasta Salad

Fold the salmon gently into the pasta mixture so it stays in nice big chunks.

1	cup packaged dried corkscrew macaroni or medium shell macaroni
1½	cups broccoli florets
4	ounces Gruyère or Swiss cheese, cut into thin, bite-size strips
¼	cup sliced radishes
⅔	cup mayonnaise or salad dressing
1	tablespoon snipped fresh basil or 1 teaspoon dried basil, crushed
2	teaspoons white wine Worcestershire sauce
⅛	teaspoon garlic salt
1	to 2 tablespoons milk
1	15½-ounce can salmon, chilled
	Leaf lettuce
	Pineapple sage flowers (optional)

In a large saucepan cook pasta in boiling salted water for 9 minutes. Add broccoli; return to boiling. Cook about 4 minutes more or until pasta and broccoli are tender. Drain the pasta and broccoli; rinse with cold water. Drain again.

In a large mixing bowl combine cooked pasta-broccoli mixture, Gruyère or Swiss cheese, and radishes.

For dressing, in a small mixing bowl stir together the mayonnaise or salad dressing, basil, white wine Worcestershire sauce, and garlic salt. Stir in enough of the milk to make desired consistency. Pour dressing over pasta mixture. Toss lightly to mix. Cover and chill for 4 to 24 hours.

Before serving, if necessary, stir a little additional milk into the pasta mixture to moisten. Drain and flake salmon, discarding skin and bones. Fold salmon into salad mixture.

Line 4 salad plates with leaf lettuce. Divide the salmon mixture among plates. If desired, garnish with pineapple sage flowers. Makes 4 servings.

Nutrition information per serving: 641 cal., 47 g total fat (12 g sat. fat), 101 mg chol., 999 mg sodium, 19 g carbo., 36 g pro.

Seafood Louis Salad

Using a blend of low-fat cottage cheese and fat-free milk, instead of the traditional mayonnaise and whipping cream, eliminates about 30 grams of fat and makes this classic salad guilt-free for fat-watchers.

1 6-ounce package frozen, peeled, cooked shrimp
½ cup low-fat cottage cheese
2 tablespoons fat-free milk
1 tablespoon tomato paste
2 tablespoons chopped red sweet pepper or diced pimiento
1 green onion, thinly sliced
⅛ teaspoon salt
⅛ teaspoon black pepper
6 cups torn romaine
1 cup shredded red cabbage
1 medium carrot, shredded (½ cup)
1 6-ounce can crabmeat, drained, flaked, and cartilage removed
2 tomatoes, cut into thin wedges
  Carrot curls (optional)

Thaw shrimp. For dressing, in a blender container or food processor bowl combine cottage cheese, milk, and tomato paste. Cover and blend or process until smooth. Transfer mixture to a small bowl. Stir in red pepper or pimiento, green onion, salt, black pepper, and enough additional fat-free milk to make dressing of desired consistency. Cover and chill till serving time.

In a large bowl toss together romaine, red cabbage, and shredded carrot. Divide among salad plates. Arrange shrimp, crabmeat, and tomatoes on each plate. Drizzle with dressing. If desired, garnish with carrot curls. Pass any remaining dressing. Makes 3 servings.

Nutrition information per serving: 207 cal., 3 g total fat (1 g sat. fat), 171 mg chol., 729 mg sodium, 14 g carbo., 31 g pro.

Blackened Fish Salad

Aromatic grilled herb bread makes a perfect partner for this crisp and hearty Cajun-style salad.

1 pound fresh or frozen catfish, cod, pollack, red snapper, or haddock fillets, ½ to ¾ inch thick

3 cups torn red-tipped leaf lettuce or leaf lettuce

3 cups torn spinach

2 medium oranges, peeled and sectioned

1 cup thinly sliced cucumber

1 small red sweet pepper, cut into thin bite-size strips (½ cup)

3 tablespoons snipped fresh basil or 1 teaspoon dried basil, crushed

1½ teaspoons snipped fresh thyme or ½ teaspoon dried thyme, crushed

1 teaspoon onion powder

1 teaspoon ground red pepper

1 teaspoon snipped fresh sage or ¼ teaspoon ground sage

½ teaspoon garlic salt

½ teaspoon white pepper

½ teaspoon black pepper

¼ cup margarine or butter, melted

⅔ cup Zesty Buttermilk Dressing

Thaw fish, if frozen. In a large salad bowl combine leaf lettuce, spinach, orange sections, cucumber slices, and pepper strips. Divide the lettuce mixture among dinner plates. Set aside.

In a small bowl combine basil, thyme, onion powder, ground red pepper, sage, garlic salt, white pepper, and black pepper. Rinse fish; pat dry with paper towels. Cut into 4 serving-size portions. Brush both sides of fish with some of the melted margarine or butter. Coat both sides with basil mixture.

Remove the rack from a charcoal grill. Place an unoiled 12-inch cast-iron skillet directly on hot coals. (If using a gas grill, place skillet on grill rack; turn heat to high.) Do not position handle over coals. Heat skillet about 5 minutes or until a drop of water sizzles.

Add fish to skillet. Carefully drizzle 2 teaspoons of the melted margarine or butter over fish. Grill for 2½ to 3 minutes or until fish is blackened. Turn fish; drizzle another 2 teaspoons melted margarine or butter over fish. Grill for 2½ to 3 minutes more or until blackened and fish flakes easily with a fork. Arrange fish on top of lettuce mixture. Serve with Zesty Buttermilk Dressing. Makes 4 servings.

Zesty Buttermilk Dressing: In a small bowl stir together ⅔ cup *mayonnaise* or *salad dressing*; ½ cup *buttermilk*; 1 tablespoon snipped *fresh basil* or 1 teaspoon *dried basil*, crushed; 1 tablespoon snipped *fresh parsley*; ½ teaspoon *seasoned salt*; ¼ teaspoon *garlic powder*; ¼ teaspoon *onion powder*; and ¼ teaspoon *black pepper*. Makes about 1¼ cups.

Nutrition information per serving: 247 cal., 14 g total fat (3 g sat. fat), 46 mg chol., 594 mg sodium, 11 g carbo., 22 g pro.

Oriental Spinach Tuna Salad

With both spinach and tuna rich in antioxidants, this salad packs a nutritious, low-fat punch.

1   9¼-ounce can chunk white tuna
      (water pack), chilled and drained
1   8-ounce can sliced water chestnuts
1   cup canned bean sprouts
6   cups torn spinach
1   large tomato, cut into wedges
1   stalk celery, chopped
1   green onion, sliced
3   tablespoons soy sauce
2   tablespoons rice vinegar
2   to 3 teaspoons toasted sesame oil
1   teaspoon sugar
⅛   teaspoon dry mustard
      Several dashes bottled hot
        pepper sauce

Break tuna into large chunks. Rinse and drain water chestnuts and bean sprouts. In a large salad bowl combine tuna, water chestnuts, bean sprouts, spinach, tomato wedges, celery, and green onion; toss gently to mix.

For dressing, in a screw-top jar combine soy sauce, rice vinegar, sesame oil, sugar, dry mustard, hot pepper sauce, and 1 tablespoon water. Cover and shake well.

Pour the dressing over the spinach mixture; toss gently to coat. Makes 4 servings.

Nutrition information per serving: 172 cal., 3 g total fat (1 g sat. fat), 12 mg chol., 1,095 mg sodium, 14 g carbo., 24 g pro.

Spanish-Style Shrimp and Rice Salad

For an authentic Spanish touch, line the serving plates with grape leaves instead of lettuce.

1   cup instant white rice
1   teaspoon instant chicken bouillon
      granules
¼   teaspoon ground turmeric
1   10-ounce package frozen peas
      with pearl onions
⅓   cup bottled Italian salad dressing
⅛   teaspoon ground red pepper
2   6-ounce packages frozen peeled,
      cooked shrimp, thawed
      Leaf lettuce

In a small saucepan bring 1 cup water to boiling. Stir in instant rice, chicken bouillon granules, and turmeric. Remove from heat. Cover and let stand for 5 minutes.

Meanwhile, cook peas with onions according to package directions. Drain. In a large bowl stir together rice mixture, peas with onions, salad dressing, and ground red pepper. Add shrimp; toss gently to coat. Cover and chill for several hours.

To serve, line dinner plates with lettuce. Divide the shrimp mixture among lettuce-lined plates. Makes 4 servings.

Nutrition information per serving: 283 cal., 10 g total fat (2 g sat. fat), 131 mg chol., 550 mg sodium, 28 g carbo., 18 g pro.

Tropical Scallop Salad

Sea scallops are larger than both bay and calico scallops. Cut any of the large scallops in half so they will cook evenly.

1 pound fresh or frozen sea scallops
1 15¼-ounce can pineapple spears (juice pack)
2 tablespoons white wine vinegar
1½ teaspoons sugar
¼ teaspoon finely shredded lime peel
1½ teaspoons lime juice
1 teaspoon cornstarch
⅛ teaspoon ground cinnamon
⅛ teaspoon ground cumin
1 cup fresh sugar snap peas
1 medium head Boston or Bibb lettuce
1 medium mango, seeded, peeled, and sliced
½ of a medium carrot, finely shredded

Thaw scallops, if frozen. Set aside.

For dressing, drain pineapple, reserving ⅓ cup of the juice. In a small saucepan combine the reserved pineapple juice, the white wine vinegar, sugar, lime peel, lime juice, cornstarch, cinnamon, and cumin. Cook and stir over medium heat until thickened and bubbly. Cook and stir for 2 minutes more. Remove from heat; cool.

In a small saucepan cook sugar snap peas in a small amount of boiling water for 1 minute. Drain and cool.

Rinse scallops; pat dry with paper towels. Cut any large scallops in half. Cook scallops in boiling, lightly salted water for 1 to 3 minutes or until scallops turn opaque. Drain.

Line dinner plates with lettuce leaves. Arrange scallops on one side of each plate. Starting from scallops, fan out pineapple spears, mango slices, and sugar snap peas on other side of each plate. Drizzle the dressing over salads. Sprinkle with carrot. Makes 4 servings.

Nutrition information per serving: 221 cal., 1 g total fat (0 g sat. fat), 34 mg chol., 178 mg sodium, 39 g carbo., 17 g pro.

Egg Salad with Fresh Veggies

This colorful salad tastes great alone or in a sandwich. For the latter, split two small pita bread rounds and line them with lettuce leaves. Each pita holds about ½ cup of the egg mixture.

8   hard-cooked eggs (see note, page 291), chopped
1   small zucchini, quartered lengthwise and sliced (1 cup)
½   cup chopped celery
½   cup shredded carrot
2   tablespoons finely chopped green onion
2   tablespoons diced pimiento
⅓   cup mayonnaise or salad dressing
2   tablespoons bottled creamy Italian or cucumber salad dressing
1   tablespoon snipped fresh dill or 1 teaspoon dried dill
1   teaspoon prepared mustard
⅛   teaspoon salt
    Boston or Bibb lettuce leaves
1   to 2 tablespoons milk (optional)
    Fresh dill sprigs (optional)

In a medium bowl combine hard-cooked eggs, zucchini, celery, carrot, green onion, and pimiento. Stir in mayonnaise or salad dressing, Italian or cucumber salad dressing, snipped fresh or dried dill, mustard, and salt. Cover and chill for 4 to 24 hours.

To serve, line dinner plates with lettuce leaves. Stir egg mixture gently. If necessary, stir in enough of the milk to moisten. Divide the egg mixture among the lettuce-lined plates. If desired, garnish with additional fresh dill. Makes 4 servings.

Nutrition information per serving: 335 cal., 28 g total fat (6 g sat. fat), 437 mg chol., 399 mg sodium, 7 g carbo., 14 g pro.

Super Salad Pizza

Choose the greens of your liking: spinach, romaine lettuce, radicchio, arugula, watercress, Bibb lettuce, or Boston lettuce.

½ of a 17.3-ounce package (1 sheet) frozen puff pastry sheets, thawed

3 cups torn mixed salad greens

½ of a 9-ounce package frozen artichoke hearts, thawed, drained, and quartered

6 cherry tomatoes, halved

1 5-ounce container semisoft cheese with garlic and herbs or ½ of an 8-ounce tub cream cheese with chives and onion

2 teaspoons Dijon-style mustard

1 to 2 tablespoons milk

2 cups shredded mozzarella cheese (8 ounces)

½ of a medium avocado, peeled and sliced

On a lightly floured surface, roll pastry into a 12-inch square; cut into a 12-inch circle. Place on a 12-inch pizza pan or large baking sheet; build up edge of pastry. Generously prick the pastry with a fork. Bake in a 375° oven for 15 to 18 minutes or until golden brown (pastry will shrink). Cool.

Meanwhile, in a large bowl combine the salad greens, artichoke hearts, and cherry tomatoes.

For dressing, in a small bowl stir together the semisoft or cream cheese and mustard. Stir in enough of the milk to make a dressing of drizzling consistency. Drizzle half of the dressing over the greens mixture; toss gently to coat.

Sprinkle 1½ cups of the mozzarella cheese evenly over the crust. Broil about 3 inches from the heat for 1 to 1½ minutes or until cheese is melted. Spoon greens mixture on top of the melted cheese. Sprinkle with the remaining mozzarella cheese. Broil for 1 to 2 minutes more or until cheese is melted.

Arrange avocado slices on top of pizza. Cut into wedges. Serve immediately with the remaining dressing. Makes 6 servings.

Nutrition information per serving: 389 cal., 28 g total fat (8 g sat. fat), 42 mg chol., 462 mg sodium, 21 g carbo., 14 g pro.

Grilled Vegetable Salad with Garlic Dressing

Vegetables, sweet and smoky from the grill, give pasta and cheese a jolt of flavor and color. By doing the grilling ahead, and storing the savory dressing in the refrigerator, this maximum-impact dish is done in the time it takes to simmer pasta.

2 red and/or yellow sweet peppers

2 Japanese eggplants, halved lengthwise

2 medium zucchini or yellow summer squash, halved lengthwise, or 8 to 10 yellow sunburst or pattypan squash*

1 tablespoon olive oil

2 cups packaged dried rigatoni or mostaccioli

Roasted Garlic Dressing

¾ cup cubed fontina cheese (3 ounces)

1 to 2 tablespoons snipped Italian flat-leaf or curly parsley

Italian flat-leaf parsley sprigs (optional)

Halve sweet peppers lengthwise; remove and discard stems, seeds, and membranes. Brush sweet peppers, eggplants, and squash with olive oil.

Grill vegetables on an uncovered grill directly over medium-hot coals for 8 to 12 minutes or until the vegetables are tender, turning occasionally. Remove vegetables from grill; cool slightly. Cut vegetables into 1-inch pieces.

Meanwhile, cook the pasta according to package directions. Drain pasta; rinse with cold water. Drain again. In a large bowl combine the pasta and grilled vegetables. Pour Roasted Garlic Dressing over pasta mixture. Toss gently to coat. Stir in fontina cheese. Sprinkle with snipped parsley. If desired, garnish with parsley sprigs. Makes 4 servings.

Roasted Garlic Dressing: In a screw-top jar combine 3 tablespoons *balsamic vinegar* or *red wine vinegar*, 2 tablespoons *olive oil*, 1 tablespoon *water*, 1 teaspoon bottled *roasted minced garlic*, ¼ teaspoon *salt*, and ¼ teaspoon *black pepper*. Cover and shake well.

*Note: If using sunburst or pattypan squash, cook the squash in a small amount of boiling water for 3 minutes before grilling.

Nutrition information per serving: 369 cal., 19 g total fat (6 g sat. fat), 61 mg chol., 317 mg sodium, 40 g carbo., 12 g pro.

Steak Soup

Sometimes called minute steaks, beef cubed steaks are thin, usually tenderized pieces of meat. They're a good choice for this soup because they cook quickly.

2   4-ounce beef cubed steaks
¼   teaspoon garlic salt
⅛   teaspoon pepper
1   tablespoon cooking oil
1   medium onion, chopped
1   stalk celery, chopped
4   cups water
1   10-ounce package frozen mixed
      vegetables
1   tablespoon instant beef bouillon
      granules
1   tablespoon Worcestershire sauce
1   teaspoon dried basil, crushed
1   7½-ounce can tomatoes, cut up
½   cup cold water
⅓   cup all-purpose flour

Sprinkle meat with garlic salt and pepper. In a large saucepan cook meat in hot oil over medium-high heat about 3 minutes or until brown, turning once. Remove meat from saucepan, reserving drippings in pan. Cut meat into cubes; set aside.

In the same saucepan cook onion and celery in the reserved drippings over medium heat until tender. Stir in meat cubes, the 4 cups water, the frozen mixed vegetables, beef bouillon granules, Worcestershire sauce, and basil.

Bring to boiling; reduce heat. Cover and simmer about 5 minutes or until vegetables are crisp-tender. Stir in undrained tomatoes.

In a screw-top jar shake together the ½ cup water and the flour; stir into meat mixture. Cook and stir until thickened and bubbly. Cook and stir for 1 minute more. Makes 5 servings.

Nutrition information per serving: 177 cal., 5 g total fat (1 g sat. fat), 29 mg chol., 784 mg sodium, 18 g carbo., 14 g pro.

TOMATO SHORTCUTS

To quickly cut up canned tomatoes, leave them in the can and use kitchen shears or scissors to snip them into small pieces. When a recipe calls for using both the cut-up tomatoes and their juice, there's no need to drain the tomatoes.

Italian Beef Soup

Italian Beef Soup

Keep the ingredients on hand for this easy soup and you'll always be prepared to whip up a hearty supper.

1 pound lean ground beef
2 14½-ounce cans beef broth
3 cups frozen pasta with broccoli, corn, and carrots in garlic seasoned sauce
1 14½-ounce can diced tomatoes
1 5½-ounce can tomato juice or ⅔ cup no-salt-added tomato juice
2 teaspoons dried Italian seasoning, crushed
¼ cup grated Parmesan cheese

In a large saucepan cook ground beef until brown. Drain fat. Stir in beef broth, pasta with vegetables, undrained tomatoes, tomato juice, and Italian seasoning.

Bring to boiling; reduce heat. Simmer, uncovered, about 10 minutes or until vegetables and pasta are tender. Ladle into soup bowls. Sprinkle each serving with Parmesan cheese. Makes 6 servings.

Nutrition information per serving: 258 cal., 14 g total fat (6 g sat. fat), 54 mg chol., 929 mg sodium, 13 g carbo., 20 g pro.

Easy Hamburger-Vegetable Soup

For a simple garnish, sprinkle with bite-size cheese or rich round crackers.

1 pound lean ground beef or pork
½ cup chopped onion
½ cup chopped green sweet pepper
4 cups beef broth
1 cup frozen whole kernel corn
1 7½-ounce can tomatoes, cut up
½ of a 9-ounce package frozen lima beans
½ cup chopped, peeled potato or ½ cup frozen hash brown potatoes
1 medium carrot, cut into julienne strips (½ cup)
1 tablespoon snipped fresh basil or 1 teaspoon dried basil, crushed
1 bay leaf
1 teaspoon Worcestershire sauce
⅛ teaspoon black pepper

In a large saucepan or Dutch oven cook ground meat, onion, and green pepper until meat is brown and onion is tender. Drain fat. Stir in beef broth, corn, undrained tomatoes, lima beans, potato, carrot, basil, bay leaf, Worcestershire sauce, and black pepper.

Bring to boiling; reduce heat. Cover and simmer for 15 to 20 minutes or until vegetables are tender. Discard bay leaf. Makes 4 servings.

Nutrition information per serving: 309 cal., 12 g total fat (5 g sat. fat), 71 mg chol., 958 mg sodium, 25 g carbo., 28 g pro.

Pork and Mushroom Stew

This hearty stew is sure to satisfy the biggest of appetites.

1 pound pork stew meat, cut into
    1-inch cubes
2 tablespoons margarine or butter
1 10½-ounce can condensed
    chicken broth
¼ cup dry white wine
3 tablespoons snipped fresh parsley
1 bay leaf
¾ teaspoon snipped fresh thyme or
    ¼ teaspoon dried thyme, crushed
¼ teaspoon garlic powder
⅛ teaspoon pepper
2 cups frozen small whole onions
1 10-ounce package frozen tiny
    whole carrots
1 4-ounce can whole mushrooms,
    drained
¾ cup cold water
¼ cup all-purpose flour
1 tablespoon lemon juice

In a large saucepan cook meat, half at a time, in hot margarine or butter until brown. Return all meat to saucepan. Stir in chicken broth, wine, parsley, bay leaf, thyme, garlic powder, and pepper. Bring to boiling; reduce heat. Cover and simmer for 40 minutes.

Stir in the frozen onions, frozen carrots, and mushrooms. Return to boiling; reduce heat. Cover and simmer about 15 minutes more or until vegetables are tender. Remove bay leaf.

In a screw-top jar shake together water and flour. Stir flour mixture and lemon juice into meat mixture. Cook and stir until thickened and bubbly. Cook and stir for 1 minute more. Makes 4 servings.

Nutrition information per serving: 361 cal., 18 g total fat (5 g sat. fat), 74 mg chol., 800 mg sodium, 20 g carbo., 26 g pro.

Ham and Bean Soup with Vegetables

Today's comfort food, ham and bean soup takes on a new look with the colorful addition of carrots, parsnips, and spinach.

1 cup dry navy beans
1¼ to 1½ pounds meaty smoked pork
    hocks or one 1- to 1½-pound
    meaty ham bone
1 cup chopped onion
½ cup sliced celery
1 tablespoon instant chicken
    bouillon granules
1 tablespoon snipped fresh parsley
1 tablespoon snipped fresh thyme or
    1 teaspoon dried thyme, crushed
¼ teaspoon pepper
2 cups chopped parsnips or rutabaga
1 cup sliced carrots
1 10-ounce package frozen chopped
    spinach, thawed and well drained

Rinse beans. In a Dutch oven combine beans and 5 cups cold water. Bring to boiling; reduce heat. Simmer, uncovered, for 2 minutes. Remove from heat. Cover and let stand for 1 hour. (Or place beans in water in Dutch oven. Cover and soak beans overnight.) Drain and rinse beans.

In the same Dutch oven combine beans, 5 cups fresh water, pork hocks or ham bone, onion, celery, bouillon granules, parsley, thyme, and pepper. Bring to boiling; reduce heat. Cover and simmer for 1¾ hours. Remove pork hocks or ham bone; set aside to cool.

Mash beans slightly. Stir parsnips or rutabaga and carrots into bean mixture. Return to boiling; reduce heat. Cover and simmer about 15 minutes or until vegetables are tender.

Meanwhile, cut meat off bones and coarsely chop. Discard bones. Stir the chopped meat and the spinach into vegetable mixture. Heat through. Makes 4 or 5 servings.

Nutrition information per serving: 347 cal., 3 g total fat (1 g sat. fat), 19 mg chol., 1,175 mg sodium, 60 g carbo., 23 g pro.

Lamb Stew with Mashed Sweet Potatoes

This spiced blend of lamb, vegetables, and fruits is incredibly delicious served over Mashed Sweet Potatoes.

2 pounds lamb stew meat, cut into 1-inch cubes
¼ teaspoon salt
¼ teaspoon pepper
2 tablespoons cooking oil
2 tablespoons all-purpose flour
2 14-ounce cans vegetable broth
1 12-ounce can apricot or mango nectar
2 inches stick cinnamon or ¼ teaspoon ground cinnamon
3 cloves garlic, minced
½ teaspoon ground cumin
½ teaspoon ground cardamom
⅛ teaspoon thread saffron, crushed
3 medium carrots, cut into ½-inch pieces (1½ cups)
1½ cups frozen small whole onions
1 cup dried apricots
1 cup dried pitted plums (prunes)
Mashed Sweet Potatoes or mashed potatoes (optional)
Fresh sage leaves (optional)

Sprinkle meat with salt and pepper. In a 4-quart Dutch oven cook meat, half at a time, in hot oil over medium-high heat until brown. Drain off fat. Return all meat to Dutch oven.

Sprinkle meat with flour, stirring to coat. Stir in vegetable broth, nectar, cinnamon, garlic, cumin, cardamom, and saffron. Bring to boiling; reduce heat. Cover and simmer about 1 hour or until meat is nearly tender.

Stir carrots, onions, dried apricots, and dried plums into meat mixture. Return to boiling; reduce heat. Cover and simmer about 30 minutes more or until meat and vegetables are tender. If using, remove stick cinnamon.

If desired, serve the meat mixture over Mashed Sweet Potatoes or mashed potatoes and garnish with fresh sage. Makes 6 servings.

Mashed Sweet Potatoes: Peel and quarter 2 pounds *sweet potatoes*. In a covered large saucepan cook sweet potatoes in a moderate amount of boiling, lightly salted water for 20 to 25 minutes or until tender; drain. Mash with a potato masher or beat with an electric mixer on low speed. Add ¼ cup *margarine* or *butter*, cut up, and ¼ cup plain *yogurt*; beat until smooth. If necessary, stir in a little *milk* to make potatoes of desired consistency.

Nutrition information per serving: 418 cal., 12 g total fat (3 g sat. fat), 96 mg chol., 773 mg sodium, 51 g carbo., 33 g pro.

Oriental Chicken-Noodle Soup

Give this soup even more of an Oriental flare by substituting four wonton skins cut into thin strips for the fine egg noodles.

2	14-ounce cans chicken broth
1	cup water
1	medium red sweet pepper, cut into ¾-inch pieces
½	cup chopped carrot
½	cup dried fine egg noodles
⅓	cup thinly sliced green onions
1	tablespoon soy sauce
1	teaspoon grated fresh ginger
⅛	teaspoon crushed red pepper
1	cup chopped cooked chicken or turkey
1	cup fresh pea pods, halved crosswise

In a large saucepan or Dutch oven combine broth, water, sweet pepper, carrot, noodles, green onions, soy sauce, ginger, and crushed red pepper. Bring to boiling; reduce heat. Cover and simmer for 4 to 6 minutes or until vegetables are crisp-tender and noodles are tender.

Stir chicken or turkey and pea pods into broth mixture. Simmer, uncovered, for 1 to 2 minutes more or until pea pods are crisp-tender. Makes 3 or 4 servings.

Nutrition information per serving: 217 cal., 6 g total fat (2 g sat. fat), 53 mg chol., 1,343 mg sodium, 15 g carbo., 24 g pro.

Easy Cheesy Chicken Chowder

This hearty chowder lives up to its name. It's easy, it only takes about 20 minutes to cook, and with a whole cup of cheddar cheese, it's definitely cheesy!

1	cup small broccoli florets
1	cup frozen whole kernel corn
½	cup water
¼	cup chopped onion
½	teaspoon dried thyme, crushed
2	cups milk
1½	cups chopped cooked chicken
1	10¾-ounce can condensed cream of potato soup
1	cup shredded cheddar cheese (4 ounces)
	Dash pepper

In a large saucepan combine broccoli, corn, water, onion, and thyme. Bring to boiling; reduce heat. Cover and simmer for 8 to 10 minutes or until vegetables are tender. Do not drain.

Stir milk, chicken, potato soup, ¾ cup of the cheddar cheese, and the pepper into vegetable mixture. Cook and stir over medium heat until cheese is melted and mixture is heated through. Sprinkle with the remaining cheese. Makes 4 servings.

Nutrition information per serving: 380 cal., 18 g total fat (9 g sat. fat), 94 mg chol., 970 mg sodium, 25 g carbo., 31 g pro.

Oriental Chicken-Noodle Soup

Easy Mulligatawny Soup

This is a simplified version of the classic, curry-flavored Indian soup.

2½ cups chicken broth
 1 cup chopped apples (2 small)
 1 cup chopped carrots (2 medium)
 1 cup water
 1 7½-ounce can tomatoes, cut up
 ½ cup chopped celery (1 stalk)
 ⅓ cup uncooked long grain rice
 ¼ cup chopped onion
 ¼ cup raisins
 1 tablespoon snipped fresh parsley
 1 to 1½ teaspoons curry powder
 1 teaspoon lemon juice
 ¼ teaspoon coarsely ground pepper
 ⅛ teaspoon ground mace or nutmeg
1½ cups chopped cooked chicken
     or turkey

In a large saucepan combine chicken broth, apples, carrots, water, undrained tomatoes, celery, uncooked rice, onion, raisins, parsley, curry powder, lemon juice, pepper, and mace or nutmeg.

Bring to boiling; reduce heat. Cover and simmer about 20 minutes or until rice is tender. Stir in the chopped chicken or turkey; heat through. Makes 4 servings.

Nutrition information per serving: 275 cal., 6 g total fat (2 g sat. fat), 51 mg chol., 677 mg sodium, 34 g carbo., 22 g pro.

Q̲UICK-COOKED POULTRY

If your recipe calls for cooked poultry and you don't have any leftovers to use, purchase a deli-roasted chicken. A roasted chicken yields 1½ to 2 cups boneless chopped meat.

Another option is to poach chicken breasts. In a large skillet place 12 ounces skinless, boneless chicken breast halves and 1½ cups water. Bring to boiling; reduce heat. Cover and simmer for 12 to 14 minutes or until chicken is no longer pink (170°). Drain well. Cut up chicken as recipe directs. The 12 ounces of boneless breasts yield about 2 cups cubed, cooked chicken.

Mexican Chicken-Tortilla Soup

This soup features cilantro, a fresh herb that looks like a flattened parsley leaf but has a pungent, almost musty odor and taste that gives a distinctive flavor to Mexican dishes.

2 whole small chicken breasts
     (about 1¼ pounds total)
3½ cups chicken broth
½ cup chopped onion
1 clove garlic, minced
½ teaspoon ground cumin
1 tablespoon cooking oil
1 14½-ounce can tomatoes, cut up
1 8-ounce can tomato sauce
1 4-ounce can whole green chile
     peppers, rinsed, seeded, and cut
     into thin bite-size strips
¼ cup snipped cilantro or parsley
1 tablespoon snipped fresh oregano or
     1 teaspoon dried oregano, crushed
6 6-inch corn tortillas
   Cooking oil
1 cup shredded cheddar or Monterey
     Jack cheese (4 ounces)

Rinse chicken. In a large saucepan or Dutch oven combine chicken and chicken broth. Bring to boiling; reduce heat. Cover and simmer about 15 minutes or until chicken is tender and no longer pink. Remove chicken. Set aside to cool. Skin, bone, and finely shred chicken. Set chicken aside. Discard skin and bones. Strain broth through a large sieve or colander lined with two layers of 100% cotton cheesecloth. Skim fat from broth and set broth aside.

In the same saucepan cook onion, garlic, and cumin in 1 tablespoon hot oil until onion is tender. Stir in strained broth, undrained tomatoes, tomato sauce, chile peppers, cilantro or parsley, and oregano. Bring to boiling; reduce heat. Cover and simmer for 20 minutes. Stir in shredded chicken. Heat through.

Meanwhile, cut tortillas in half, then cut crosswise into ½-inch-wide strips. In a heavy medium skillet heat ¼ inch oil. Cook strips in hot oil, half at a time, about 1 minute or until crisp and light brown. Remove with a slotted spoon; drain on paper towels.

Divide fried tortilla strips among soup bowls. Ladle soup over tortilla strips. Sprinkle each serving with shredded cheese. Serve immediately. Makes 4 servings.

Nutrition information per serving: 496 cal., 24 g total fat (8 g sat. fat), 85 mg chol., 1,658 mg sodium, 33 g carbo., 38 g pro.

White Chili with Salsa Verde

This wintertime dish looks like navy bean soup and tastes like a mild-flavored chili. Unlike ordinary chili, however, it's topped with a spicy Mexican salsa that's made with tomatillos.

12 ounces uncooked ground turkey
½   cup chopped onion
1   clove garlic, minced
3   cups water
1   15-ounce can Great Northern or
      white kidney (cannellini) beans,
      rinsed and drained
1   4-ounce can diced green chile
      peppers
2   teaspoons instant chicken
      bouillon granules
1   teaspoon ground cumin
¼   teaspoon black pepper
¼   cup water
2   tablespoons all-purpose flour
1   cup shredded Monterey Jack cheese
      (4 ounces)
    Salsa Verde

In a large saucepan or Dutch oven cook ground turkey, onion, and garlic until turkey is brown. Drain off fat, if necessary. Stir in the 3 cups water, the beans, undrained chile peppers, chicken bouillon granules, cumin, and black pepper.

Bring to boiling; reduce heat. Cover and simmer for 30 minutes. Stir together the ¼ cup water and the flour; stir into bean mixture. Cook and stir until thickened and bubbly. Cook and stir for 1 minute more. Top each serving with cheese and Salsa Verde. Makes 4 servings.

Salsa Verde: In a medium bowl stir together 5 or 6 *fresh tomatillos* (6 to 8 ounces), husks removed and finely chopped, or one 13-ounce *can tomatillos*, rinsed, drained, and finely chopped; 2 tablespoons finely chopped *onion*; 2 fresh *serrano* or *jalapeño peppers*, seeded and finely chopped; 1 tablespoon snipped *fresh cilantro* or *parsley*; 1 teaspoon finely shredded *lime peel*; and ½ teaspoon *sugar*. Cover and chill up to 2 days or freeze; thaw before using.

Nutrition information per serving: 319 cal., 16 g total fat (7 g sat. fat), 57 mg chol., 927 mg sodium, 24 g carbo., 26 g pro.

Quick-to-Fix Turkey and Rice Soup

Turn your leftover Thanksgiving turkey into a meal your family will love.

4   cups chicken broth

1   cup water

1   teaspoon snipped fresh rosemary
    or ¼ teaspoon dried rosemary,
    crushed

¼   teaspoon pepper

1   10-ounce package frozen mixed
    vegetables

1   cup instant white rice

2   cups chopped cooked turkey
    or chicken

1   14½-ounce can tomatoes, cut up

In a large saucepan or Dutch oven combine broth, water, rosemary, and pepper. Bring to boiling. Stir in mixed vegetables and rice.

Return to boiling; reduce heat. Cover and simmer for 10 to 15 minutes or until vegetables and rice are tender. Stir in turkey or chicken and undrained tomatoes. Heat through. Makes 6 servings.

Nutrition information per serving: 209 cal., 4 g total fat (1 g sat. fat), 36 mg chol., 699 mg sodium, 24 g carbo., 20 g pro.

Chunky Vegetable-Cod Soup

This fish soup will win your family's approval—hook, line, and sinker!

1 pound fresh or frozen skinless cod
   fillets or steaks
½ cup chopped red sweet pepper
¼ cup chopped onion
1 tablespoon margarine or butter
3½ cups vegetable broth or chicken
   broth
1 cup frozen cut green beans
1 cup coarsely chopped cabbage
½ cup sliced carrot
1 teaspoon snipped fresh basil
1 teaspoon snipped fresh thyme
½ teaspoon snipped fresh rosemary
¼ teaspoon black pepper
   Lemon wedges (optional)

Thaw fish, if frozen. Rinse fish. Cut into 1-inch pieces. In a large saucepan or Dutch oven cook red pepper and onion in margarine or butter until tender.

Stir in the broth, green beans, cabbage, carrot, basil, thyme, rosemary, and black pepper. Bring to boiling; reduce heat. Cover and simmer for 8 to 10 minutes or until vegetables are nearly tender.

Stir fish into broth mixture. Return to boiling; reduce heat. Cover and simmer about 5 minutes or until fish flakes easily with a fork, stirring once. If desired, serve with lemon wedges. Makes 4 servings.

Nutrition information per serving: 140 cal., 5 g total fat (1 g sat. fat), 45 mg chol., 922 mg sodium, 9 g carbo., 20 g pro.

Manhattan Fish Chowder

Manhattan-style chowders are tomato-based and may contain other vegetables in place of the potatoes found in milk-based New England-style chowders.

12 ounces fresh or frozen fish fillets
1 24-ounce can vegetable juice
1 11-ounce can whole kernel corn
   with sweet peppers
½ cup sliced green onions
¼ cup chicken broth
1½ teaspoons snipped fresh thyme or
   ½ teaspoon dried thyme, crushed
1 teaspoon Worcestershire sauce
   Several dashes bottled hot
     pepper sauce

Thaw fish, if frozen. Rinse fish. Cut fish into ¾-inch pieces. In a large saucepan combine vegetable juice, corn, green onions, broth, thyme, Worcestershire sauce, and hot pepper sauce. Bring to boiling; reduce heat. Cover and simmer for 8 minutes.

Stir fish into juice mixture. Return to boiling; reduce heat. Cover and simmer for 3 to 5 minutes more or until fish flakes easily with a fork, stirring once. Makes 4 servings.

Nutrition information per serving: 164 cal., 1 g total fat (0 g sat. fat), 34 mg chol., 995 mg sodium, 22 g carbo., 16 g pro.

Chunky Vegetable-Cod Soup

Fresh Tomato Soup with Tortellini

Quick Asian Fish Soup

Skimp on time, not taste, when you cook up this intriguing Oriental-inspired soup.

12 ounces fresh or frozen monkfish,
    cusk, cod, or croaker fillets,
    ½ inch thick
 1 10¾-ounce can condensed chicken
    with rice soup
1½ cups water
 2 tablespoons reduced-sodium soy
    sauce
⅛ teaspoon ground red pepper
1½ cups loose-pack frozen broccoli, red
    pepper, onions, and mushrooms
 1 tablespoon lemon juice

Thaw fish, if frozen. Rinse fish; pat dry with paper towels. Cut fish into ½-inch pieces. Set aside.

In a large saucepan combine soup, water, soy sauce, and ground red pepper. Bring to boiling. Stir in frozen vegetables. Return to boiling; reduce heat. Cover and simmer for 5 minutes. Stir in fish.

Cover and cook for 3 to 5 minutes more or until fish flakes easily with a fork. Stir in lemon juice. Makes 3 servings.

Nutrition information per serving: 155 cal., 2 g total fat (1 g sat. fat), 48 mg chol., 1,152 mg sodium, 10 g carbo., 23 g pro.

Fresh Tomato Soup with Tortellini

Add your favorite brand of tortellini, a hat-shaped pasta filled with meat or cheese, to this fresh tomato-sage-flavored soup.

 1 cup chopped onion
 1 tablespoon olive oil or cooking oil
 2 pounds ripe tomatoes (6 medium),
    peeled, seeded, and cut up
1½ cups reduced-sodium chicken broth
1½ cups water
 1 8-ounce can low-sodium tomato
    sauce
 1 tablespoon snipped fresh sage or
    1 teaspoon dried sage, crushed
¼ teaspoon salt
¼ teaspoon pepper
 4 ounces dried tortellini
    Fresh sage sprigs (optional)
¼ cup finely shredded Parmesan cheese

In a large saucepan or Dutch oven cook onion in hot oil until tender. Stir in tomatoes, chicken broth, water, tomato sauce, snipped fresh or dried sage, salt, and pepper. Bring to boiling; reduce heat. Cover and simmer for 30 minutes. Remove from heat; cool slightly. Meanwhile, cook tortellini according to package directions; drain.

Press the tomato mixture through a food mill. (Or place one-third to one-half of the mixture at a time in a blender container or food processor bowl. Cover and blend or process until smooth.) Return tomato mixture to saucepan. Stir in cooked tortellini; heat through. If desired, garnish each serving with fresh sage sprigs. Pass the Parmesan cheese. Makes 4 servings.

Nutrition information per serving: 266 cal., 9 g total fat (2 g sat. fat), 5 mg chol., 744 mg sodium, 35 g carbo., 12 g pro.

Beef & PORK

Contents

GARLIC-SAGE-MARINATED BEEF
POT ROAST (recipe, page 95)

Garlic Steaks with Nectarine-Onion Relish

What's better than the smell of steak on the grill in the summertime? The aroma of garlic-studded beef on the grill. Serve this steak with some crusty bread to soak up the delicious juices.

4 boneless beef top loin steaks, cut
   1 inch thick
6 cloves garlic, thinly sliced
2 medium onions, coarsely chopped
1 teaspoon olive oil
2 tablespoons cider vinegar
1 tablespoon honey
1 medium nectarine, chopped
2 teaspoons snipped fresh applemint,
   pineapplemint, or spearmint
  Fresh applemint, pineapplemint,
   or spearmint sprigs (optional)

Trim fat from steaks. With the point of a paring knife, make small slits in steaks. Insert half of the garlic slices into slits.

Wrap the steaks in plastic wrap; let stand at room temperature up to 20 minutes. (For more intense flavor, chill steaks up to 8 hours.) Sprinkle the steaks with salt and pepper.

Meanwhile, for relish, in a large nonstick skillet cook onions and remaining garlic in hot oil over medium heat about 10 minutes or until onions are a deep golden color (but not brown), stirring occasionally. Stir in vinegar and honey. Stir in nectarine and the snipped mint. Heat through.

Grill steaks on an uncovered grill directly over medium coals to desired doneness, turning once. (Allow 8 to 12 minutes for medium rare or 12 to 15 minutes for medium.) Serve the relish with steaks. If desired, garnish with mint sprigs. Makes 4 servings.

Nutrition information per serving: 272 cal., 9 g total fat (3 g sat. fat), 97 mg chol., 108 mg sodium, 13 g carbo., 34 g pro.

ⓄLIVE OIL OPTIONS

All olive oils are not the same. This versatile oil, made from pressed olives, is sold by grade from "pure" (a blend of lower- and higher-quality oils) to "extra virgin" (the richest in aroma and flavor). Color also indicates a flavor difference. Green to greenish gold olive oil tastes slightly sharp. Golden olive oil has a more delicate flavor.

Grilled Rump Roast with Curried Mustard

A mixture of mustard, honey, curry powder, and chives makes a glistening glaze for the roast. Stir more of the same mustard mixture into sour cream for a refreshing sauce.

1 3-pound boneless beef round rump
    roast
2 tablespoons Dijon-style mustard
1 tablespoon honey
1 teaspoon curry powder
1 teaspoon snipped fresh chives
½ cup dairy sour cream
    Snipped fresh chives (optional)

Trim fat from meat. In a small bowl stir together mustard, honey, curry powder, and the 1 teaspoon chives. Remove about 1 tablespoon of the mustard mixture; brush over meat. Insert an oven-going meat thermometer into center of meat.

For sauce, in a small bowl combine the remaining mustard mixture and the sour cream. Cover and chill until serving time.

In a covered grill arrange medium coals around a drip pan. Test for medium-low heat above the pan. Place meat on grill rack over drip pan. Cover and grill to desired doneness. [Allow 1¼ to 1¾ hours for medium rare (140°) or 1¾ to 2¼ hours for medium (155°).]

Remove meat from grill and cover with foil. Let stand for 15 minutes before slicing. (The meat's temperature will rise 5° during standing.)

Serve the meat with sauce and, if desired, additional snipped chives. Makes 12 servings.

Nutrition information per serving: 202 cal., 9 g total fat (4 g sat. fat), 81 mg chol., 108 mg sodium, 2 g carbo., 26 g pro.

Weeknight Steak with Vegetables

Sautéeing the vegetables gives them a robust flavor and keeps most of the work for this dish in one pan.

- 2 tablespoons olive oil
- 2 medium zucchini and/or yellow summer squash, cut into 1-inch chunks
- 2 stalks celery, cut into 1-inch slices
- 1 large onion, cut into thick wedges
- 3 cloves garlic, peeled
- 1 teaspoon dried rosemary, crushed
- 1 pound boneless beef top sirloin steak, cut ¾ inch thick
- ½ cup Zinfandel or other fruity dry red wine
- 1 14½-ounce can diced tomatoes with basil, oregano, and garlic

In a large skillet heat 1 tablespoon of the oil over medium heat. Cook the squash, celery, onion, garlic, and rosemary in the hot oil for 6 to 7 minutes or just until vegetables are crisp-tender, stirring occasionally. Remove from skillet.

Trim fat from steak. Cut steak into 4 serving-size portions. Add remaining oil to skillet. Add steak to hot skillet; sprinkle with salt and pepper. Cook over medium-high heat for 4 to 5 minutes or until medium rare (145°), turning once. Remove steak from skillet. Cover and keep warm.

Add the wine to skillet, scraping up any browned bits on bottom. Stir in undrained tomatoes. Bring to boiling. Boil gently, uncovered, about 5 minutes or until slightly thickened. Return cooked vegetables to skillet. Cook and stir just until heated through. Serve the vegetable mixture over steak. Makes 4 servings.

Nutrition information per serving: 388 cal., 23 g total fat (7 g sat. fat), 74 mg chol., 362 mg sodium, 16 g carbo., 24 g pro.

USING A MEAT THERMOMETER

To ensure perfectly cooked meat, check for doneness with a meat thermometer. For thinner foods, such as steaks, burgers, and chops, insert an instant-read thermometer through the side of the meat to get an accurate reading. Do not leave this type of thermometer in the food while it is cooking.

BLT Steak

A loaf of crusty bread and a bottle of red wine complete this bistro-style dinner.

2 12-ounce boneless beef top loin
   steaks, cut 1¼ inches thick
2 slices bacon, cut into quarters
½ cup bottled balsamic vinaigrette
   salad dressing
12 thin slices red and/or yellow
   tomatoes
2 cups mixed baby salad greens
   Fresh Italian flat-leaf parsley sprigs
   (optional)

Trim fat from steaks. Place steaks on the rack of an uncovered grill directly over medium coals. Grill to desired doneness, turning once. [Allow 13 to 15 minutes for medium rare (145°) or 16 to 18 minutes for medium (160°).]

Meanwhile, in a large skillet cook bacon pieces over medium heat until crisp. Drain bacon, reserving 1 tablespoon drippings in skillet. Add the balsamic vinaigrette dressing to reserved drippings in skillet. Cook and stir over high heat for 1 minute, scraping up any browned bits on bottom of skillet.

To serve, cut each steak in half. Arrange the steak portions on dinner plates. Top with tomato slices, bacon, mixed greens, and dressing from the skillet. If desired, garnish with parsley. Makes 4 servings.

Nutrition information per serving: 556 cal., 42 g total fat (14 g sat. fat), 122 mg chol., 636 mg sodium, 5 g carbo., 38 g pro.

Peppered Steak with Mushroom Gravy

Tenderloin is one of the leanest cuts of beef. To keep these prized steaks at their moist and juicy best, don't overcook them.

6 beef tenderloin steaks or 3 beef top loin steaks, cut 1 inch thick (about 1½ pounds total)

1½ teaspoons dried whole green peppercorns, crushed, or ½ teaspoon coarsely ground black pepper

½ teaspoon dried thyme, crushed

½ teaspoon dried oregano, crushed

¼ teaspoon salt
Nonstick spray coating

⅓ cup water

½ teaspoon instant beef bouillon granules

¾ cup sliced fresh shiitake mushrooms or other fresh mushrooms

¾ cup fat-free milk

2 tablespoons all-purpose flour

½ teaspoon dried thyme, crushed

⅔ cup fat-free or light dairy sour cream
Fresh thyme sprigs (optional)

Trim fat from steaks. In a small bowl stir together the peppercorns or pepper, ½ teaspoon dried thyme, oregano, and salt. Sprinkle both sides of steaks with pepper mixture, pressing into meat.

Spray an unheated large nonstick skillet with nonstick coating. Preheat over medium heat. Add steaks and cook to desired doneness, turning once. (Allow 8 to 11 minutes for medium rare or 12 to 14 minutes for medium.) Remove from skillet. Cover and keep warm.

For sauce, add water and bouillon granules to skillet. Bring to boiling. Add the mushrooms. Cook about 2 minutes or until tender. Stir together milk, flour, and ½ teaspoon dried thyme. Add to mushroom mixture. Cook and stir until thickened and bubbly. Stir in sour cream. Heat through, but do not boil.

To serve, spoon the sauce over steaks. If desired, garnish with fresh thyme. Makes 6 servings.

Nutrition information per serving: 206 cal., 7 g total fat (3 g sat. fat), 64 mg chol., 243 mg sodium, 9 g carbo., 25 g pro.

Midwest Swiss Steak with Tomato Gravy

Serve this satisfying entrée with a tossed green salad and crusty sourdough rolls.

1½ pounds boneless beef round steak
2 tablespoons all-purpose flour
   Nonstick spray coating
2 large onions, sliced
2 cups chopped peeled parsnips
1 14½-ounce can low-sodium tomatoes, cut up
1 large red sweet pepper, chopped
1 cup beef broth
1 teaspoon salt-free seasoning blend
1 teaspoon dried basil, crushed
1 clove garlic, minced
¼ teaspoon black pepper
1 tablespoon cold water
1 teaspoon cornstarch
2 tablespoons snipped parsley

Trim fat from meat. Cut the meat into 6 serving-size pieces. Sprinkle both sides of the meat with flour. With a meat mallet, pound the flour into the meat.

Spray an unheated 12-inch skillet with nonstick coating. Preheat over medium heat. Add meat and cook until brown on both sides. Add the onions, parsnips, undrained tomatoes, sweet pepper, beef broth, seasoning blend, basil, garlic, and black pepper.

Bring to boiling; reduce heat. Cover and simmer about 1¼ hours or until meat and vegetables are tender. Transfer meat and vegetables to a platter. Cover and keep warm while preparing sauce.

For sauce, skim fat from pan drippings. Stir together water and cornstarch. Stir into pan drippings. Cook and stir until thickened and bubbly. Cook and stir for 2 minutes more. Stir in parsley. Serve sauce over meat and vegetables. Makes 6 servings.

Nutrition information per serving: 211 cal., 5 g total fat (2 g sat. fat), 60 mg chol., 321 mg sodium, 16 g carbo., 25 g pro.

SNIPPING SAVVY

Snipping parsley and other fresh herbs takes only a few moments. Loosely pack the cleaned and dried leaves in a glass measuring cup. Use kitchen shears to cut them into small uniform pieces. This method eliminates the work of washing a cutting board.

Garlic-Sage-Marinated Beef Pot Roast

Red wine, tomato paste, and garlic give this fork-tender roast a robust, well-rounded flavor.

1 2- to 2½-pound boneless beef chuck pot roast
¾ cup dry red wine or tomato juice
2 tablespoons tomato paste
1 tablespoon snipped fresh sage or ½ teaspoon ground sage
10 cloves garlic, halved
2 teaspoons instant beef bouillon granules
¼ teaspoon pepper
1 tablespoon cooking oil
1¼ pounds tiny new potatoes or 4 medium potatoes
4 medium carrots, cut into 2-inch pieces
2 small onions, cut into wedges
2 stalks celery, bias-sliced into 1-inch pieces
½ cup cold water
¼ cup all-purpose flour

Trim fat from meat. Place meat in a plastic bag and set the bag into a shallow dish. For marinade, in a small bowl combine the red wine or tomato juice, tomato paste, sage, garlic, beef bouillon granules, and pepper. Pour over meat; seal bag. Marinate in the refrigerator for 6 to 24 hours, turning bag occasionally. Drain meat, reserving the marinade.

In a Dutch oven brown the meat on both sides in hot oil. Drain fat. Pour the marinade over meat. Bring to boiling; reduce heat. Cover and simmer for 1 hour.

Remove a narrow strip of peel from around the center of each new potato. (Or, peel and quarter each medium potato.) Add potatoes, carrots, onions, and celery to meat. Cover and simmer for 45 to 60 minutes or until meat and vegetables are tender, adding some water if necessary. Transfer meat and vegetables to a platter. Cover and keep warm while preparing gravy.

For gravy, measure pan juices; skim fat. If necessary, add water to equal 1¾ cups liquid; return to Dutch oven. Combine the ½ cup water and flour; stir into juices. Cook and stir until thickened and bubbly. Cook and stir for 1 minute more. Season to taste with salt and pepper. Serve gravy with meat and vegetables. Makes 8 servings.

Nutrition information per serving: 321 cal., 8 g total fat (3 g sat. fat), 78 mg chol., 345 mg sodium, 28 g carbo., 29 g pro.

Horseradish-Dill Beef Stroganoff

Follow this quick-prep method to make a classic Old World recipe. The horseradish-sour cream sauce is an imperial touch.

3	cups dried wide noodles
3	cups broccoli florets (12 ounces)
½	cup light dairy sour cream
1½	teaspoons prepared horseradish
½	teaspoon snipped fresh dill
1	pound beef ribeye steak
1	small onion, cut into ½-inch slices
1	clove garlic, minced
1	tablespoon cooking oil
4	teaspoons all-purpose flour
½	teaspoon pepper
1	14-ounce can beef broth
3	tablespoons tomato paste
1	teaspoon Worcestershire sauce

Cook noodles according to package directions, adding broccoli the last 5 minutes of cooking; drain. Cover and keep warm.

Meanwhile, for sauce, in a small bowl stir together the sour cream, horseradish, and dill. Cover and chill until serving time.

Trim fat from meat. Slice meat across the grain into bite-size strips. In a large skillet cook half of the meat, the onion, and garlic in hot oil over medium-high heat about 3 minutes or until meat is slightly pink in center. Remove from skillet. Repeat with the remaining meat. Return all meat mixture to skillet.

Sprinkle meat with flour and pepper; stir to coat. Stir in the beef broth, tomato paste, and Worcestershire sauce. Cook and stir until thickened and bubbly. Cook and stir for 1 minute more.

To serve, divide the noodle mixture among bowls or dinner plates. Spoon the meat mixture on top of noodle mixture. Spoon the sauce on top of meat mixture. Makes 4 servings.

Nutrition information per serving: 368 cal., 15 g total fat (5 g sat. fat), 81 mg chol., 454 mg sodium, 32 g carbo., 29 g pro.

Szechwan Beef Stir-Fry

To partially freeze the meat, place it in the freezer for about 20 minutes. If you're starting with frozen meat, thaw it until it's soft but still icy.

12 ounces boneless beef sirloin steak or top round steak
1 8¾-ounce can whole baby corn, drained
3 tablespoons dry sherry or dry white wine
3 tablespoons soy sauce
2 tablespoons water
2 tablespoons bottled hoisin sauce
2 teaspoons cornstarch
2 teaspoons grated fresh ginger
1 teaspoon sugar
2 cloves garlic, minced
½ teaspoon crushed red pepper
¼ teaspoon black pepper (optional)
1 tablespoon cooking oil
1 cup thinly sliced carrots (2 medium)
1 red sweet pepper, cut into 1-inch pieces (1 cup)
2 cups hot cooked rice
Lime peel curls (optional)

Trim fat from meat. Partially freeze meat. Thinly slice across the grain into bite-size strips. Set aside. If desired, cut baby corn in half crosswise. Set aside.

For sauce, in a small bowl stir together sherry or wine, soy sauce, water, hoisin sauce, cornstarch, ginger, sugar, garlic, red pepper, and, if desired, black pepper. Set aside.

Add cooking oil to a wok or large skillet. Preheat over medium-high heat (add more oil if necessary during cooking). Stir-fry carrots in hot oil for 2 minutes. Add baby corn and sweet pepper. Stir-fry for 1 to 2 minutes more or until crisp-tender. Remove vegetables from wok.

Add meat to wok. Stir-fry for 2 to 3 minutes or until meat is slightly pink in center. Push meat from center of wok.

Stir sauce. Add sauce to center of wok. Cook and stir until thickened and bubbly. Return cooked vegetables to wok. Stir all ingredients together to coat. Cook and stir for 1 to 2 minutes more or until mixture is heated through. Serve immediately over hot cooked rice. If desired, garnish with lime peel. Makes 4 servings.

Nutrition information per serving: 363 cal., 11 g total fat (4 g sat. fat), 57 mg chol., 1,396 mg sodium, 36 g carbo., 25 g pro.

Spicy Thai Ginger Beef

Thai cooking is strongly influenced by both Chinese and Indian cuisines. In fact, the Thai people migrated from China's Yunnan province in the 13th century.

12   ounces beef top round steak
 1   tablespoon fish sauce
 1   tablespoon water
 1   teaspoon finely shredded lime peel
 1   tablespoon lime juice
 1   teaspoon sugar
 1   tablespoon cooking oil
 2   medium zucchini, cut into thin
       bite-size strips (2 cups)
 6   green onions, bias-sliced into 1-inch
       pieces (1 cup)
 1   fresh, pickled, or canned jalapeño
       pepper, seeded and finely chopped
 3   cloves garlic, minced
 2   teaspoons grated fresh ginger
 2   cups hot cooked rice sticks or rice
 2   tablespoons snipped fresh cilantro

Trim fat from meat. Partially freeze meat. Thinly slice meat across the grain into bite-size strips. Set aside.

For sauce, in a small bowl stir together fish sauce, water, lime peel, lime juice, and sugar. Set aside.

Add cooking oil to a wok or large skillet. Preheat over medium-high heat (add more oil if necessary during cooking). Stir-fry zucchini in hot oil for 1 to 2 minutes or until crisp-tender. Remove zucchini from wok. Add green onions to wok. Stir-fry for 1½ minutes. Remove green onions from wok.

Add jalapeño pepper, garlic, and ginger to wok. Stir-fry for 15 seconds. Add meat. Stir-fry for 2 to 3 minutes or until meat is slightly pink in center. Return the cooked zucchini and green onions to wok.

Add sauce to center of wok. Cook and stir about 2 minutes or until heated through. Serve immediately with hot cooked rice sticks or rice. Sprinkle with cilantro. Makes 3 servings.

Nutrition information per serving: 339 cal., 10 g total fat (3 g sat. fat), 74 mg chol., 242 mg sodium, 30 g carbo., 31 g pro.

Beef Strips with Vermicelli

Strips of top round steak make a lean choice for this sauce whether you're counting calories or pennies.

8 ounces boneless beef top
    round steak
4 ounces dried vermicelli or spaghetti
1 tablespoon cooking oil
1 medium onion, chopped
1 14½-ounce can tomato wedges
1 9-ounce package frozen cut Italian-
    style green beans or green beans
1 4-ounce can sliced mushrooms,
    drained
½ of a 6-ounce can (⅓ cup) Italian-
    style tomato paste
½ teaspoon fennel seeds, crushed
    (optional)
¼ teaspoon pepper
1 tablespoon grated Parmesan cheese
    Grated Parmesan cheese (optional)

Trim fat from meat. Partially freeze meat. Thinly slice meat across the grain into bite-size strips. Cook pasta according to package directions; drain. Cover and keep warm.

Meanwhile, in a large skillet heat oil over medium-high heat. Add meat and onion. Cook and stir about 2 minutes or until meat is brown. Stir in undrained tomato wedges, green beans, mushrooms, tomato paste, fennel seeds (if desired), and pepper. Bring to boiling; reduce heat. Simmer, uncovered, for 7 to 8 minutes or until slightly thickened, stirring frequently. Stir in the 1 tablespoon cheese.

To serve, arrange pasta on dinner plates or a large platter. Spoon the meat mixture over pasta. If desired, sprinkle with additional Parmesan cheese. Makes 4 servings.

Nutrition information per serving: 278 cal., 7 g total fat (2 g sat. fat), 28 mg chol., 488 mg sodium, 38 g carbo., 18 g pro.

Marinated Steak Fajitas

It's easy to make tasty beef fajitas at home with this simple recipe. For extra flavor, top them with sour cream, chopped tomato, and fresh cilantro.

1	pound beef flank steak
3	tablespoons bottled chili sauce
2	tablespoons water
1	tablespoon Worcestershire sauce
1	teaspoon dried oregano, crushed
½	teaspoon chili powder
⅛	teaspoon garlic powder
⅛	teaspoon black pepper
10	7-inch flour tortillas
	Nonstick cooking spray
2	small red, yellow, and/or green sweet peppers, cut into thin bite-size strips
1	small onion, cut into thin wedges

Trim fat from meat. Thinly slice meat across the grain into bite-size strips. Place meat in a plastic bag set in a shallow dish. For marinade, in a small bowl stir together chili sauce, water, Worcestershire sauce, oregano, chili powder, garlic powder, and black pepper. Pour over meat; seal bag. Marinate in the refrigerator for 4 to 24 hours, turning bag occasionally.

Stack tortillas; wrap in foil. Bake in a 350° oven about 10 minutes or until warm. (Or just before serving, microwave tortillas, covered with a paper towel, on 100% power [high] about 1 minute.)

Coat a large nonstick skillet with cooking spray. Heat over medium-high heat. Add half of the meat mixture. Cook and stir for 2 to 3 minutes or until meat is slightly pink in center. Remove meat from skillet. Repeat with remaining meat mixture (add 1 teaspoon cooking oil if necessary). Remove meat from skillet, reserving juices in skillet.

Add the pepper strips and onion wedges to reserved juices in skillet. Bring to boiling; reduce heat. Cover and simmer for 3 to 4 minutes or until vegetables are crisp-tender. Stir the meat into vegetable mixture. Heat through.

To serve, place about ½ cup of the meat mixture on each tortilla. Roll up tortillas. Makes 5 servings.

Nutrition information per serving: 388 cal., 12 g total fat (4 g sat. fat), 43 mg chol., 541 mg sodium, 45 g carbo., 24 g pro.

Southwest Beef-Linguine Toss

A jar of picante sauce makes an easy, yet flavor-packed sauce in this one-dish meal.

4 ounces packaged dried linguine
12 ounces beef top round steak
1 tablespoon cooking oil
2 teaspoons chili powder
1 clove garlic, minced
1 small onion, sliced and separated
   into rings
1 red or green sweet pepper, cut into
   strips
1 10-ounce package frozen whole
   kernel corn
¼ cup picante sauce
   Cilantro sprigs (optional)

Cook pasta according to package directions. Drain pasta; rinse with warm water. Drain again. Meanwhile, trim fat from meat. Cut meat into thin, bite-size strips.

Add cooking oil to a wok or large skillet. Preheat over medium-high heat (add more oil if necessary during cooking). Stir-fry chili powder and garlic in hot oil for 15 seconds. Add onion; stir-fry for 1 minute. Add sweet pepper; stir-fry for 1 to 2 minutes more or until vegetables are crisp-tender. Remove from wok.

Add meat to wok. Stir-fry for 2 to 3 minutes or until meat is slightly pink in center. Return vegetables to wok. Stir in corn and picante sauce. Add the cooked pasta. Toss all ingredients together to coat. Cook and stir until heated through. Serve immediately. If desired, garnish with cilantro. Makes 4 servings.

Nutrition information per serving: 351 cal., 9 g total fat (2 g sat. fat), 54 mg chol., 166 mg sodium, 43 g carbo., 27 g pro.

STIR-FRYING GARLIC

To evenly distribute garlic flavor to stir-fry ingredients, season the oil by cooking the garlic first. Cook the garlic in the hot oil, keeping it moving constantly so it doesn't burn. After about 15 seconds, begin adding the other stir-fry ingredients to the oil.

Double Salsa Burgers

A fresh tomato salsa flavors the beef mixture and also serves as a colorful topping for these zesty burgers.

1 large tomato, seeded and finely chopped

½ cup finely chopped green sweet pepper

¼ cup finely chopped red onion

2 jalapeño peppers, seeded and finely chopped

1 tablespoon snipped cilantro

1 clove garlic, minced

¼ teaspoon salt

1½ pounds lean ground beef

2 cups shredded lettuce

⅓ cup shredded cheddar cheese

¼ cup dairy sour cream and/or guacamole

For salsa, in a medium bowl combine tomato, green pepper, onion, jalapeño peppers, cilantro, garlic, and salt. Set aside 2 tablespoons of the salsa. Cover and chill the remaining salsa until serving time.

In another medium bowl combine ground beef and the 2 tablespoons salsa; mix well. Shape mixture into six ½-inch-thick oval patties.

Grill patties on an uncovered grill directly over medium coals for 12 to 14 minutes or until meat is done (160°), turning once.

Arrange shredded lettuce on dinner plates. Top with patties, remaining salsa, and cheddar cheese. Serve with sour cream and/or guacamole. Makes 6 servings.

Nutrition information per serving: 298 cal., 19 g total fat (9 g sat. fat), 87 mg chol., 350 mg sodium, 6 g carbo., 24 g pro.

Handle with care

Because hot peppers contain oils that can burn your eyes, lips, and skin, protect yourself when working with the peppers by covering one or both hands with plastic bags (or wear plastic gloves). Be sure to wash your hands thoroughly before touching your eyes or face.

Pepper-Bacon Burgers

The All-American burger gets a spicy makeover with the addition of serrano or jalapeño peppers.

1   beaten egg
¼   cup fine dry bread crumbs
6   slices crisp-cooked bacon, crumbled
4   to 6 fresh serrano peppers or 2 to
     3 fresh jalapeño peppers, seeded and
     finely chopped (3 tablespoons)
2   tablespoons milk
1   pound lean ground beef
1   fresh Anaheim pepper or mild green
     chile pepper, seeded and sliced
1   small onion, thinly sliced and
     separated into rings
2   tablespoons margarine or butter
4   kaiser rolls or hamburger buns,
     split and toasted
4   lettuce leaves (optional)

In a large bowl combine egg, bread crumbs, bacon, serrano or jalapeño peppers, and milk. Add ground beef; mix well. Form into four ¾-inch-thick patties.

Place patties on the rack of an uncovered grill directly over medium coals. Grill for 14 to 18 minutes or until done (160°), turning once.

Meanwhile, in a small saucepan cook the Anaheim or green chile pepper and onion in hot margarine or butter about 10 minutes or until onion is tender.

If desired, line bottoms of rolls or buns with lettuce. Top with burgers and onion mixture. Replace roll or bun tops. Makes 4 servings.

Nutrition information per serving: 550 cal., 29 g total fat (9 g sat. fat), 132 mg chol., 733 mg sodium, 38 g carbo., 32 g pro.

Meatballs in Pasta Nests

These tiny meatballs, inspired by the Italian classic osso buco, tuck into a bed of pasta. Unlike the original, a chunky sauce of carrots, onion, and fennel tops this Americanized version.

1 slightly beaten egg
¼ cup fine dry bread crumbs
3 large cloves garlic, minced
1 teaspoon dried sage, crushed
½ teaspoon salt
¼ teaspoon pepper
1 pound ground veal or lean ground beef
2 tablespoons olive oil
6 dried vermicelli nests (6 ounces total)
2 tablespoons snipped fennel tops
1 tablespoon finely shredded lemon peel
   Lemony Vegetable Sauce
   Snipped fresh parsley and/or fennel tops (optional)

For meatballs, in a large bowl combine egg, bread crumbs, garlic, sage, salt, and pepper. Add ground veal or beef; mix well. Form into 36 meatballs, about 1 inch in size.

In a large skillet heat oil. Add meatballs; cook for 8 to 10 minutes or until brown on all sides and meat is done (160°). Remove meatballs from skillet, reserving drippings for use in Lemony Vegetable Sauce. Cover meatballs; keep warm.

In a large saucepan or Dutch oven cook vermicelli nests according to package directions, stirring the 2 tablespoons fennel tops and the lemon peel into cooking water. Using a slotted spoon, carefully transfer nests to a colander to drain. Cover and keep warm. Prepare Lemony Vegetable Sauce.

To serve, divide the pasta nests among dinner plates. Spoon meatballs into nests. Spoon the sauce over meatballs and pasta nests. If desired, sprinkle with parsley and/or additional fennel tops. Makes 6 servings.

Lemony Vegetable Sauce: Add 2 tablespoons *olive oil* to the reserved drippings in skillet used for meatballs. Add 1 cup finely chopped *onion*, 1 cup finely chopped *fennel*, 1 cup finely chopped *carrots*, ¼ teaspoon *salt*, and ¼ teaspoon *pepper*. Cook and stir over medium heat for 2 minutes. Remove from heat. Stir in ⅓ cup snipped fresh *parsley* and 1 tablespoon finely shredded *lemon peel*.

Nutrition information per serving: 352 cal., 16 g total fat (4 g sat. fat), 97 mg chol., 411 mg sodium, 31 g carbo., 21 g pro.

Easy Taco Pizza

This hearty south-of-the border pizza is popular with both kids and adults alike.

Cornmeal Pizza Dough
12 ounces lean ground beef
1 cup chopped onion
1 8-ounce can tomato sauce
1 2¼-ounce can sliced pitted ripe
    olives, drained
1 1¼-ounce envelope taco
    seasoning mix
2 cups shredded cheddar cheese
    (8 ounces)
2 cups shredded lettuce
2 cups chopped tomatoes
2 medium avocados, seeded, peeled,
    and chopped
1 8-ounce carton dairy sour cream
    Chili powder (optional)

Prepare Cornmeal Pizza Dough. Grease two 11- to 13-inch pizza pans or baking sheets. On a lightly floured surface, roll each half of dough into a circle 1 inch larger than pizza pan. Transfer dough to pans. Build up edges slightly. If desired, flute edges. Prick crusts well with a fork. Do not let rise. Bake in a 425° oven for 10 to 12 minutes or until crusts are lightly browned.

Meanwhile, in a large skillet cook ground beef and onion until meat is brown and onion is tender. Drain fat. Stir in tomato sauce, olives, and taco seasoning mix. Heat through.

Spread meat mixture over hot crusts. Sprinkle with cheese. Bake about 12 minutes more or until cheese is melted. Top with lettuce, tomatoes, avocados, and sour cream. If desired, sprinkle sour cream with chili powder. Makes 6 servings.

Cornmeal Pizza Dough: In a large bowl combine 1¼ cups *all-purpose flour*, 1 package *active dry yeast*, and ¼ teaspoon *salt*. Add 1 cup *warm water* (120° to 130°) and 2 tablespoons *cooking oil*. Beat with an electric mixer on low speed for 30 seconds. Beat on high speed for 3 minutes. Using a spoon, stir in ¾ cup *yellow cornmeal* and as much of ¾ to 1¼ cups additional *all-purpose flour* as you can. On a lightly floured surface, knead in enough of the remaining flour to make a moderately stiff dough that is smooth and elastic (6 to 8 minutes total). Divide in half. Cover and let rest for 10 minutes.

Nutrition information per serving: 726 cal., 45 g total fat (15 g sat. fat), 90 mg chol., 1,274 mg sodium, 56 g carbo., 32 g pro.

Zippy Beef, Mac, and Cheese

Zippy Beef, Mac, and Cheese

Nothing goes better with this old favorite than a fresh side salad. Simply peel and section oranges and cut jicama into strips; arrange on a lettuce leaf and drizzle with an oil-and-vinegar dressing.

6	ounces dried elbow macaroni or corkscrew pasta (about 1½ cups)
12	ounces lean ground beef, lean ground pork, or uncooked ground turkey
1	15-ounce can tomato sauce
1	14½-ounce can stewed tomatoes or Mexican-style stewed tomatoes
4	ounces American or sharp American cheese, cut into small pieces
1	tablespoon chili powder
	Finely shredded or grated Parmesan cheese

In a 3-quart saucepan cook pasta according to package directions; drain. Meanwhile, in a large skillet cook ground meat until brown. Drain off fat.

Stir ground meat, tomato sauce, undrained tomatoes, American cheese, and chili powder into cooked pasta. Cook and stir over medium heat for 6 to 8 minutes or until heated through. Sprinkle each serving with Parmesan cheese. Makes 4 servings.

Nutrition information per serving: 342 cal., 15 g total fat (7 g sat. fat), 55 mg chol., 957 mg sodium, 32 g carbo., 20 g pro.

Easy Shepherd's Pie

Frozen mashed potatoes make quick work of this family-style ground meat- and soup-based skillet supper.

1	28-ounce package frozen mashed potatoes
1¾	cups milk
1	10-ounce package frozen mixed vegetables
1	pound lean ground beef, uncooked ground turkey, or uncooked ground chicken
¼	cup water
1	teaspoon dried minced onion
1	10¾-ounce can condensed tomato soup
1	teaspoon Worcestershire sauce
¼	teaspoon dried thyme, crushed
½	cup shredded cheddar cheese

Prepare the potatoes according to package directions using 4 cups of the frozen potatoes and the milk. Meanwhile, run cold water over frozen vegetables to separate. In a large skillet cook ground meat until brown. Drain off any fat. Stir in mixed vegetables, water, and onion.

Bring to boiling; reduce heat. Cover and simmer for 5 to 10 minutes or until vegetables are tender. Stir in soup, Worcestershire sauce, and thyme. Return to boiling. Drop potatoes in mounds on top of hot mixture. Sprinkle with cheese; reduce heat. Cover and simmer about 5 minutes or until heated through. Makes 6 servings.

Nutrition information per serving: 342 cal., 16 g total fat (7 g sat. fat), 62 mg chol., 541 mg sodium, 30 g carbo., 19 g pro.

Pasta Pizza

This hybrid recipe uses favorite casserole ingredients to create an outstanding dish that looks and tastes like pizza.

5   ounces dried corkscrew pasta (2 cups)
1   beaten egg
¼   cup milk
2   tablespoons grated Parmesan cheese
8   ounces lean ground beef
1   small onion, chopped (⅓ cup)
1   clove garlic, minced
1   14½-ounce can Italian-style stewed
      tomatoes
1   cup green and/or yellow sweet
      pepper cut into 2-inch strips
½   teaspoon dried Italian seasoning,
      crushed
1   4½-ounce jar sliced mushrooms,
      drained
¼   teaspoon crushed red pepper
1   cup shredded mozzarella cheese
      (4 ounces)

Cook pasta according to package directions; drain. Rinse with cold water; drain again.

For pasta crust, in a large bowl combine egg, milk, and Parmesan cheese. Stir in cooked pasta. Spread pasta mixture evenly in a greased 12-inch pizza pan. Bake in a 350° oven for 20 minutes.

Meanwhile, in a large skillet cook meat, onion, and garlic until meat is brown. Drain off fat. Stir in undrained tomatoes (cut up any large pieces), sweet pepper, and Italian seasoning. Bring to boiling; reduce heat. Simmer, uncovered, for 10 to 12 minutes or until sweet pepper is crisp-tender and most of the liquid is evaporated, stirring once or twice. Stir in mushrooms and crushed red pepper.

Spoon the meat mixture over pasta crust. Sprinkle with mozzarella cheese. Bake for 10 to 12 minutes more or until pizza is heated through and cheese is melted. To serve, cut the pizza into wedges. Makes 6 servings.

Nutrition information per serving: 259 cal., 9 g total fat (4 g sat. fat), 72 mg chol., 479 mg sodium, 27 g carbo., 18 g pro.

Plum Good Pork Chops

Plum Good Pork Chops

Plum preserves make this glistening glaze simple to make. Try it with grilled chicken or lamb, too.

3 tablespoons plum preserves
1 green onion, thinly sliced
1 tablespoon soy sauce
2 teaspoons lemon juice
⅛ teaspoon curry powder
   Dash ground cinnamon
   Dash ground red pepper
4 pork loin or rib chops, cut
   1¼ inches thick
   (about 2 pounds total)
1 clove garlic, halved
   Plum wedges (optional)

For sauce, in a small saucepan heat and stir plum preserves, green onion, soy sauce, lemon juice, curry powder, cinnamon, and red pepper over medium heat until bubbly. Trim fat from chops. Rub both sides of chops with cut sides of garlic.

Grill chops on an uncovered grill directly over medium coals for 25 to 30 minutes or until slightly pink in center and juices run clear, turning once. Brush with sauce during the last 10 minutes of grilling. If desired, garnish with plum wedges. Makes 4 servings.

Nutrition information per serving: 224 cal., 11 g total fat (4 g sat. fat), 66 mg chol., 283 mg sodium, 11 g carbo., 20 g pro.

Spicy Fruit and Pork Kabobs

Tangy pineapple and cool cantaloupe complement the spicy flavor of this pork on a stick.

1½ pounds lean boneless pork
 2 tablespoons olive oil or cooking oil
 2 tablespoons balsamic vinegar
 1 teaspoon finely shredded orange
     peel
 2 tablespoons orange juice
 1 clove garlic, minced
 ¼ teaspoon salt
 ¼ teaspoon ground cumin
12 1½-inch cubes fresh pineapple
12 1½-inch cubes cantaloupe

Trim fat from meat. Cut into 1½-inch cubes. Place meat in a plastic bag and set bag into a shallow dish. For marinade, combine oil, balsamic vinegar, orange peel, orange juice, garlic, salt, and cumin. Pour over meat; seal bag.

Marinate in the refrigerator for 2 to 4 hours, turning bag once. Drain meat, reserving marinade. Alternately thread meat, pineapple, and cantaloupe onto 6 long metal skewers.

Grill kabobs on an uncovered grill directly over medium coals for 14 to 16 minutes or until meat is slightly pink in center and juices run clear, turning and brushing once with marinade halfway through grilling. Makes 6 servings.

Nutrition information per serving: 181 cal., 10 g total fat (3 g sat. fat), 51 mg chol., 87 mg sodium, 6 g carbo., 16 g pro.

Spicy Pork Chops

Vegetable juice is the base for this zippy marinade. Add more hot pepper sauce if you like extra heat.

4 boneless pork top loin chops, cut
   ½ inch thick (about 1¼ pounds
   total)
1 6-ounce can (⅔ cup) vegetable juice
2 tablespoons sliced green onion
2 tablespoons canned diced green
   chile peppers
1 teaspoon Worcestershire sauce
1 clove garlic, minced
½ teaspoon dried basil, crushed
   Few dashes bottled hot pepper sauce
2 cups hot cooked orzo or rice

Trim fat from pork chops. Place the chops in a plastic bag set in a shallow bowl.

For marinade, in a small bowl combine the vegetable juice, green onion, green chile peppers, Worcestershire sauce, garlic, basil, and hot pepper sauce. Pour over the chops; seal bag. Marinate in the refrigerator for 2 to 24 hours, turning bag occasionally. Drain chops, reserving marinade.

Place chops on the unheated rack of a broiler pan. Broil 3 to 4 inches from the heat for 5 to 7 minutes or until chops are slightly pink in center and juices run clear (160°), turning once.

In a small saucepan bring the marinade to boiling. Boil gently, uncovered, for 1 minute. Serve the hot marinade with pork chops and hot cooked orzo or rice. Makes 4 servings.

Nutrition information per serving: 273 cal., 11 g total fat (4 g sat. fat), 63 mg chol., 241 mg sodium, 21 g carbo., 22 g pro.

Broiling Basics

To make sure food is placed correctly for even broiling, use a ruler to measure the distance from the surface of the food to the heating element. If the distance does not match the guidelines in your recipe, adjust the broiler pan or oven rack. *Be sure to measure before turning on the broiler.* To keep cleanup to a minimum, line the broiler pan with foil before sliding the broiler rack into position.

Pork Scaloppine with Mustard and Rosemary

To keep the pork warm while you prepare the mushroom mixture, place the cooked pork slices on a warm serving platter. Cover with foil and place the platter in a 300° oven.

1   pound pork tenderloin
⅓   cup all-purpose flour
½   teaspoon pepper
¼   teaspoon salt
2   teaspoons margarine or butter
1   tablespoon olive oil or cooking oil
1   cup sliced fresh mushrooms
1   tablespoon snipped fresh rosemary
     or 1 teaspoon dried rosemary,
     crushed
2   cloves garlic, minced
¾   cup chicken broth
2   tablespoons Dijon-style mustard
1   teaspoon finely shredded lemon peel
1   tablespoon lemon juice
     Lemon wedges (optional)
     Fresh rosemary sprigs (optional)

Trim any fat from meat. Cut meat crosswise into ½-inch slices. Place each slice between two pieces of plastic wrap. With the heel of your hand, press each slice until about ⅛ inch thick. Remove plastic wrap.

In a shallow dish combine flour, pepper, and salt. Coat meat with flour mixture, shaking off excess.

In a large skillet heat margarine or butter and oil over medium-high heat. Add half of the meat; cook for 3 to 4 minutes or until slightly pink in center, turning once. Remove from skillet, reserving drippings in skillet. Cover and keep warm. Repeat with the remaining meat.

Reduce heat to medium. Add mushrooms, snipped fresh or dried rosemary, and garlic to reserved drippings in skillet. Cook and stir just until mushrooms are tender. Add broth, scraping up any browned bits on bottom. Bring to boiling. Boil gently, uncovered, about 5 minutes or until reduced by half. Stir in Dijon mustard, lemon peel, and lemon juice. Heat through.

Serve the mushroom mixture over meat. If desired, garnish with lemon wedges and fresh rosemary sprigs. Makes 4 servings.

Nutrition information per serving: 287 cal., 14 g total fat (3 g sat. fat), 81 mg chol., 594 mg sodium, 10 g carbo., 28 g pro.

Pork Tenderloin with Raspberry Sauce

This special-occasion dish features pork tenderloin with a spicy fruit sauce, fresh star fruit, and berries. Choose a seedless jam for the prettiest appearance.

1 pound pork tenderloin
¼ teaspoon black pepper
2 tablespoons margarine or butter
⅓ cup seedless raspberry or strawberry
   ⸰ jam
2 tablespoons red wine vinegar
2 teaspoons prepared horseradish
1 clove garlic, minced
¼ teaspoon ground red pepper
   Sliced star fruit (optional)
   Raspberries (optional)

Trim any fat from meat. Cut meat crosswise into 1-inch slices. Place each slice between two pieces of plastic wrap. With the heel of your hand, press each slice until about ½ inch thick. Remove plastic wrap. Sprinkle meat with black pepper.

In a 12-inch skillet heat margarine or butter over medium-high heat. Add meat and cook for 4 to 6 minutes or until slightly pink in center, turning once. Remove from skillet, reserving drippings in skillet. Cover and keep warm.

For sauce, stir raspberry or strawberry jam, vinegar, horseradish, garlic, and ground red pepper into reserved drippings in skillet. Cook and stir until bubbly. Cook and stir about 1 minute more or until slightly thickened.

Serve the sauce over meat. If desired, garnish with star fruit and raspberries. Makes 4 servings.

Nutrition information per serving: 282 cal., 10 g total fat (3 g sat. fat), 81 mg chol., 157 mg sodium, 22 g carbo., 25 g pro.

Rhubarb-Glazed Pork Roast

Make this in the spring when rhubarb is in season or buy frozen sliced rhubarb for convenience. You also can make Ginger-Apricot-Glazed Pork Roast (see below).

1 2- to 3-pound boneless pork top loin roast (single loin)
4 cups fresh or frozen sliced rhubarb
½ of a 12-ounce can frozen cranberry-apple juice concentrate
2 tablespoons cornstarch
2 tablespoons cold water
⅓ cup honey
2 tablespoons Dijon-style mustard
1 tablespoon wine vinegar
   Fresh rosemary sprigs (optional)

Place meat on a rack in a shallow roasting pan. Insert an oven-going meat thermometer into center of meat. Roast in a 325° oven for 1¼ to 1¾ hours or until the thermometer registers 155°.

Meanwhile, for glaze, in a 2-quart saucepan combine rhubarb and cranberry-apple juice concentrate. Bring to boiling; reduce heat. Cover and simmer about 15 minutes or until rhubarb is very tender. Pour mixture through a wire strainer placed over a 2-cup liquid measure, pressing out liquid with the back of a spoon. Add enough water to rhubarb liquid to equal 1¼ cups. Discard pulp.

In the same saucepan stir together cornstarch and cold water. Stir in rhubarb liquid. Cook and stir over medium heat until thickened and bubbly. Cook and stir for 2 minutes more. Stir in honey, mustard, and vinegar. Heat through.

Brush some of the glaze onto the meat the last 30 minutes of roasting. Cover meat with foil; let stand for 15 minutes before slicing. (The meat's temperature will rise 5° during standing.) Heat the remaining glaze; serve with meat. If desired, garnish with rosemary sprigs. Makes 6 to 8 servings.

Nutrition information per serving: 264 cal., 8 g total fat (3 g sat. fat), 51 mg chol., 137 mg sodium, 31 g carbo., 17 g pro.

Ginger-Apricot-Glazed Pork Roast: Prepare as above, except substitute apricot glaze for rhubarb glaze. For apricot glaze, in a small saucepan combine ⅔ cup *apricot preserves*, 4 teaspoons *lime juice*, 2 teaspoons *soy sauce*, ¼ teaspoon grated *fresh ginger* or ⅛ teaspoon *ground ginger*, and dash *ground red pepper*. Cook and stir until mixture is bubbly.

Easy Everyday Cooking • BEEF & PORK 123

Mustard-Orange Pork Tenderloin

A mixture of vegetables, such as cut-up red onions, baby carrots, and chunks of zucchini, can be roasted alongside the meat. Just spray the vegetables with olive oil-flavored nonstick spray coating before placing them in the pan around the meat.

12 ounces pork tenderloin
½ cup apricot preserves or orange
    marmalade
 3 tablespoons Dijon-style mustard
    Nonstick spray coating
 2 cups sliced fresh mushrooms
½ cup sliced green onions
 2 tablespoons orange juice

Trim fat from meat. Place meat on a rack in a shallow roasting pan. Insert a meat thermometer into the center of meat. Roast, uncovered, in a 425° oven for 10 minutes.

Meanwhile, in a small bowl stir together preserves or marmalade and mustard. Spoon half of the mustard mixture over the meat. Set the remaining mustard mixture aside.

Roast for 15 to 25 minutes more or until the meat thermometer registers 155°. Transfer the meat to a warm platter and cover with foil. Let stand for 10 minutes before slicing. (The meat's temperature will rise 5° during standing.)

Meanwhile, spray a medium saucepan with nonstick coating. Add mushrooms and green onions. Cook and stir for 2 to 3 minutes or until mushrooms are tender. Stir in the remaining mustard mixture and orange juice. Cook and stir until heated through.

To serve, thinly slice the meat. Spoon the mushroom mixture over meat. Makes 4 servings.

Nutrition information per serving: 240 cal., 4 g total fat (1 g sat. fat), 60 mg chol., 334 mg sodium, 32 g carbo., 21 g pro.

Szechwan Pork with Peppers

Green and red sweet peppers and the spicy sweetness of hoisin sauce contrast nicely with the pleasant heat of this dish. But if you prefer more heat than sweet, simply add more hot bean sauce.

12 ounces lean boneless pork
3 tablespoons bottled hoisin sauce
1 tablespoon hot bean sauce or hot bean paste
1 tablespoon soy sauce
1 teaspoon sugar
1 tablespoon cooking oil
4 cloves garlic, thinly sliced
1 teaspoon grated fresh ginger
2 medium red sweet peppers, cut into 1-inch pieces (2 cups)
2 medium green sweet peppers, cut into 1-inch pieces (2 cups)
2 cups hot cooked noodles or rice

Trim fat from meat. Partially freeze meat. Thinly slice across the grain into bite-size strips. Set aside. For sauce, in a small bowl stir together hoisin sauce, bean sauce or paste, soy sauce, and sugar. Set aside.

Add cooking oil to a wok or large skillet. Preheat over medium-high heat (add more oil if necessary during cooking). Stir-fry garlic and ginger in hot oil for 15 seconds. Add sweet peppers; stir-fry for 3 to 4 minutes or until crisp-tender. Remove pepper mixture from wok.

Add meat to wok. Stir-fry for 2 to 3 minutes or until meat is slightly pink in center. Push meat from center of wok. Add sauce to center of wok. Cook and stir until bubbly.

Return pepper mixture to wok. Stir all ingredients together to coat. Cook and stir about 1 minute more or until heated through. Serve immediately over hot cooked noodles or rice. Makes 4 servings.

Nutrition information per serving: 292 cal., 10 g total fat (3 g sat. fat), 63 mg chol., 1,324 mg sodium, 32 g carbo., 18 g pro.

*G*REAT-TASTING GINGER

Many stir-fries depend on spicy-sweet ginger for its tempting flavor. Look for this knobby root in your supermarket's produce section. Grate or slice as much as you need (peeling isn't necessary). Wrap the remaining root in paper towels and refrigerate it up to 1 week. Or cut up the ginger and place it in a small jar. Fill the jar with dry sherry or wine and refrigerate it, covered, up to 3 months.

Jamaican Pork and Sweet Potato Stir-Fry

Take a vacation from the postwork, predinner rush with this Jamaica-inspired dish, which features two of the easygoing island's favorite ingredients: lean pork and golden sweet potatoes. For flavor, pick up Jamaican jerk seasoning at the grocery store or make your own seasoning.

1½ cups instant white rice

2 green onions, thinly sliced (¼ cup)

1 large sweet potato (about 12 ounces)

1 medium tart apple (such as Granny Smith), cored

12 ounces lean boneless pork strips for stir-frying

2 to 3 teaspoons purchased Jamaican jerk seasoning or Homemade Jamaican Jerk Seasoning

1 tablespoon cooking oil

⅓ cup apple juice or water

Prepare rice according to package directions. Stir half of the green onions into cooked rice.

Meanwhile, peel sweet potato. Cut into quarters lengthwise, then thinly slice crosswise. Place in a microwave-safe pie plate or shallow dish. Cover with vented plastic wrap. Microwave on 100% power (high) for 3 to 4 minutes or until tender, stirring once. Cut apple into 16 wedges. Sprinkle meat strips with jerk seasoning; toss to coat.

Add cooking oil to a wok or large skillet. Preheat over medium-high heat (add more oil if necessary during cooking). Stir-fry meat in hot oil for 2 minutes. Add apple and remaining green onions. Stir-fry for 1 to 2 minutes more or until meat is slightly pink in center.

Stir in sweet potato and apple juice or water. Bring to boiling; reduce heat. Simmer, uncovered, for 1 minute. Serve immediately over hot cooked rice mixture. Makes 4 servings.

Homemade Jamaican Jerk Seasoning: In a small bowl combine 1 teaspoon *crushed red pepper;* ½ teaspoon *ground allspice;* ¼ teaspoon *curry powder;* ¼ teaspoon coarsely *ground black pepper;* ⅛ teaspoon *dried thyme,* crushed; ⅛ teaspoon *ground red pepper;* and ⅛ teaspoon *ground ginger.*

Nutrition information per serving: 365 cal., 9 g total fat (2 g sat. fat), 38 mg chol., 131 mg sodium, 54 g carbo., 16 g pro.

Country-Style Oven Ribs

The secret ingredient in the sweet dark basting sauce keeps your family guessing—it's root beer! For a complete meal, serve the ribs with a side dish of crisp, refreshing vegetables or coleslaw.

1½ teaspoons salt
1 teaspoon ground cumin
1 teaspoon paprika
½ teaspoon pepper
½ teaspoon ground cinnamon
¼ teaspoon ground cloves
3½ pounds pork country-style ribs
4 cups root beer (not low calorie)
⅓ cup bottled barbecue sauce
2 tablespoons tomato paste
1 tablespoon vinegar
2 teaspoons Dijon-style mustard
1 teaspoon Worcestershire sauce

In a small bowl combine the salt, cumin, paprika, pepper, cinnamon, and cloves. Sprinkle ribs with spice mixture, rubbing it over entire surface. Place ribs, bone sides up, in a shallow roasting pan. Cover and bake in a 350° oven for 1¼ hours.

Meanwhile, for sauce, in a large saucepan bring root beer to boiling. Boil gently, uncovered, for 20 to 25 minutes or until root beer is reduced to 1¼ cups. Remove from heat. Stir in the barbecue sauce, tomato paste, vinegar, mustard, and Worcestershire sauce. Return to boiling. Boil gently, uncovered, for 1 minute. Remove from heat.

Drain fat from ribs. Turn ribs meaty sides up. Spoon about half of the sauce over ribs. Bake for 45 minutes more, basting once or twice with more of the sauce. To serve, spoon the remaining sauce over ribs. Makes 4 servings.

Nutrition information per serving: 549 cal., 24 g total fat (8 g sat. fat), 99 mg chol., 1,186 mg sodium, 32 g carbo., 49 g pro.

Ham, Spinach, and Mostaccioli Casserole

Just before serving, be sure to give the casserole a good stir to distribute the rich and creamy sauce.

8 ounces packaged dried mostaccioli, cut ziti, or elbow macaroni
3 tablespoons margarine or butter
3 medium onions, cut into thin wedges, or 5 medium leeks, sliced
2 cloves garlic, minced
¼ cup all-purpose flour
½ teaspoon dried thyme, crushed
⅛ teaspoon pepper
1½ cups half-and-half, light cream, or milk
1½ cups chicken broth
1½ cups cubed fully cooked ham
1 10-ounce package frozen chopped spinach, thawed and drained

Cook pasta according to package directions. Drain pasta; rinse with cold water. Drain again.

In a large saucepan melt margarine or butter. Add onions or leeks and garlic. Cover and cook about 5 minutes or until onions are tender, stirring occasionally. Stir in flour, thyme, and pepper. Add half-and-half, light cream, or milk and the chicken broth all at once. Cook and stir until thickened and bubbly. Cook and stir for 1 minute more. Stir in pasta, ham, and spinach. Spoon mixture into a 3-quart casserole.

Cover and bake in a 350° oven for 30 to 35 minutes or until heated through. Let stand for 5 minute and stir gently before serving. Makes 6 servings.

Nutrition information per serving: 388 cal., 16 g total fat (6 g sat. fat), 42 mg chol., 719 mg sodium, 44 g carbo., 18 g pro.

THAWING SPINACH

When you forget to thaw frozen spinach ahead of time, place the unwrapped frozen block of spinach in a colander and run hot water over it, breaking up the block with a fork. If you prefer, you can micro-thaw spinach by placing the unwrapped block in a bowl and micro-cooking it on 30% power (medium-low) for 2 to 4 minutes or until soft enough to break into chunks. Continue to cook the spinach on 30% power for 3 to 5 minutes or until thawed.

Provolone and Ham Melt

This sandwich satisfies both children and adults. Variations include cheese, ham, and fruit, or red sweet pepper and prosciutto.

8 slices thick-cut multigrain, whole wheat, poppy seed, white, or pumpernickel bread
   Margarine or butter, softened
4 teaspoons mayonnaise or salad dressing
4 ounces provolone and/or cheddar cheese, thinly sliced
½ of a 7-ounce jar roasted red sweet peppers, well drained
½ of a small pear or apple, thinly sliced, or 2 canned pineapple rings, well drained and patted dry
4 ounces thinly sliced cooked ham or prosciutto
2 tablespoons mango chutney
   Fresh fruit (such as sliced pears or apples, pineapple wedges, and/or grapes) (optional)

Spread one side of each bread slice with margarine or butter. Place 4 bread slices, buttered sides down, on a griddle. Spread mayonnaise or salad dressing on the slices on griddle. Top with provolone and/or cheddar cheese. Top 2 of the bread slices with roasted red peppers and the other 2 slices with sliced pear or apple or pineapple rings. Top all bread slices on griddle with ham or prosciutto.

Cut up large pieces of chutney; spread the unbuttered sides of the remaining 4 bread slices with chutney. Place, buttered sides up, on top of bread slices on griddle.

Cook sandwiches over medium heat about 8 minutes or until bread is toasted and cheese is melted, turning once. If desired, serve with additional fruit. Makes 4 servings.

Nutrition information per serving: 398 cal., 22 g total fat (10 g sat. fat), 53 mg chol., 970 mg sodium, 35 g carbo., 17 g pro.

Cheesy Ham and Linguine

Make this meal even easier by buying cut-up vegetables from your grocery store's salad bar.

6 ounces dried spinach and/or plain linguine	In a Dutch oven or large saucepan cook pasta and carrots in a large amount of boiling salted water for 7 minutes, stirring occasionally. Add broccoli florets. Return to boiling and cook for 3 to 5 minutes more or until pasta is tender but slightly firm and vegetables are crisp-tender; drain. Cover and keep warm.
2 medium carrots, cut into ½-inch pieces (1 cup)	
1 cup broccoli florets	
1 cup sliced fresh mushrooms	
2 tablespoons margarine or butter	Meanwhile, in a medium saucepan cook mushrooms in hot margarine or butter until tender. Stir in flour, parsley, and basil. Add milk all at once. Cook and stir until thickened and bubbly. Add ham and cheddar cheese, stirring until cheese is melted. Pour cheese mixture over pasta and vegetables; toss gently to coat. Makes 4 servings.
2 tablespoons all-purpose flour	
1 tablespoon snipped fresh parsley	
½ teaspoon dried basil, crushed	
1¼ cups milk	
6 ounces sliced cooked ham, cut into bite-size strips	
½ cup shredded cheddar cheese (2 ounces)	

Nutrition information per serving: 417 cal., 15 g total fat (6 g sat. fat), 33 mg chol., 711 mg sodium, 47 g carbo., 23 g pro.

Sausage, Broccoli, and Pasta Toss

No time to cook? Here's a quick-and-easy dish to serve in a pinch.

1 cup dried tricolor or plain tortellini (about ½ of a 7-ounce package)	In a Dutch oven or large saucepan cook tortellini in a large amount of boiling salted water for 10 minutes, stirring occasionally. Add broccoli and sausage. Return to boiling and cook about 5 minutes more or until pasta is tender but slightly firm and broccoli is crisp-tender; drain. Cover and keep warm.
3 cups broccoli florets	
8 ounces cooked smoked Polish sausage, halved lengthwise and thinly bias-sliced	
1 tablespoon margarine or butter	Meanwhile, in a medium saucepan melt margarine or butter. Stir in flour and caraway seeds. Add milk all at once. Cook and stir until thickened and bubbly. Add Swiss cheese and mustard, stirring until cheese is melted. Pour over the tortellini mixture; toss gently to coat. Makes 4 servings.
1 tablespoon all-purpose flour	
1 teaspoon caraway seeds	
1 cup milk	
1 cup shredded process Swiss cheese (4 ounces)	
1 tablespoon coarse-grain brown mustard	

Nutrition information per serving: 482 cal., 31 g total fat (12 g sat. fat), 70 mg chol., 925 mg sodium, 25 g carbo., 26 g pro.

Sausage and Bean Rigatoni

Reminiscent of a wonderful baked Italian casserole that comes bubbling from the oven, this dish cooks on the stovetop instead, so it's ready for the table in less than half the time.

8   ounces dried rigatoni pasta
1   15-ounce can white kidney (cannellini), Great Northern, or navy beans, rinsed and drained
1   14½-ounce can Italian-style stewed tomatoes
6   ounces light cooked smoked sausage or turkey sausage, sliced ½ inch thick
⅓   cup finely shredded or snipped fresh basil
¼   cup shaved or finely shredded Asiago cheese (1 ounce)

Cook pasta according to package directions, except omit any salt; drain. Cover and keep warm.

Meanwhile, in a large saucepan combine beans, undrained tomatoes, and sausage; heat through. Add bean mixture and basil to cooked pasta; toss gently to mix. Sprinkle each serving with Asiago cheese. Makes 4 servings.

Nutrition information per serving: 401 cal., 6 g total fat (1 g sat. fat), 32 mg chol., 964 mg sodium, 67 g carbo., 25 g pro.

Italian Pizza Sandwiches

Some like it hot! If you do, choose the hot sausage. For those with less adventurous palates, choose the mild or sweet sausage. You may want to grill some of each.

1   medium green sweet pepper, cut into thin strips
1   medium onion, thinly sliced
1   tablespoon margarine or butter
4   uncooked mild or hot Italian sausage links (12 to 16 ounces total)
½   cup pizza sauce
4   individual French-style rolls, split
2   tablespoons grated Parmesan cheese

Fold a 36×18-inch piece of heavy foil in half to make an 18-inch square. Place green pepper and onion in the center of the foil. Dot with margarine or butter.

Bring up two opposite edges of foil and seal with a double fold. Then fold remaining ends to completely enclose vegetables, leaving space for steam to build. Prick the sausage links in several places with a fork or the tip of a sharp knife.

In a covered grill arrange medium-hot coals around a drip pan. Test for medium heat above the pan. Place sausage links and vegetable packet on grill rack over drip pan. Cover and grill for 20 to 25 minutes or until sausage juices run clear and vegetables are tender.

Meanwhile, in a small saucepan heat pizza sauce. Toast cut sides of French rolls on grill.

To serve, halve the sausage links lengthwise, cutting to, but not through, the other side. Place sausage links in the toasted rolls. Top with the grilled vegetables and warm pizza sauce. Sprinkle with Parmesan cheese. Makes 4 servings.

Nutrition information per serving: 376 cal., 22 g total fat (7 g sat. fat), 51 mg chol., 1,067 mg sodium, 26 g carbo., 18 g pro.

Bow Ties with Sausage & Peppers

You will be amazed that so few ingredients generate so much flavor. To reduce the fat, use Italian-style ground turkey sausage.

8	ounces packaged dried large bow-tie pasta
12	ounces spicy Italian sausage links
2	medium red sweet peppers, cut into ¾-inch pieces
½	cup vegetable broth or beef broth
¼	teaspoon coarsely ground black pepper
¼	cup snipped Italian flat-leaf parsley

Cook pasta according to package directions. Drain; keep warm. Meanwhile, cut the sausage into 1-inch pieces. In a large skillet cook sausage and sweet peppers over medium-high heat until sausage is brown. Drain fat.

Stir the vegetable or beef broth and black pepper into sausage mixture. Bring to boiling; reduce heat. Simmer, uncovered, for 5 minutes. Remove from heat. Pour the sausage mixture over pasta; add parsley. Toss gently to coat. Makes 4 servings.

Nutrition information per serving: 397 cal., 18 g total fat (6 g sat. fat), 94 mg chol., 713 mg sodium, 38 g carbo., 24 g pro.

Greek-Style Pasta Skillet

Lamb, cinnamon, and feta cheese add a Greek twist to this macaroni casserole.

12	ounces ground lamb or lean ground beef
1	medium onion, chopped (½ cup)
1	14½-ounce can diced tomatoes
1	5½-ounce can tomato juice
½	cup water
½	teaspoon instant beef bouillon granules
½	teaspoon ground cinnamon
⅛	teaspoon garlic powder
1	cup packaged dried medium shell macaroni or elbow macaroni
1	cup loose-pack frozen cut green beans
½	cup crumbled feta cheese

In a large skillet cook ground meat and onion until meat is brown. Drain fat. Stir in the undrained tomatoes, tomato juice, water, bouillon granules, cinnamon, and garlic powder.

Bring to boiling. Stir the uncooked pasta and green beans into meat mixture. Return to boiling; reduce heat. Cover and simmer about 15 minutes or until pasta and green beans are tender. Sprinkle with feta cheese. Makes 4 servings.

Nutrition information per serving: 362 cal., 16 g total fat (7 g sat. fat), 70 mg chol., 647 mg sodium, 33 g carbo., 22 g pro.

Greek-Style Pasta Skillet

Grecian Kabobs

Take your pick—lamb or pork. Both meats are equally delicious when speared on these herb-scented kabobs.

1 pound lean boneless lamb or pork
2 tablespoons olive oil or cooking oil
2 tablespoons lemon juice
1 tablespoon snipped fresh chives or
    1 teaspoon dried chives
1 tablespoon snipped fresh oregano or
    1 teaspoon dried oregano, crushed
1 tablespoon water
1 clove garlic, minced
1 medium red onion, cut into wedges
1 medium green sweet pepper, cut
    into 1-inch squares
2 cups fresh mushrooms
   Hot cooked couscous (optional)*
   Fresh oregano sprigs (optional)

Trim fat from meat. Cut meat into 1-inch cubes. Place meat in a plastic bag and set the bag into a shallow dish. For marinade, in a small bowl combine olive or cooking oil, lemon juice, chives, snipped fresh or dried oregano, water, and garlic. Pour over meat; seal bag. Marinate in the refrigerator for 4 to 24 hours, turning the bag occasionally.

Meanwhile, cook onion wedges in a small amount of boiling water for 3 minutes. Drain and cool slightly.

Drain meat, reserving marinade. On 8 short or 4 long metal skewers, alternately thread meat cubes, onion, green pepper, and mushrooms, leaving about ¼ inch space between pieces.

Grill the kabobs on an uncovered grill directly over medium coals for 12 to 14 minutes or until meat is slightly pink in center, turning and brushing once with marinade halfway through grilling.

(Or, in a covered grill arrange medium-hot coals around a drip pan. Test for medium heat above pan. Place kabobs on grill rack over drip pan. Cover and grill for 16 to 18 minutes, brushing once with marinade halfway through grilling)

If desired, serve over hot cooked couscous and garnish with fresh oregano sprigs. Makes 4 servings.

*Note: If you like, stir 1 small tomato, chopped, and 2 green onions, thinly sliced, into the boiling water with the couscous.

Nutrition information per serving: 177 cal., 9 g total fat (3 g sat. fat), 57 mg chol., 46 mg sodium, 5 g carbo., 19 g pro.

Poultry

Contents

CHICKEN WITH GOLDEN
RAISINS AND PINE NUTS
(recipe, page 150)

Ruby-Glazed Chicken Breasts

These chicken breasts have such a rich flavor from the currant and apple glaze that you would never guess they are low in fat—only 3 grams per serving.

⅓ cup apple juice
3   tablespoons currant jelly
1   teaspoon cornstarch
¼   teaspoon salt
⅛   teaspoon dried marjoram, crushed
3   whole small chicken breasts
     (about 2¼ pounds total),
     halved lengthwise

For sauce, in a small saucepan combine apple juice, currant jelly, cornstarch, and salt. Cook and stir over medium heat until thickened and bubbly. Cook and stir for 2 minutes more. Remove from heat. Stir in the marjoram. Set aside.

If desired, skin chicken. Rinse chicken; pat dry with paper towels.

Grill chicken, bone side up, on an uncovered grill directly over medium coals for 35 to 45 minutes or until chicken is tender and no longer pink, turning and brushing once with sauce.

(Or, in a covered grill arrange medium-hot coals around a drip pan. Test for medium heat above the pan. Place chicken, bone side down, on grill rack over drip pan. Cover and grill for 50 to 60 minutes. Brush occasionally with sauce during the last 20 minutes of grilling.)

Brush the grilled chicken with any remaining sauce before serving. Makes 6 servings.

Nutrition information per serving: 167 cal., 3 g total fat (1 g sat. fat), 69 mg chol., 150 mg sodium, 9 g carbo., 25 g pro.

Keys-Style Citrus Chicken

The tropical-island-inspired cooking of the Florida Keys draws on the best of both worlds. Here, it combines fresh Florida citrus with the Caribbean penchant for fiery peppers. Soak up the delicious juice with hot cooked rice.

4 medium skinless, boneless
      chicken breast halves (about
      1 pound total)
2 or 3 cloves garlic, peeled and
      thinly sliced
1 tablespoon butter or margarine
1 teaspoon finely shredded lime peel
2 tablespoons lime juice
¼ teaspoon ground ginger
⅛ teaspoon crushed red pepper
1 orange
    Hot cooked rice (optional)
    Lime wedges (optional)

Rinse chicken; pat dry with paper towels. In a large skillet cook chicken and garlic in butter or margarine over medium heat for 8 to 10 minutes or until chicken is tender and no longer pink, turning chicken once and stirring garlic occasionally.

Meanwhile, in a small bowl combine lime peel, lime juice, ginger, and red pepper; set aside. Peel orange. Reserving juice, cut orange in half lengthwise, then cut crosswise into slices. Add any reserved orange juice and the lime juice mixture to skillet.

Place the orange slices on top of chicken. Cover and cook for 1 to 2 minutes more or until heated through.

To serve, spoon any reserved drippings over chicken. If desired, serve with cooked rice and garnish with lime wedges. Makes 4 servings.

Nutrition information per serving: 167 cal., 6 g total fat (3 g sat. fat), 67 mg chol., 84 mg sodium, 5 g carbo., 22 g pro.

Chicken with Peas and Potatoes

Save clean-up time with this chicken meal-in-a-skillet featuring tiny potatoes and peas in a rosemary-scented sauce.

1	2½- to 3 pound cut up broiler fryer chicken or 2 pounds chicken thighs
1	pound small new potatoes, quartered
2	tablespoons margarine or butter
¾	cup chicken broth
1	teaspoon dried rosemary, crushed
¼	teaspoon pepper
4	green onions, thinly sliced
1	10-ounce package frozen peas
¼	cup snipped parsley
1	8-ounce carton dairy sour cream
2	tablespoons all-purpose flour

Skin chicken, if desired. Rinse and pat dry with paper towels. Scrub the potatoes.

In a 12-inch skillet cook chicken in hot margarine or butter over medium heat about 15 minutes or until chicken is browned, turning to brown evenly. Add potatoes, broth, rosemary, and pepper. Bring to boiling; reduce heat. Cover and simmer for 30 minutes.

Add green onion, peas, and ¼ cup parsley to skillet. Cover and simmer about 10 minutes more or until the chicken and potatoes are tender and chicken is no longer pink. Using a slotted spoon, transfer chicken and vegetables to a platter; keep warm.

Remove skillet from heat. Stir together sour cream and flour; stir into broth in skillet. Cook and stir until thickened and bubbly; cook and stir for 1 minute more. Spoon sauce over chicken and vegetables. Makes 6 servings.

Nutrition information per serving: 491 cal., 27 g total fat (10 g sat. fat), 106 mg chol., 286 mg sodium, 28 g carbo., 34 g pro.

Honeyed Chicken

For a zippy appetizer, use this glaze for 10 to 12 chicken wings (cut the wings at the joints and discard tips).

8	chicken drumsticks and/or thighs (about 2 pounds total)
¼	cup finely chopped green onions
¼	cup honey
¼	teaspoon garlic powder
	Dash ground red pepper

Arrange washed chicken in a 15×10×1-inch baking pan so the pieces don't touch. Bake in a 400° oven for 30 minutes.

Meanwhile, combine the chopped green onions, honey, garlic powder, and ground red pepper. Brush over chicken. Bake for 15 to 20 minutes more or until chicken is tender and no longer pink. Makes 4 servings.

Nutrition information per serving: 327 cal., 15 g total fat (4 g sat. fat), 103 mg chol., 98 mg sodium, 17 g carbo., 29 g pro.

Chicken with Golden Raisins and Pine Nuts

Italians frequently use pine nuts, also called pignoli, in pasta sauces, pesto, rice dishes, and cookies. Refrigerate pine nuts in an airtight container up to two months or freeze them up to six months to prevent them from turning rancid.

1	medium onion, cut into thin slivers
2	cloves garlic, minced
1	tablespoon olive oil
1½	pounds meaty chicken pieces (breast halves, thighs, and drumsticks), skinned
½	cup white wine vinegar
¼	teaspoon salt
⅛	teaspoon pepper
1	cup reduced-sodium chicken broth
½	cup golden raisins
2	teaspoons snipped fresh thyme or ½ teaspoon dried thyme, crushed
1	teaspoon snipped fresh rosemary or ¼ teaspoon dried rosemary, crushed
1	tablespoon cold water
1½	teaspoons cornstarch
2	tablespoons pine nuts, toasted

In a large nonstick skillet cook onion and garlic in hot oil over medium heat for 1 minute. Add chicken pieces and cook for 10 to 15 minutes or until brown, turning to brown evenly. Drain well.

Add the vinegar, salt, and pepper to chicken in skillet. Bring to boiling. Cook, uncovered, over high heat about 5 minutes or until vinegar is nearly evaporated, turning chicken once. Carefully add broth, raisins, thyme, and rosemary. Bring to boiling; reduce heat. Cover and simmer for 30 to 35 minutes or until chicken is no longer pink (170° for breasts; 180° for thighs and drumsticks).

To serve, transfer chicken to a serving platter. For sauce, combine cold water and cornstarch; stir into broth mixture in skillet. Cook and stir until thickened and bubbly. Cook and stir for 2 minutes more. Spoon some of the sauce over chicken; pass the remaining sauce. Sprinkle the chicken with pine nuts. Makes 4 servings.

Nutrition information per serving: 269 cal., 10 g total fat (2 g sat. fat), 71 mg chol., 334 mg sodium, 22 g carbo., 24 g pro.

Quick Chicken Mole

Declare a Mexican theme night by serving this dish with warm flour tortillas, tomato salsa seasoned with snipped fresh cilantro, and sliced oranges layered with coconut for dessert.

6   medium chicken breast halves
        (about 3 pounds total)
2   tablespoons olive oil or cooking oil
1   small onion, chopped
1½ teaspoons chili powder
1   teaspoon sesame seeds
1   clove garlic, minced
¼   teaspoon salt
¼   teaspoon ground cumin
¼   teaspoon ground cinnamon
1   small tomato, chopped
1   tomatillo, peeled and cut into wedges,
        or 1 small tomato, chopped
½   cup chicken broth
½   cup tomato sauce
2   tablespoons raisins
2   teaspoons unsweetened cocoa
        powder
     Several dashes bottled hot pepper
        sauce
     Hot cooked rice
     Pumpkin seeds or slivered almonds,
        toasted (optional)

Skin chicken. In a large skillet cook chicken in hot oil over medium heat about 10 minutes or until light brown, turning to brown evenly. Add onion, chili powder, sesame seeds, garlic, salt, cumin, and cinnamon. Cook and stir for 30 seconds.

Stir in tomato, tomatillo, chicken broth, tomato sauce, raisins, cocoa powder, and hot pepper sauce. Bring to boiling; reduce heat. Simmer, uncovered, about 15 minutes or until chicken is no longer pink (170°). Using a slotted spoon, remove chicken pieces from skillet. Simmer the tomato mixture, uncovered, for 4 to 5 minutes or to desired consistency.

To serve, spoon tomato mixture over chicken and rice. If desired, sprinkle with pumpkin seeds or almonds. Makes 6 servings.

Nutrition information per serving: 367 cal., 9 g total fat (2 g sat. fat), 76 mg chol., 543 mg sodium, 37 g carbo., 33 g pro.

GARLIC HINTS

Working with garlic is easy if you know how to handle it. Loosen the garlic skin quickly by crushing each clove with the flat side of a chef's knife. The skin will slip off. To mince the peeled garlic, place it in a garlic press or use a sharp knife to cut it into tiny pieces. If you prefer, use bottled minced garlic (usually found in your supermarket's produce section) instead of the cloves.

Chicken with Peach Salsa

If fresh peaches or papayas aren't in season, thaw and chop 1 cup frozen unsweetened peach slices.

2   tablespoons lime juice
4   teaspoons teriyaki sauce or soy sauce
4   medium skinless, boneless chicken
      breast halves (about 1 pound
      total)
1   medium peach, peeled, pitted,
      and chopped, or ½ of a medium
      papaya, peeled, seeded, and
      chopped (about 1 cup)
1   small tomato, chopped (½ cup)
2   tablespoons sliced green onion
1   tablespoon lime juice
1   teaspoon grated fresh ginger or
      ¼ teaspoon ground ginger
¼   teaspoon bottled minced garlic or
      ⅛ teaspoon garlic powder
    Hot cooked rice (optional)
    Fresh thyme sprigs (optional)

For marinade, in a small bowl stir together the 2 tablespoons lime juice and the teriyaki sauce or soy sauce. Brush both sides of chicken with marinade. Cover and marinate at room temperature for 30 minutes or in the refrigerator up to 2 hours.

For salsa, in a medium bowl stir together peach or papaya, tomato, green onion, the 1 tablespoon lime juice, the ginger, and garlic or garlic powder. Cover and let stand at room temperature for 30 minutes or chill up to 2 hours.

Place the chicken on the unheated rack of a broiler pan. Broil 4 to 5 inches from the heat for 12 to 15 minutes or until no longer pink (170°), turning once.

If desired, serve chicken and salsa over hot cooked rice and garnish with thyme. Makes 4 servings.

Nutrition information per serving: 146 cal., 3 g total fat (1 g sat. fat), 59 mg chol., 287 mg sodium, 6 g carbo., 22 g pro.

Southwest Chicken Breasts

To transform this dish into a salad, slice the chicken breasts and arrange them on plates lined with shredded lettuce. Top with the avocado mixture for a chunky dressing and add some shredded Monterey Jack cheese.

6 medium skinless, boneless chicken breast halves (about 1½ pounds total)
¼ cup dry white wine
2 tablespoons olive oil or cooking oil
2 teaspoons snipped fresh tarragon or ¼ teaspoon dried tarragon, crushed
¼ teaspoon salt
2 avocados, seeded, peeled, and chopped
1 tomato, chopped
2 green onions, finely chopped
2 tablespoons finely chopped, seeded green chile peppers (such as jalapeño, serrano, or Anaheim)
1 tablespoon snipped cilantro
1 tablespoon honey
1 tablespoon lemon juice
1 clove garlic, minced
Lettuce leaves (optional)

Rinse chicken; pat dry with paper towels. Place chicken in a plastic bag and set the bag into a shallow dish. For marinade, in a small bowl combine the white wine, oil, tarragon, and salt. Pour over chicken; seal bag. Marinate in the refrigerator for 2 to 24 hours, turning bag occasionally.

Meanwhile, combine avocados, tomato, green onions, chile peppers, cilantro, honey, lemon juice, and garlic. Toss gently to mix. Cover and chill up to 2 hours.

Drain chicken, reserving marinade. Grill chicken on an uncovered grill directly over medium coals for 12 to 15 minutes or until tender and no longer pink, turning and brushing once with marinade halfway through grilling.

(Or, in a covered grill arrange medium-hot coals around a drip pan. Test for medium heat above the pan. Place chicken on grill rack over drip pan. Cover and grill for 15 to 18 minutes. Brush occasionally with marinade up to the last 5 minutes of grilling.)

Serve the grilled chicken with avocado mixture and, if desired, lettuce leaves. Makes 6 servings.

Nutrition information per serving: 239 cal., 16 g total fat (1 g sat. fat), 50 mg chol., 130 mg sodium, 5 g carbo., 20 g pro.

Pollo Relleno

Expect oohs and aahs when you serve these chicken rolls; each has a cheese-stuffed chile pepper inside.

6 medium skinless, boneless chicken breast halves (about 1½ pounds total)

⅓ cup yellow cornmeal

½ of a 1¼-ounce package (2 tablespoons) taco seasoning mix

1 egg

1 4-ounce can whole green chile peppers, rinsed, seeded, and cut in half lengthwise (6 pieces total)

2 ounces Monterey Jack cheese, cut into six 2×½-inch sticks

2 tablespoons snipped fresh cilantro or parsley

¼ teaspoon black pepper

¼ teaspoon crushed red pepper

1 8-ounce jar taco sauce or salsa

½ cup shredded Monterey Jack or cheddar cheese (optional)

Fresh cilantro sprigs (optional)

Place each chicken piece between two pieces of plastic wrap. Pound lightly with the flat side of a meat mallet until about ⅛ inch thick. Remove plastic wrap.

In a shallow bowl combine cornmeal and taco seasoning mix. Place egg in another shallow bowl; beat lightly.

For each chicken roll, place a chile pepper half on a chicken piece near an edge. Place a cheese stick on top of chile pepper. Sprinkle with some of the snipped cilantro or parsley, black pepper, and red pepper. Fold in sides; starting from edge with cheese, roll up chicken.

Dip chicken rolls into egg and roll in cornmeal mixture to coat. Place rolls, seam sides down, in a shallow baking pan. Bake in a 375° oven for 25 to 30 minutes or until chicken is no longer pink.

Heat taco sauce or salsa. If desired, sprinkle chicken rolls with shredded cheese. Serve with taco sauce or salsa. If desired, garnish with cilantro sprigs. Makes 6 servings.

Nutrition information per serving: 235 cal., 10 g total fat (3 g sat. fat), 103 mg chol., 769 mg sodium, 13 g carbo., 28 g pro.

Chicken and Mushrooms

Whether to slice the mushrooms or not depends on their size. If they're larger than 1½ inches in diameter, slice them. Otherwise leave them whole.

4 chicken thighs
4 chicken drumsticks
¼ cup all-purpose flour
¼ teaspoon salt
¼ teaspoon pepper
¼ teaspoon paprika
2 tablespoons cooking oil
2 cups whole or sliced fresh
   mushrooms
1 medium red sweet pepper, cut into
   1-inch strips
1 medium onion, sliced
3 cloves garlic, minced
½ cup dry red wine or beef broth
2 tablespoons balsamic vinegar
1 14½-ounce can diced tomatoes
2 teaspoons dried Italian seasoning,
   crushed
¼ cup half-and-half or light cream
1 tablespoon all-purpose flour
   Hot cooked pasta (optional)
¼ cup snipped fresh Italian flat-leaf
   parsley

Skin chicken. In a large self-sealing plastic bag combine the ¼ cup flour, the salt, pepper, and paprika. Add 2 or 3 pieces of chicken to the bag at a time. Seal and shake to coat well.

In a very large skillet heat the 2 tablespoons oil over medium heat. Cook the chicken in hot oil for 10 to 15 minutes or until brown, turning to brown evenly. Remove chicken from skillet, reserving drippings in skillet.

Add mushrooms, sweet pepper, onion, and garlic to the reserved drippings in skillet. Cook and stir for 2 minutes. Add red wine or beef broth and balsamic vinegar. Cook and stir for 5 minutes more. Stir in undrained tomatoes and Italian seasoning.

Bring to boiling, scraping up any browned bits on bottom of skillet. Return chicken to skillet; reduce heat. Cover and simmer about 20 minutes or until chicken is no longer pink (180°). Remove chicken; cover and keep warm.

Stir together half-and-half or light cream and the 1 tablespoon flour; stir into tomato mixture. Cook and stir until slightly thickened and bubbly. Cook and stir for 1 minute more. Return chicken to skillet; heat through. If desired, serve over hot cooked pasta. Sprinkle with parsley. Makes 4 to 6 servings.

Nutrition information per serving: 323 cal., 13 g total fat (3 g sat. fat), 89 mg chol., 400 mg sodium, 21 g carbo., 25 g pro.

Chicken and Prosciutto Roll-Ups

This pretty dish takes the Italian technique braciola—wrapping thin slices of meat around savories such as Italian ham, cheese, artichokes, spinach, and herbs—and applies it to chicken. Serve these attractive spirals with spinach fettuccine.

¼ cup dry white wine
2 teaspoons snipped fresh thyme or
   ½ teaspoon dried thyme, crushed
4 medium skinless, boneless chicken
   breast halves (about 1 pound
   total)
4 thin slices prosciutto (about
   1 ounce total), trimmed of fat
2 ounces fontina cheese, thinly sliced
½ of a 7-ounce jar roasted red sweet
   peppers, cut into thin strips
   (about ½ cup)
   Fresh thyme sprigs (optional)

For sauce, in a small bowl combine wine and the snipped fresh or dried thyme. Set aside.

Place each chicken piece between two pieces of plastic wrap. Pound lightly with the flat side of a meat mallet until about ⅛ inch thick. Remove plastic wrap.

For each chicken roll, place a slice of prosciutto and one-fourth of the cheese on a chicken piece near an edge. Arrange one-fourth of the roasted pepper strips on top of cheese. Fold in the sides; starting from edge with pepper strips, roll up chicken. Secure with wooden toothpicks. (If desired, wrap each chicken roll in plastic wrap and chill up to 4 hours.)

Place chicken rolls on the rack of an uncovered grill directly over medium coals. Grill for 15 to 17 minutes or until chicken is no longer pink, turning to cook evenly and brushing twice with sauce. Remove the toothpicks. If desired, garnish chicken rolls with fresh thyme sprigs. Makes 4 servings.

Nutrition information per serving: 214 cal., 9 g total fat (4 g sat. fat), 76 mg chol., 294 mg sodium, 2 g carbo., 27 g pro.

Fruit-Stuffed Roasted Chicken

While the bird roasts to perfection, tuck some rice pudding in the oven to bake alongside.

1 4½- to 5-pound whole roasting chicken
¼ cup margarine or butter, melted
¼ cup dry sherry
4½ teaspoons snipped fresh thyme or 1½ teaspoons dried thyme, crushed
2 teaspoons finely shredded orange peel
2 medium apples, cored and chopped (2 cups)
1 medium onion, chopped (½ cup)
½ cup chopped celery
2 cups French bread cut into ¾-inch cubes
10 pitted dried plums (prunes) or dried apricots, cut up
1 cup seedless green grapes, halved
2 tablespoons orange juice

Rinse chicken; pat dry with paper towels. Sprinkle body cavity with salt and pepper. In a small bowl combine 2 tablespoons of the melted margarine or butter, 2 tablespoons of the sherry, 1 tablespoon of the fresh thyme or 1 teaspoon of the dried thyme, and 1 teaspoon of the orange peel. Brush chicken with sherry mixture.

For stuffing, in a medium skillet cook apples, onion, and celery in the remaining melted margarine or butter about 5 minutes or until tender. In a large bowl combine apple mixture, French bread, dried plums or apricots, grapes, orange juice, remaining sherry, remaining fresh or dried thyme, and remaining orange peel. (Stuffing will become more moist while cooking.)

Spoon some of the stuffing loosely into neck cavity of chicken. Pull neck skin to back; fasten with a small skewer. Lightly spoon the remaining stuffing into body cavity. Tuck drumsticks under band of skin that crosses tail. If there is no band, tie drumsticks to tail. Twist wing tips under chicken. Place chicken, breast side up, on a rack in a shallow roasting pan. Insert an oven-going meat thermometer into center of an inside thigh muscle, not touching bone.

Roast in a 375° oven for 1¼ hours. Cut band of skin or string between drumsticks so thighs will cook evenly. Roast for 30 minutes to 1 hour more or until drumsticks move easily in their sockets and thermometer registers 180°. (Center of stuffing should reach 165°.)

Remove from oven. Cover the chicken with foil; let stand for 10 to 15 minutes before carving. Makes 10 servings.

Nutrition information per serving: 393 cal., 18 g total fat (5 g sat. fat), 93 mg chol., 250 mg sodium, 22 g carbo., 33 g pro.

Skewered Chicken with Papaya Chutney

To round out this meal, accompany chicken kabobs with steamed rice spiked with dried crushed red pepper.

Papaya Chutney
1 medium onion, cut into 8 wedges
1 tablespoon curry powder
2 tablespoons olive oil or cooking oil
2 tablespoons lemon juice
1 tablespoon water
½ teaspoon salt
¼ teaspoon pepper
1 pound skinless, boneless chicken breast halves or thighs
1 red or green sweet pepper, cut into 1-inch pieces
12 fresh or canned pineapple chunks

Prepare Papaya Chutney. In a small saucepan cook onion in a small amount of boiling water for 4 minutes; drain. Set aside.

Meanwhile, in a small skillet cook and stir curry powder in hot oil for 30 seconds. Remove from heat. Stir in lemon juice, water, salt, and pepper. Set aside.

Cut chicken into 1-inch pieces. Alternately thread chicken, red or green sweet pepper, pineapple, and onion onto 4 long metal skewers. Stir curry mixture; brush over kabobs.

Place kabobs on the rack of an uncovered grill directly over medium coals. Grill for 12 to 14 minutes or until chicken is no longer pink, turning occasionally to brown evenly. (Or place on the unheated rack of a broiler pan. Broil 4 to 5 inches from the heat for 10 to 12 minutes, turning occasionally to brown evenly.) Serve the kabobs with chutney. Makes 4 servings.

Papaya Chutney: In a medium saucepan combine 1 cup chopped, peeled apple; 1 cup chopped, peeled *papaya*; ¼ cup packed *brown sugar*; 2 tablespoons *raisins*; 2 tablespoons chopped *green sweet pepper*; 2 tablespoons *vinegar*; 2 tablespoons *water*; 2 teaspoons *lemon juice*; and dash *salt*. Bring to boiling; reduce heat. Simmer, uncovered, about 15 minutes or until fruit is tender and chutney is desired consistency, stirring occasionally.

Nutrition information per serving: 337 cal., 11 g total fat (2 g sat. fat), 59 mg chol., 384 mg sodium, 40 g carbo., 23 g pro.

Texas-Style Barbecued Chicken Legs

Cut lengthwise strips of assorted sweet peppers and grill to perfection alongside the chicken.

1	medium onion, finely chopped (½-cup)
2	cloves garlic, minced
1	teaspoon chili powder
¼	teaspoon ground sage
1	tablespoon margarine or butter
½	cup catsup
2	tablespoons water
2	tablespoons vinegar
1	tablespoon sugar
1	tablespoon lemon juice
1	tablespoon Worcestershire sauce
½	teaspoon salt
½	teaspoon bottled hot pepper sauce
¼	teaspoon cracked black pepper
6	chicken legs (thigh-drumstick pieces) (3 to 3½ pounds total)

For sauce, in a small saucepan cook onion, garlic, chili powder, and sage in margarine or butter until onion is tender. Stir in catsup, water, vinegar, sugar, lemon juice, Worcestershire sauce, salt, hot pepper sauce, and black pepper. Bring to boiling; reduce heat. Simmer, uncovered, for 5 minutes, stirring occasionally.

Meanwhile, rinse chicken; pat dry with paper towels. Grill chicken, skin side down, on an uncovered grill directly over medium coals for 35 to 40 minutes or until chicken is tender and no longer pink, turning once. (Or, place chicken on the unheated rack of a broiler pan. Broil 5 to 6 inches from the heat for 28 to 32 minutes, turning once.) Brush with sauce during the last 10 minutes of grilling or broiling.

Heat the remaining sauce until bubbly. Pass the sauce with chicken. Makes 6 servings.

Nutrition information per serving: 276 cal., 15 g total fat (4 g sat. fat), 86 mg chol., 596 mg sodium, 11 g carbo., 25 g pro.

TEST THE TEMPERATURE

Before you grill, check the temperature of the coals. Hold your hand, palm side down, in the location you plan to place the food. Count "one thousand one, one thousand two," etc., for as long as you can hold your hand there. Two seconds means the coals are hot, three is medium-hot, four is medium, five is medium-slow, and six is slow.

Minnesota Apple- and Wild Rice-Stuffed Chicken

Team up this bird with a chicory and red onion salad dressed with a blue cheese vinaigrette.

1 6-ounce package long grain and wild rice mix
8 ounces sliced fresh mushrooms (3 cups)
2 medium cooking apples (such as Granny Smith or Jonathan), cored and chopped
1 cup shredded carrot
½ cup thinly sliced green onions
½ teaspoon pepper
1 5- to 6-pound whole roasting chicken
2 to 3 tablespoons apple jelly, melted
Apple wedges (optional)

For stuffing, cook rice according to package directions, except add mushrooms, apples, shredded carrot, green onions, and pepper to rice before cooking.

Meanwhile, rinse chicken; pat dry with paper towels. Spoon some of the stuffing loosely into the neck cavity. Pull neck skin to back; fasten with a small skewer. Lightly spoon the remaining stuffing into the body cavity. Tuck the drumsticks under the band of skin that crosses the tail. If there is no band, tie the drumsticks to tail. Twist the wing tips under the chicken.

Place stuffed chicken, breast side up, on a rack in a shallow roasting pan. Insert meat thermometer into the center of an inside thigh muscle. The bulb should not touch the bone.

Roast, uncovered, in a 325° oven for 1¾ to 2½ hours or until meat thermometer registers 180°. At this time, chicken is no longer pink and the drumsticks move easily in their sockets. When the bird is two-thirds done, cut the band of skin or string between drumsticks so thighs will cook evenly. Brush chicken with melted jelly once or twice during the last 10 minutes of roasting.

Remove the chicken from oven; cover with foil. Let stand for 10 to 20 minutes before carving. Transfer chicken to a serving platter. Spoon some of the stuffing around the chicken. If desired, garnish with apple wedges. Pass the remaining stuffing. Makes 10 servings.

Nutrition information per serving: 332 cal., 13 g total fat (4 g sat. fat), 93 mg chol., 365 mg sodium, 19 g carbo., 34 g pro.

Curried Chicken Thighs

You also can use skinless, boneless chicken thighs in this Indian-style recipe. Just reduce the cooking time to 10 minutes after adding the chicken broth.

8   chicken thighs (about 2½ pounds
       total)
2   tablespoons cooking oil
1   cup sliced fresh mushrooms
1   medium onion, chopped (½ cup)
1   clove garlic, minced
3   to 4 teaspoons curry powder
¼   teaspoon salt
¼   teaspoon ground cinnamon
¾   cup chicken broth
1   medium apple, cored and
       chopped
1   cup half-and-half, light cream,
       or milk
2   tablespoons all-purpose flour
3   cups hot cooked rice
     Assorted condiments: raisins,
       chopped hard-cooked egg, pea-
       nuts, chopped tomato, chopped
       green sweet pepper, toasted coco-
       nut, chutney,
       cut-up fruits (optional)

Skin chicken. Rinse chicken; pat dry with paper towels. In a 10-inch skillet cook chicken in hot oil over medium heat about 10 minutes or until lightly browned, turning to brown evenly. Remove chicken. If necessary, add 1 tablespoon additional cooking oil to skillet.

Add mushrooms, onion, and garlic to skillet; cook until vegetables are tender. Add curry powder, salt, and cinnamon; cook and stir for 1 minute. Add chicken broth and apple. Return chicken to skillet. Bring to boiling; reduce heat. Cover and simmer about 15 minutes or until chicken is tender and no longer pink.

Transfer chicken to platter; keep warm. Stir the half-and-half, light cream, or milk into the flour. Stir into pan juices. Cook and stir until thickened and bubbly. Cook and stir for 1 minute more. Spoon some sauce over chicken. Pass remaining sauce. Serve with rice and, if desired, pass condiments. Makes 4 servings.

Nutrition information per serving: 695 cal., 32 g total fat (10 g sat. fat), 158 mg chol., 829 mg sodium, 45 g carbo., 54 g pro.

Pacific Rim Stir-Fry

Adjust the hotness of this stir-fry by reducing or increasing the amount of chile oil used.

3 ounces rice sticks (also called rice noodles) or packaged dried vermicelli, broken

12 ounces skinless, boneless chicken thighs or breast halves

½ cup chicken broth

2 tablespoons snipped fresh basil or 2 teaspoons dried basil, crushed

2 tablespoons soy sauce

2 teaspoons cornstarch

1 teaspoon chile oil or ½ teaspoon crushed red pepper

½ teaspoon ground turmeric

1 tablespoon cooking oil

2 medium carrots, cut into julienne strips

2 cups broccoli florets

1 red or green sweet pepper, cut into lengthwise strips

¼ cup cashew halves or peanuts

In a saucepan cook rice sticks in boiling water for 3 minutes. (Or, cook vermicelli according to package directions.) Drain; keep warm.

Meanwhile, rinse chicken; pat dry with paper towels. Cut chicken thighs or breasts into thin, bite-size strips; set aside.

For sauce, in a small bowl combine chicken broth, basil, soy sauce, cornstarch, chile oil or crushed red pepper, and turmeric; set aside.

Add cooking oil to a wok or 12-inch skillet. Preheat over medium-high heat (add more oil if necessary during cooking). Stir-fry carrot strips in hot oil for 1 minute. Add broccoli; stir-fry for 2 minutes. Add sweet pepper strips; stir-fry for 1½ to 3 minutes more or until crisp-tender. Remove from wok. Add the chicken to wok; stir-fry for 2 to 3 minutes or until tender and no longer pink. Push from center of wok.

Stir sauce; add to center of wok. Cook and stir until thickened and bubbly. Return cooked vegetables to wok. Stir all ingredients together to coat. Cook and stir about 2 minutes more or until heated through. Serve immediately over hot rice sticks or vermicelli. Top with cashews or peanuts. Makes 4 servings.

Nutrition information per serving: 309 cal., 13 g total fat (3 g sat. fat), 41 mg chol., 748 mg sodium, 32 g carbo., 17 g pro.

Chicken and Apple Stir-Fry

This sweet-spiced dish includes an array of colorful peppers, plus dried mushrooms, crunchy almonds, and crisp, tart apple slices.

6 dried mushrooms (such as shiitake or wood ear mushrooms)
12 ounces skinless, boneless chicken breast halves or turkey breast tenderloin steaks
¾ cup cold water
3 tablespoons frozen orange, apple, or pineapple juice concentrate, thawed
2 tablespoons soy sauce
2 teaspoons cornstarch
¼ teaspoon ground ginger
¼ teaspoon ground cinnamon
⅛ to ¼ teaspoon ground red pepper
¼ cup sliced or slivered almonds
1 tablespoon cooking oil
2 medium green, red, orange, and/or yellow sweet peppers, cut into thin strips
2 medium apples, thinly sliced
2 cups hot cooked brown rice

In a small bowl cover mushrooms with warm water. Let soak for 30 minutes. Rinse and squeeze the mushrooms to drain thoroughly. Discard stems. Thinly slice mushrooms. Set aside.

Meanwhile, rinse chicken or turkey; pat dry with paper towels. Cut into 1-inch pieces. Set aside.

For sauce, in a small mixing bowl stir together the cold water, juice concentrate, soy sauce, cornstarch, ginger, cinnamon, and ground red pepper. Set aside.

Preheat a wok or large skillet over medium-high heat. Add almonds; stir-fry for 2 to 3 minutes or until golden. Remove almonds from wok. Let wok cool slightly.

Add cooking oil to wok. Preheat over medium-high heat (add more oil if necessary during cooking). Stir-fry mushrooms, sweet peppers, and apples in hot oil for 1 to 2 minutes or until peppers and apples are crisp-tender. Remove apple mixture from wok.

Add chicken to wok. Stir-fry for 3 to 4 minutes or until tender and no longer pink. Push chicken from center of wok. Stir sauce; add to center of wok. Cook and stir until thickened and bubbly. Return apple mixture to wok. Stir all ingredients together to coat. Cook and stir for 1 to 2 minutes more or until heated through.

Stir in toasted almonds. Serve immediately over hot cooked brown rice. Makes 4 servings.

Nutrition information per serving: 370 cal., 11 g total fat (2 g sat. fat), 45 mg chol., 563 mg sodium, 48 g carbo., 22 g pro.

Chicken, Bean, and Tomato Stir-Fry

If you think good taste is hard to measure, consider cooking with Chinese long beans. A star of Asian stir-fries, these dark green, pencil-thin legumes average 1½ feet of crunchy flavor.

6 ounces dried wide rice noodles or egg noodles

12 ounces skinless, boneless chicken breast halves

1 teaspoon Cajun seasoning or other spicy seasoning blend

4 teaspoons cooking oil

2 cloves garlic, minced

1 pound whole Chinese long beans or green beans, cut into 3-inch pieces

¼ cup water

2 medium tomatoes, cut into thin wedges

2 tablespoons raspberry vinegar

Cook rice noodles in boiling, lightly salted water for 3 to 5 minutes or until tender. (Or cook egg noodles according to package directions.) Drain; cover and keep warm. Meanwhile, cut chicken into thin bite-size strips. Combine chicken and Cajun or other seasoning blend; toss to coat. Set aside.

Add 2 teaspoons of the oil to a large skillet. Preheat over medium-high heat. Stir-fry garlic in hot oil for 15 seconds. Add beans. Stir-fry for 2 minutes. Add water; reduce heat to low. Cover and simmer for 6 to 8 minutes or until beans are crisp-tender. Remove from skillet.

Add the remaining oil to skillet. Add chicken. Stir-fry for 2 to 3 minutes or until no longer pink. Return cooked beans to skillet. Add tomatoes and vinegar. Stir all ingredients together to coat. Cook and stir for 1 to 2 minutes more or until heated through. Serve immediately over hot cooked noodles. Makes 4 servings.

Nutrition information per serving: 361 cal., 5 g total fat (1 g sat. fat), 45 mg chol., 334 mg sodium, 54 g carbo., 25 g pro.

STIR-FRYING GARLIC

To evenly distribute garlic flavor to stir-fry ingredients, season the oil first. Add the garlic to the hot oil, moving it constantly so it doesn't burn. After about 15 seconds, begin adding the other stir-fry ingredients to the oil.

Polynesian Chicken Kabobs

Fresh pineapple adds a special flavor to these colorful kabobs. To save time and effort, look for peeled, fresh pineapple in the produce department of your supermarket.

1 pound skinless, boneless chicken
   breast halves or thighs
¼ cup soy sauce
2 tablespoons lemon juice
2 cloves garlic, minced
1 teaspoon grated gingerroot or
   ⅛ teaspoon ground ginger
⅛ teaspoon dry mustard
1 medium green sweet pepper
1 medium red sweet pepper
1 cup fresh pineapple chunks or one
   8-ounce can pineapple chunks,
   drained
   Hot cooked rice (optional)
   Green onion fans (optional)

Rinse chicken; pat dry with paper towels. Cut into 1-inch pieces. Place chicken in a plastic bag and set the bag into a shallow dish. For marinade, in a small bowl combine soy sauce, lemon juice, garlic, ginger, and mustard. Pour over chicken; seal bag. Marinate in the refrigerator for 2 to 24 hours, turning bag occasionally.

Drain chicken, reserving marinade. Cut green and red peppers into 1-inch pieces. On 12 short metal skewers, alternately thread chicken, pineapple, green pepper, and red pepper.

Grill kabobs on an uncovered grill directly over medium coals for 12 to 14 minutes or until chicken is tender and no longer pink, turning and brushing once with marinade halfway through grilling.

(Or, in a covered grill arrange medium-hot coals around a drip pan. Test for medium heat above the pan. Place kabobs on grill rack over drip pan. Cover and grill for 16 to 18 minutes. Brush occasionally with marinade up to the last 5 minutes of grilling.)

If desired, serve the kabobs over hot cooked rice and garnish with green onion fans. Makes 6 servings.

Nutrition information per serving: 110 cal., 2 g total fat (1 g sat. fat), 40 mg chol., 723 mg sodium, 7 g carbo., 15 g pro.

Chicken Fajitas with Guacamole

Make this chunky guacamole up to four hours before serving. Just keep it covered and refrigerated so it won't darken.

12 ounces skinless, boneless chicken
    breast halves
¼ cup snipped fresh cilantro or parsley
¼ cup olive oil or cooking oil
1 teaspoon finely shredded lemon peel
2 tablespoons lemon juice
1 teaspoon chili powder
½ teaspoon ground cumin
½ teaspoon pepper
8 8-inch flour tortillas
2 cups shredded lettuce
1 cup shredded cheddar cheese
    (4 ounces)
1 large tomato, chopped
½ cup sliced pitted ripe olives
    Guacamole

Place chicken in a plastic bag set in a shallow dish. For marinade, in a small bowl combine cilantro or parsley, oil, lemon peel, lemon juice, chili powder, cumin, and pepper. Pour over chicken; seal bag. Marinate in the refrigerator for 1 hour, turning bag occasionally. Drain chicken, reserving marinade.

Place chicken on the rack of an uncovered grill directly over medium coals. Grill for 12 to 15 minutes or until chicken is no longer pink (170°), turning and brushing once with reserved marinade. (Or place on the unheated rack of a broiler pan. Broil 4 to 5 inches from the heat for 12 to 15 minutes, turning and brushing once with reserved marinade.) Stack tortillas; wrap in foil. Heat on grill or in oven the last 5 minutes of cooking.

Cut chicken into bite-size strips. To assemble fajitas, arrange chicken strips, lettuce, cheese, tomato, and olives on warm tortillas. Fold or roll up tortillas. Serve with Guacamole. Makes 4 servings.

Guacamole: Seed and peel 1 ripe *avocado*. In a small bowl coarsely mash avocado. Stir in 1 medium *tomato*, seeded, chopped, and drained; 2 tablespoons finely chopped *onion*; 1 tablespoon *lemon juice*; and ¼ teaspoon *salt*. Cover the surface with plastic wrap and chill up to 4 hours.

Nutrition information per serving: 576 cal., 32 g total fat (10 g sat. fat), 74 mg chol., 745 mg sodium, 45 g carbo., 30 g pro.

Chicken Fingers with Honey Sauce

Serve your favorite barbecue sauce as a quick alternative to the honey sauce.

12 ounces skinless, boneless chicken
    breast halves
2 slightly beaten egg whites
1 tablespoon honey
2 cups cornflakes, crushed
¼ teaspoon pepper
¼ cup honey
4 teaspoons prepared mustard or
    Dijon-style mustard
¼ teaspoon garlic powder

Cut chicken into 3×¾-inch strips. In a small bowl combine egg whites and the 1 tablespoon honey. In a shallow dish combine crushed cornflakes and pepper. Dip chicken strips in egg white mixture and roll in cornflake mixture to coat.

Place chicken in a single layer on an ungreased baking sheet. Bake in a 450° oven for 11 to 13 minutes or until chicken is no longer pink.

Meanwhile, for sauce, in a small bowl stir together the ¼ cup honey, the mustard, and garlic powder. Serve the chicken strips with sauce. Makes 4 servings.

Nutrition information per serving: 230 cal., 2 g total fat (1 g sat. fat), 45 mg chol., 275 mg sodium, 31 g carbo., 19 g pro.

Fruity Chicken Salad Sandwiches

For a special touch, pick up a hearty wheat bread from your favorite bakery.

2 cups chopped cooked chicken breast
    (10 ounces)
1 small Red Delicious or Granny
    Smith apple, cored and chopped
⅓ cup sliced celery
¼ cup raisins
1 green onion, thinly sliced
¼ cup plain fat-free yogurt
¼ cup bottled reduced-calorie ranch
    salad dressing
    Red-tipped leaf lettuce
8 slices whole wheat or other bread

In a large bowl stir together the chicken, apple, celery, raisins, and green onion. In a small bowl combine yogurt and ranch salad dressing. Pour over chicken mixture; toss gently to coat.

Arrange lettuce leaves on half of the bread slices. Spread chicken mixture on lettuce. Top with the remaining bread. Makes 4 servings.

Nutrition information per serving: 332 cal., 8 g total fat (1 g sat. fat), 65 mg chol., 590 mg sodium, 38 g carbo., 29 g pro.

Chicken Fingers with Honey Sauce

Swiss Chicken Bundles

This tarragon-laced lasagna makes an elegant dish for a bridal or baby shower.

8 dried lasagna noodles
1 beaten egg
2 cups ricotta cheese or cream-style cottage cheese, drained
1½ cups chopped cooked chicken or turkey
1½ teaspoons snipped fresh tarragon or basil or ¼ teaspoon dried tarragon or basil, crushed
2 tablespoons margarine or butter
2 tablespoons all-purpose flour
½ teaspoon dry mustard
¼ teaspoon salt
⅛ teaspoon pepper
1½ cups milk
1½ cups shredded process Swiss cheese (6 ounces)
Paprika or snipped fresh parsley (optional)
Fresh tarragon sprigs (optional)

Cook lasagna noodles according to package directions; drain. Rinse with cold water; drain again.

Meanwhile, for filling, in a medium bowl stir together egg, ricotta or cottage cheese, chicken or turkey, and the snipped fresh or dried tarragon or basil.

Grease a 2-quart rectangular baking dish; set aside. To assemble bundles, spread about ⅓ cup of the filling over each lasagna noodle. Starting from a short end, roll up lasagna noodles. Place the bundles, seam sides down, in the prepared baking dish; set aside.

For sauce, in a medium saucepan melt margarine or butter. Stir in flour, mustard, salt, and pepper. Add milk all at once. Cook and stir until thickened and bubbly. Gradually add cheese, stirring until melted after each addition. Pour sauce over lasagna bundles.

Cover and bake in a 375° oven for 30 to 35 minutes or until heated through. Let stand for 10 minutes. Transfer lasagna bundles to dinner plates. Stir sauce in baking dish; spoon the sauce over bundles. If desired, sprinkle with paprika or parsley and garnish with fresh tarragon sprigs. Makes 8 servings.

Nutrition information per serving: 347 cal., 17 g total fat (8 g sat. fat), 92 mg chol., 523 mg sodium, 22 g carbo., 25 g pro.

Saucy Chicken Rigatoni

While cooking this single-saucepan dinner, stir every now and then to prevent the pasta from sticking to the pan.

1 medium onion, chopped (½ cup)
1 clove garlic, minced
1 tablespoon cooking oil
1 14½-ounce can tomatoes, cut up
1 7½-ounce can tomatoes, cut up
2 cups dried rigatoni pasta or elbow macaroni
1¼ cups water
1 2½-ounce jar sliced mushrooms, drained
1 teaspoon dried Italian seasoning, crushed
⅛ teaspoon ground red pepper (optional)
1½ cups chopped cooked chicken or turkey
    Fresh basil leaves (optional)

In a large saucepan cook onion and garlic in hot oil until tender. Stir in both cans of undrained tomatoes, the pasta, water, mushrooms, Italian seasoning, and, if desired, ground red pepper.

Bring to boiling; reduce heat. Cover and simmer about 20 minutes or until pasta is tender but still firm, stirring occasionally.

Stir chicken or turkey into pasta mixture; heat through. If desired, garnish with basil. Makes 4 servings.

Nutrition information per serving: 293 cal., 9 g total fat (2 g sat. fat), 51 mg chol., 399 mg sodium, 32 g carbo., 22 g pro.

Pasta with Chicken and Pepper-Cheese Sauce

Ground red, white, and black and jalapeño peppers multiply the hotness by four in this zippy cream sauce.

8 ounces packaged dried spaghetti or fettuccine
3 small skinless, boneless chicken breast halves (about 8 ounces total)
1 tablespoon all-purpose flour
½ teaspoon salt
¼ to ½ teaspoon ground red pepper
⅛ to ¼ teaspoon ground white pepper
⅛ to ¼ teaspoon ground black pepper
1 tablespoon cooking oil
1 medium red or green sweet pepper, chopped (1 cup)
1 medium onion, chopped (½ cup)
1 tablespoon chopped, seeded jalapeño pepper
2 cloves garlic, minced
2 tablespoons all-purpose flour
¾ cup chicken broth
½ cup milk
1 teaspoon Worcestershire sauce
1 cup shredded Monterey Jack or cheddar cheese (4 ounces)
¼ cup dairy sour cream
1 jalapeño pepper, thinly sliced (optional)

Cook pasta according to package directions. Drain; keep warm.

Rinse chicken; pat dry with paper towels. Cut into 1-inch pieces. In a small mixing bowl combine the 1 tablespoon flour, salt, ground red pepper, white pepper, and black pepper. Toss flour mixture with chicken to coat. Set aside.

In a large skillet heat the oil over medium-high heat. (Add more oil as necessary during cooking.) Add sweet pepper, onion, chopped jalapeño pepper, and garlic; cook and stir until vegetables are tender. Remove the vegetables with a slotted spoon; set aside.

Add chicken to the skillet. Cook and stir for 3 to 4 minutes or until chicken is tender and no longer pink. Remove chicken from skillet.

Stir 2 tablespoons flour into drippings in skillet. Add chicken broth, milk, and Worcestershire sauce. Cook and stir until thickened and bubbly. Add the Monterey Jack or cheddar cheese, stirring until cheese melts. Stir 1 cup of the hot mixture into the sour cream; return all of the sour cream mixture to skillet. Stir in chicken and vegetables. Cook until heated through. Do not boil.

Arrange pasta on individual plates or a large platter. Spoon the chicken mixture over pasta. If desired, garnish with jalapeño pepper slices. Makes 4 servings.

Nutrition information per serving: 512 cal., 19 g total fat (9 g sat. fat), 64 mg chol., 660 mg sodium, 56 g carbo., 29 g pro.

Chicken Manicotti with Chive-Cream Sauce

Broccoli and roasted red peppers or pimiento add vivid colors to the tasty chicken filling that spills from these pasta shells.

12 packaged dried manicotti shells
 1 8-ounce container soft-style cream
       cheese with chives and onion
⅔ cup milk
¼ cup grated Romano or Parmesan
       cheese
 2 cups chopped cooked chicken
       (10 ounces)
 1 10-ounce package frozen chopped
       broccoli, thawed and drained
½ of a 7-ounce jar roasted red
       sweet peppers, drained and sliced,
       or one 4-ounce jar diced
       pimiento, drained
¼ teaspoon black pepper
       Paprika

Cook manicotti shells according to package directions. Drain shells; rinse with cold water. Drain again.

Meanwhile, for sauce, in a small heavy saucepan melt cream cheese over medium-low heat, stirring constantly. Slowly add milk, stirring until smooth. Stir in Romano or Parmesan cheese. Remove from heat.

For filling, in a medium mixing bowl stir together ¾ cup of the sauce, chicken, broccoli, roasted red sweet peppers or pimiento, and black pepper. Using a small spoon, carefully fill each manicotti shell with about ⅓ cup of the filling.

Arrange the filled shells in a 3-quart rectangular baking dish. Pour the remaining sauce over the shells. Sprinkle with paprika. Cover with foil. Bake in a 350° oven for 25 to 30 minutes or until heated through. Makes 6 servings.

Nutrition information per serving: 396 cal., 18 g total fat (9 g sat. fat), 92 mg chol., 257 mg sodium, 31 g carbo., 25 g pro.

Deep-Dish Chicken Pie

To save time with the same delicious results, you can easily substitute one folded refrigerated unbaked piecrust for the Pastry for Single-Crust Pie. Just put the chicken mixture in a 2-quart round casserole and top with the piecrust. Flute, brush, and bake as directed in the recipe.

Pastry for Single-Crust Pie
- 3 medium leeks or 1 large onion, chopped
- 1 cup sliced fresh mushrooms
- ¾ cup sliced celery
- ½ cup chopped red sweet pepper
- 2 tablespoons margarine or butter
- ⅓ cup all-purpose flour
- 1 teaspoon poultry seasoning
- ¼ teaspoon salt
- ¼ teaspoon black pepper
- 1½ cups chicken broth
- 1 cup half-and-half, light cream, or milk
- 2½ cups chopped cooked chicken
- 1 cup frozen peas
- 1 slightly beaten egg

Prepare Pastry for Single-Crust Pie. On a lightly floured surface, roll pastry into a rectangle ⅛ inch thick. Trim to a rectangle 1 inch larger than a 2-quart rectangular baking dish. Using a sharp knife or small cookie cutter, cut some shapes out of center of pastry.

In a large saucepan cook leeks or onion, mushrooms, celery, and sweet pepper in margarine or butter over medium heat until tender. Stir in the flour, poultry seasoning, salt, and black pepper. Add the broth and half-and-half, light cream, or milk all at once. Cook and stir until thickened and bubbly. Stir in the cooked chicken and peas. Pour into the baking dish.

Place pastry over the hot chicken mixture in dish; turn edges of pastry under and flute to top edges of dish. Brush with the egg. Place reserved pastry shapes on top of pastry. Brush again with egg.

Bake in a 400° oven for 30 to 35 minutes or until the crust is golden brown. Cool about 20 minutes before serving. Makes 6 servings.

Pastry for Single-Crust Pie: In a medium bowl stir together 1¼ cups *all-purpose flour* and ¼ teaspoon *salt*. Using a pastry blender, cut in ⅓ cup *shortening* until pieces are pea-size. Using 4 to 5 tablespoons *cold water,* sprinkle 1 tablespoon water at a time over mixture, gently tossing with a fork until all is moistened. Form dough into a ball.

Nutrition information per serving: 484 cal., 26 g total fat (8 g sat. fat), 107 mg chol., 538 mg sodium, 35 g carbo., 27 g pro.

Cincinnati-Style Chicken Chili

If desired, sprinkle this Midwestern favorite with freshly shredded cheddar cheese before serving.

1	pound uncooked ground chicken or turkey
1	large onion, chopped
1	clove garlic, minced
3	tablespoons chili powder
2	teaspoons paprika
1	teaspoon ground cumin
½	teaspoon salt
½	teaspoon ground cinnamon
⅛	teaspoon ground cloves
⅛	teaspoon ground red pepper
1	bay leaf
1	14½-ounce can stewed tomatoes
1	8-ounce can tomato sauce
½	cup water
1	tablespoon red wine vinegar
1	tablespoon molasses
1	15-ounce can red kidney beans
	Hot cooked spaghetti

In a 4½-quart Dutch oven cook ground chicken or turkey, onion, and garlic over medium heat for 5 to 7 minutes or until chicken is brown. Drain off fat, if necessary.

Add chili powder, paprika, cumin, salt, cinnamon, cloves, ground red pepper, and bay leaf. Cook and stir for 3 minutes.

Stir in undrained stewed tomatoes, tomato sauce, water, red wine vinegar, and molasses. Bring to boiling; reduce heat. Cover and simmer for 45 minutes, stirring occasionally. Uncover and simmer to desired consistency. Discard bay leaf.

In a medium saucepan heat undrained kidney beans; drain. To serve, spoon the chicken mixture and beans over hot cooked spaghetti. Makes 4 servings.

Nutrition information per serving: 402 cal., 8 g total fat (2 g sat. fat), 54 mg chol., 1,223 mg sodium, 61 g carbo., 30 g pro.

SERVING CINCINNATI-STYLE

Visit Cincinnati and you can sample chili that's unlike any you'll find in Texas or the Southwest. Cincinnati natives love their chili served over spaghetti or other pasta. They often sprinkle it with shredded cheese, chopped onion, and other toppers.

Cornish Hens with Basil-Wild Rice Stuffing

A combination of wild rice and basil makes for a nutty-tasting stuffing. The stuffing cooks in a handy foil packet on the grill.

1 tablespoon olive oil or cooking oil
¼ cup chopped onion
1 clove garlic, minced
2 cups cooked brown rice
1 cup cooked wild rice
¼ cup snipped fresh basil
2 tablespoons grated Parmesan cheese
½ teaspoon salt
Dash ground nutmeg
2 1¼- to 1½-pound Cornish
game hens
2 tablespoons honey
2 teaspoons Dijon-style mustard

For stuffing, in a large skillet heat oil over medium heat. Add onion and garlic; cook until onion is tender. Stir in brown rice, wild rice, basil, Parmesan cheese, salt, and nutmeg.

Fold a 36×18-inch piece of heavy foil in half to make an 18-inch square. Place stuffing in the center of the foil. Bring up two opposite edges of foil and seal with a double fold. Fold remaining ends to completely enclose the stuffing, leaving space for steam to build. Chill the packet until ready to grill.

Rinse Cornish hens; pat dry with paper towels. Twist wing tips under hens. Tie legs to tails. Insert an oven-going meat thermometer into center of an inside thigh muscle, not touching bone. In a small bowl stir together honey and mustard.

In a covered grill arrange medium-hot coals around a drip pan. Test for medium heat above the pan. Place hens, breast sides up, on grill rack over drip pan. Cover and grill for 50 to 60 minutes or until the thermometer registers 180°, brushing occasionally with mustard mixture the last 10 minutes of grilling. Meanwhile, place the foil packet of stuffing on grill rack directly over coals. Grill for 15 to 20 minutes or until heated through.

To serve, cut hens in half lengthwise with poultry shears. Serve with stuffing. Makes 4 servings.

Nutrition information per serving: 523 cal., 24 g total fat (5 g sat. fat), 102 mg chol., 470 mg sodium, 41 g carbo., 36 g pro.

Turkey Breast with Raspberry Salsa

Raspberry jam and prepared salsa team up for a sweet sauce with just a little kick.

⅓ cup seedless raspberry jam
1 tablespoon Dijon-style mustard
1 teaspoon finely shredded orange
   peel
½ cup mild salsa
1 2- to 2½-pound bone-in turkey
   breast half
   Orange peel strips (optional)

Stir together raspberry jam, mustard, and 1 teaspoon orange peel. Stir 3 tablespoons of the jam mixture into salsa. Cover and chill jam mixture and salsa mixture. If desired, skin turkey breast. Rinse turkey; pat dry with paper towels. Insert a meat thermometer into the center of turkey breast.

In a covered grill arrange medium-hot coals around a drip pan. Test for medium heat above the pan. Place turkey, bone side down, on grill rack over drip pan. Cover and grill for 1 to 1¼ hours or until meat thermometer registers 170°, brushing occasionally with jam mixture during the last 30 minutes of grilling.

Remove turkey from grill and cover with foil. Let stand for 15 minutes before slicing. Serve turkey with salsa mixture. If desired, garnish with orange peel strips. Makes 8 servings.

Nutrition information per serving: 149 cal., 3 g total fat (2 g sat. fat), 46 mg chol., 147 mg sodium, 11 g carbo., 20 g pro.

HANDLING POULTRY SAFELY

Follow these simple guidelines to safely handle fresh poultry.
- Always wash your hands, work surfaces, and utensils in hot soapy water after handling raw poultry to prevent spreading bacteria to other foods.
- When cutting raw poultry, use a plastic cutting board because it's easier to clean and disinfect than a wooden one.
- When grilling, never use the same plate to transfer raw and cooked poultry to and from the grill.
- Always marinate poultry in the refrigerator.
- Serve poultry immediately after cooking it. Refrigerate leftovers as soon as possible.

Stuffed Turkey Tenderloins

There's more than one way to stuff a turkey. Fresh spinach and tangy goat cheese make a melt-in-your-mouth filling in these turkey tenderloins. When sliced, the rosy-red, spicy crust on the meat yields to a juicy, tender interior.

2 8-ounce turkey breast tenderloins
2 cups chopped spinach leaves
3 ounces semisoft goat cheese
      (chèvre) or feta cheese, crumbled
      (about ¾ cup)
½ teaspoon black pepper
1 tablespoon olive oil
1 teaspoon paprika
½ teaspoon salt
⅛ to ¼ teaspoon ground red pepper

Rinse turkey; pat dry with paper towels. Make a pocket in each tenderloin by cutting lengthwise from one side almost to, but not through, the opposite side. Set aside.

For stuffing, in a medium bowl combine spinach, goat or feta cheese, and black pepper. Spoon stuffing into pockets. Tie 100% cotton string around each tenderloin in 3 or 4 places to hold in stuffing. In a small bowl combine oil, paprika, salt, and ground red pepper. Brush evenly over turkey.

Grill turkey on lightly greased rack of an uncovered grill directly over medium coals for 16 to 20 minutes or until turkey is tender and no longer pink in center of the thickest part, turning once.

Remove and discard the strings. Slice turkey tenderloins crosswise. Makes 4 servings.

Nutrition information per serving: 220 cal., 12 g total fat (4 g sat. fat), 68 mg chol., 458 mg sodium, 1 g carbo., 26 g pro.

CLEANING YOUR GRILL

To make the job easier, clean your grill rack right after cooking. Let it cool until easily handled, then soak it in hot sudsy water to loosen cooked-on grime. If the rack is too large for your sink, let it stand about 1 hour wrapped in wet paper towels, then wipe clean. If necessary, use a stiff brush to remove stubborn burned-on food.

Curry-Glazed Turkey Thighs

Curry-Glazed Turkey Thighs

Turn economical turkey thighs into a company-pleasing entrée by glazing them with orange marmalade and dressing them with a yogurt sauce.

⅓ cup orange marmalade
1 tablespoon Dijon-style mustard
½ to 1 teaspoon curry powder
⅛ teaspoon salt
½ cup plain yogurt
2 small turkey thighs (about 2 pounds total)
   Hot cooked rice (optional)
   Raisins, peanuts, and/or chopped apple (optional)

For glaze, stir together marmalade, mustard, curry powder, and salt. For sauce, stir 3 tablespoons of the glaze into yogurt. Cover and chill until serving time. If desired, skin turkey. Insert an oven-going meat thermometer into center of a turkey thigh, not touching bone.

In a covered grill arrange medium-hot coals around a drip pan. Test for medium heat above the pan. Place turkey thighs on grill rack over drip pan. Cover and grill for 50 to 60 minutes or until the thermometer registers 180°, brushing once or twice with glaze the last 10 minutes of grilling. Slice turkey. Serve over hot cooked rice (if desired) and top with sauce. If desired, serve with raisins, peanuts, and/or apple. Makes 4 servings.

Nutrition information per serving: 157 cal., 4 g total fat (1 g sat. fat), 30 mg chol., 209 mg sodium, 21 g carbo., 9 g pro.

Turkey Parmigiana

Can't find turkey tenderloin steaks? Buy two whole turkey tenderloins and cut each in half horizontally to make four steaks.

8 ounces dried spaghetti
4 turkey breast tenderloin steaks (about 1 pound total)
1 tablespoon margarine or butter
2 tablespoons grated Parmesan cheese
1 14-ounce jar tomato and herb pasta sauce
¾ cup shredded mozzarella cheese (3 ounces)

Cook spaghetti according to package directions; drain. Cover and keep warm. Meanwhile, in a large skillet cook turkey in hot margarine or butter over medium heat for 8 to 10 minutes or until no longer pink (170°), turning once. Sprinkle with Parmesan cheese. Top with sauce. Cover and cook for 1 to 2 minutes or until heated through.

Sprinkle turkey with mozzarella cheese. Cover and let stand for 1 to 2 minutes or until cheese is melted. Serve with the hot cooked spaghetti. Makes 4 servings.

Nutrition information per serving: 518 cal., 12 g total fat (4 g sat. fat), 64 mg chol., 561 mg sodium, 62 g carbo., 37 g pro.

Turkey Tetrazzini

Tetrazzini is a quick supper when cooked in a wok—there's plenty of room for tossing the spaghetti with the turkey, mushrooms, and creamy sauce.

12 ounces turkey breast tenderloin
1⅔ cups milk
2 tablespoons all-purpose flour
2 teaspoons instant chicken bouillon granules
⅛ teaspoon pepper
¼ cup slivered almonds
1 tablespoon cooking oil
1 cup sliced fresh mushrooms
2 green onions, sliced (¼ cup)
2 tablespoons dry white wine, dry sherry, or milk
4 ounces dried thin spaghetti, cooked and drained
¼ cup finely shredded Parmesan cheese
2 tablespoons snipped fresh parsley
Tomato slices (optional)
Fresh parsley sprigs (optional)

Cut turkey into thin bite-size strips. For sauce, in a small bowl stir together the 1⅔ cups milk, the flour, chicken bouillon granules, and pepper. Set aside.

Preheat a wok or large skillet over medium-high heat. Stir-fry almonds in hot wok for 2 to 3 minutes or until golden brown. Remove almonds from wok. Let wok cool slightly.

Add cooking oil to cooled wok. Preheat over medium-high heat (add more oil if necessary during cooking). Stir-fry mushrooms and green onions in hot oil for 1 to 2 minutes or until tender. Remove the mushroom mixture from wok.

Add turkey to wok. Stir-fry for 2 to 3 minutes or until no longer pink. Push turkey from center of wok. Stir sauce; add to center of wok. Cook and stir until thickened and bubbly. Cook and stir for 2 minutes more.

Stir in wine, sherry, or milk. Return cooked mushroom mixture to wok. Add cooked spaghetti, Parmesan cheese, and the snipped parsley. Toss all ingredients together to coat. Cook and stir for 1 to 2 minutes more or until heated through. Sprinkle with toasted almonds. Serve immediately. If desired, garnish with tomato and parsley sprigs. Makes 4 servings.

Nutrition information per serving: 376 cal., 13 g total fat (4 g sat. fat), 50 mg chol., 637 mg sodium, 34 g carbo., 28 g pro.

Turkey Lasagna Rolls

For this robust lasagna-style entrée, roll the noodles around a cheesy spinach filling and then top them with a ground turkey and tomato sauce.

8	ounces ground raw turkey
1	medium onion, chopped (½ cup)
2	cloves garlic, minced
1	cup sliced fresh mushrooms
1	cup water
1	7½-ounce can tomatoes, cut up
1	6-ounce can tomato paste
1½	teaspoons dried oregano, crushed
1	teaspoon dried basil, crushed
8	packaged dried lasagna noodles
1	beaten egg
1	15-ounce carton ricotta cheese
1	10-ounce package frozen chopped spinach, thawed and drained
1½	cups shredded mozzarella cheese (6 ounces)
1	cup grated Parmesan cheese Fresh parsley sprigs (optional)

For sauce, in a large skillet cook turkey, onion, and garlic until turkey is no longer pink; drain fat. Stir in mushrooms, water, undrained tomatoes, tomato paste, oregano, and basil. Bring to boiling; reduce heat. Cover and simmer for 25 minutes.

Meanwhile, cook the lasagna noodles according to package directions. Drain noodles; rinse with cold water. Drain again.

For filling, in a mixing bowl stir together egg, ricotta cheese, spinach, 1 cup of the mozzarella cheese, and ¾ cup of the Parmesan cheese.

To assemble rolls, spread about ½ cup of the filling over each lasagna noodle. Roll up noodles, starting from a short end. Place lasagna rolls, seam sides down, in a 2-quart rectangular baking dish. Pour sauce over lasagna rolls. Cover dish with foil.

Bake in a 375° oven for 25 minutes. Remove foil. Sprinkle with remaining mozzarella cheese. Bake for 5 to 10 minutes more or until heated through. Let stand 5 minutes before serving. Sprinkle with remaining Parmesan cheese and, if desired, garnish with parsley sprigs. Makes 8 servings.

Nutrition information per serving: 345 cal., 15 g total fat (8 g sat. fat), 75 mg chol., 511 mg sodium, 28 g carbo., 26 g pro.

Spaghetti with Turkey Meatballs

We updated everyone's favorite pasta dish by using ground turkey instead of ground beef.

1 large onion, chopped (1 cup)
1 medium green sweet pepper, coarsely chopped (1 cup)
1 medium carrot, coarsely chopped (½ cup)
1 stalk celery, sliced (½ cup)
1 tablespoon cooking oil
4 large ripe tomatoes, peeled and chopped (4 cups), or two 14½-ounce cans tomatoes, cut up
1 6-ounce can (⅔ cup) tomato paste
2 teaspoons dried Italian seasoning, crushed
½ teaspoon sugar
½ teaspoon salt
½ teaspoon garlic powder
   Turkey Meatballs
12 ounces packaged dried spaghetti or mostaccioli

For sauce, in a Dutch oven cook onion, green pepper, carrot, and celery in hot oil until tender. Stir in fresh or undrained canned tomatoes, tomato paste, Italian seasoning, sugar, salt, and garlic powder. Bring to boiling.

Add the Turkey Meatballs; reduce heat. Cover and simmer for 30 minutes. If necessary, uncover and simmer for 10 to 15 minutes more or until sauce is desired consistency, stirring occasionally.

Meanwhile, cook the pasta according to package directions. Drain.

Arrange pasta on individual plates or a large platter. Spoon the meatballs and sauce over pasta. Makes 6 servings.

Turkey Meatballs: In a medium mixing bowl combine 1 beaten *egg* and 2 tablespoons *milk*. Stir in ¼ cup *fine dry bread crumbs;* ½ teaspoon *salt;* ½ teaspoon *dried Italian seasoning,* crushed; and ½ teaspoon *pepper.* Add 1 pound *ground raw turkey;* mix well. With wet hands, shape mixture into twenty-four 1-inch meatballs. Place the meatballs in a greased 13×9×2-inch baking pan. Bake in a 375° oven about 20 minutes or until turkey is done (165°). Drain fat.

Nutrition information per serving: 442 cal., 11 g total fat (2 g sat. fat), 64 mg chol., 686 mg sodium, 65 g carbo., 22 g pro.

Hot Turkey Sub Sandwich

Pair this hefty sandwich with bowls of tomato soup.

1 tablespoon olive oil
1 teaspoon dried basil, crushed
1 clove garlic, minced, or ⅛ teaspoon
   garlic powder
1 8-ounce loaf or ½ of a 16-ounce loaf
   French bread
6 ounces sliced mozzarella cheese
4 ounces sliced smoked turkey
2 tablespoons sliced pitted ripe olives
2 tomatoes, thinly sliced
⅛ teaspoon coarsely ground pepper

In a small bowl stir together the olive oil, basil, and garlic or garlic powder. Cut the French bread in half horizontally. Using a spoon, hollow out the top half, leaving a ¾-inch shell. Brush the cut sides of both bread halves with the olive oil mixture.

On the bottom half of the French bread, layer half of the mozzarella cheese, all of the smoked turkey, the olives, the remaining cheese, and the tomato slices. Sprinkle with pepper. Replace the bread top.

Wrap in heavy foil. Bake in a 375° oven about 10 minutes or until heated through. Cut into 4 serving-size portions. Makes 4 servings.

Nutrition information per serving: 335 cal., 13 g total fat (5 g sat. fat), 36 mg chol., 849 mg sodium, 33 g carbo., 22 g pro.

Parmesan-Turkey Sandwiches

Keep the ingredients you need for this sandwich on hand, and you'll be prepared every time your teenager invites friends for dinner.

1 slightly beaten egg
½ cup crushed cornflakes or rich round
   crackers
¼ cup grated Parmesan cheese
⅛ teaspoon garlic powder
⅛ teaspoon pepper
4 turkey breast tenderloin steaks
   (about 1 pound total)
2 tablespoons margarine or butter
4 lettuce leaves
4 hoagie buns, split and toasted
¼ cup bottled creamy Parmesan or
   buttermilk ranch salad dressing
2 tomatoes, thinly sliced

In a shallow dish beat together egg and 1 tablespoon water. In another shallow dish stir together crushed cornflakes or crackers, Parmesan cheese, garlic powder, and pepper. Dip turkey in egg mixture and roll in cornflake mixture to coat.

In a large skillet cook turkey in hot margarine or butter over medium heat for 8 to 10 minutes or until no longer pink (170°), turning once.

To assemble sandwiches, place lettuce on bottom halves of hoagie buns. Top with turkey, salad dressing, and tomato slices. Replace bun tops. Makes 4 servings.

Nutrition information per serving: 686 cal., 21 g total fat (5 g sat. fat), 112 mg chol., 1,177 mg sodium, 83 g carbo., 39 g pro.

Hot Turkey Sub Sandwich

Hawaiian Turkey Burgers

These unusual burgers are even better served with pineapple spritzers. Simply pour unsweetened pineapple juice over ice, filling a tall glass about one-third full, and top with carbonated water.

1 beaten egg
¼ cup seasoned fine dry bread crumbs
3 tablespoons chopped water
    chestnuts
¾ teaspoon ground ginger
¼ teaspoon salt
¼ teaspoon pepper
1 pound uncooked ground turkey or
    chicken
¼ cup bottled sweet-and-sour sauce
4 canned pineapple rings
    Shredded spinach
4 kaiser rolls or hamburger buns,
    split and toasted

In a medium bowl combine egg, bread crumbs, water chestnuts, ginger, salt, and pepper. Add ground turkey or chicken; mix well. Form into four ¾-inch-thick patties.

Place patties on the rack of an uncovered grill directly over medium coals. Grill for 14 to 18 minutes or until done (165°), turning once and brushing with sweet-and-sour sauce the last 5 minutes of grilling. Meanwhile, place pineapple slices on grill rack. Grill for 5 minutes, turning occasionally.

To serve, place shredded spinach on the bottoms of rolls or buns. Top with burgers. Brush the burgers with sweet-and-sour sauce and top with pineapple slices. Replace roll or bun tops. Makes 4 servings.

Nutrition information per serving: 331 cal., 9 g total fat (2 g sat. fat), 108 mg chol., 1,092 mg sodium, 37 g carbo., 23 g pro.

Firecracker Turkey Burgers

Cool and creamy garlic sauce helps tame the fire brought on by spices and peppers in these smoky grilled patties.

½ cup mayonnaise or salad dressing
¼ cup dairy sour cream
1 clove garlic, minced
½ teaspoon cracked black pepper
¼ cup fine dry bread crumbs
2 tablespoons water
1 tablespoon chili powder
1 or 2 canned chipotle peppers
    in adobo sauce, drained and
    chopped (reserve 2 tablespoons
    adobo sauce)
2 cloves garlic, minced
¼ teaspoon salt
1 pound uncooked ground turkey or
    chicken
4 poppy seed rolls or hamburger buns,
    split and toasted
4 lettuce leaves
4 tomato slices
8 to 12 avocado slices (optional)

For sauce, in a small bowl stir together the mayonnaise or salad dressing, sour cream, the 1 clove garlic, and the black pepper. Cover and chill until serving time.

In a large bowl combine bread crumbs, water, chili powder, chipotle peppers, the 2 cloves garlic, and the salt. Add ground turkey or chicken; mix well. Form into four ¾-inch-thick patties.

Place patties on the rack of an uncovered grill directly over medium coals. Grill for 14 to 18 minutes or until done (165°), turning once.

To serve, spread the bottoms of rolls or buns with adobo sauce. Top with burgers and sauce. Add lettuce leaves, tomato slices, and, if desired, avocado slices. Replace roll or bun tops. Makes 4 servings.

Nutrition information per serving: 517 cal., 32 g total fat (8 g sat. fat), 111 mg chol., 700 mg sodium, 31 g carbo., 25 g pro.

Fish & SEAFOOD

Contents

STIR-FRIED SHRIMP AND BROCCOLI
(recipe, page 249)

Grilled Tuna with Tuscan Beans

Tuna and beans—tonno e fagioli—is a favorite combination in Italian coastal towns. Using canned beans makes our version fast and easy.

1 pound fresh or frozen tuna, swordfish, halibut, shark, or salmon steaks
2 cloves garlic, minced
1 tablespoon olive oil
1 14½-ounce can Italian-style stewed tomatoes, cut up
2 teaspoons snipped fresh sage or ¼ teaspoon ground sage
1 15-ounce can small white beans, rinsed and drained
2 teaspoons olive oil
2 teaspoons lemon juice
⅛ teaspoon pepper
   Fresh sage sprigs (optional)

Thaw fish, if frozen. In a large skillet cook the garlic in 1 tablespoon hot oil for 15 seconds. Stir in the undrained tomatoes and snipped fresh or dried sage. Bring to boiling; reduce heat. Simmer, uncovered, for 5 minutes. Stir in beans; heat through.

Meanwhile, rinse fish; pat dry with paper towels. Cut fish into 4 serving-size portions. Brush both sides of fish with the 2 teaspoons oil and the lemon juice. Sprinkle with pepper.

Grill fish on the greased rack of an uncovered grill directly over medium coals until fish flakes easily with a fork, gently turning once (allow 4 to 6 minutes per ½-inch thickness).

[Or, place fish on the greased unheated rack of a broiler pan. Broil 4 inches from heat, gently turning once (allow 4 to 6 minutes per ½-inch thickness).]

To serve, remove the skin from fish. Spoon the bean mixture onto dinner plates and top with fish. If desired, garnish with sage sprigs. Makes 4 servings.

Nutrition information per serving: 298 cal., 7 g total fat (1 g sat. fat), 49 mg chol., 536 mg sodium, 25 g carbo., 33 g pro.

Pesto Sole Roll-Ups

Walleyed pike is often called the "sole" of fresh waters and has long been a favorite of fishermen. It works equally as well as sole or flounder in these carrot-and-pesto filled bundles.

4 4-ounce fresh or frozen sole or
   flounder fillets, ¼ to ½ inch thick
⅔ cup refrigerated pesto sauce
1 medium carrot, shredded (½ cup)
1 tablespoon margarine or butter,
   melted
3 tablespoons fine dry bread crumbs
1 teaspoon finely shredded lemon peel
6 ounces hot cooked fettuccine
1 tablespoon lemon juice
   Lemon wedges (optional)
   Carrot curls (optional)
   Fresh basil sprigs (optional)

Thaw fish, if frozen. Rinse fish; pat dry with paper towels. Spread one side of each fillet with about 1 tablespoon of the pesto. Sprinkle each fillet with 2 tablespoons of the shredded carrot. Starting from a short end, roll up fish around the carrot. Place fish rolls, seam sides down, in a 2-quart square baking dish. Brush fish rolls with melted margarine or butter.

Toss together bread crumbs and lemon peel; sprinkle over fish rolls. Bake, uncovered, in a 375° oven for 20 to 25 minutes or until fish flakes easily with a fork.

Toss together the remaining pesto, hot pasta, and lemon juice. Divide the pasta mixture evenly among dinner plates and top each with a fish roll. If desired, garnish with lemon wedges, carrot curls, and basil sprigs. Makes 4 servings.

Nutrition information per serving: 607 cal., 32 g total fat (1 g sat. fat), 59 mg chol., 475 mg sodium, 47 g carbo., 31 g pro.

Halibut with Creamy Dijon Sauce

Feel like having a barbecue instead of cooking these fish steaks indoors? Grill the fish on a greased rack of an uncovered grill directly over medium coals for 8 to 12 minutes or until fish is done, turning fish and brushing once with the basting sauce.

4	fresh or frozen halibut or sea bass steaks, cut 1 inch thick (about 1½ pounds)
1	tablespoon margarine or butter, melted
¼	teaspoon onion salt
¼	teaspoon dried marjoram, crushed
¼	teaspoon dried thyme, crushed
½	cup dairy sour cream
1	tablespoon all-purpose flour
1	tablespoon Dijon-style mustard
⅛	teaspoon salt
⅛	teaspoon pepper
⅛	teaspoon dried thyme, crushed
½	cup chicken or vegetable broth
4	cups shredded spinach (5 ounces)
1	medium carrot, shredded (½ cup)
	Lemon wedges (optional)

Thaw fish, if frozen. Rinse fish; pat dry with paper towels. Set aside.

For basting sauce, combine margarine or butter, onion salt, marjoram, and ¼ teaspoon thyme.

Place fish steaks on the rack of an unheated broiler pan. Brush with basting sauce. Broil 4 inches from the heat for 8 to 12 minutes or until fish flakes easily with a fork, turning and brushing once with the remaining basting sauce halfway through broiling.

Meanwhile, for Dijon sauce, in a small saucepan stir together the sour cream, flour, mustard, salt, pepper, and ⅛ teaspoon thyme. Add chicken or vegetable broth, stirring until well mixed. Cook and stir over medium heat till thickened and bubbly. Cook and stir for 1 minute more. Keep warm.

Toss together spinach and carrot. Line dinner plates with the spinach mixture. Arrange fish on spinach mixture. Top with Dijon sauce. If desired, garnish with lemon wedges. Makes 4 servings.

Nutrition information per serving: 282 cal., 9 g total fat (2 g sat. fat), 59 mg chol., 549 mg sodium, 9 g carbo., 39 g pro.

Salmon with Wilted Greens

This dinner packs in all the vitamin C and almost half of the vitamin A you need for an entire day—all for under 300 calories.

4 fresh or frozen salmon steaks, cut ¾ inch thick (about 1 pound)
3 tablespoons orange juice concentrate
3 tablespoons water
2 tablespoons reduced-sodium soy sauce
1 tablespoon honey
2 teaspoons cooking oil
1 teaspoon toasted sesame oil
½ teaspoon grated gingerroot or ¼ teaspoon ground ginger
6 cups torn mixed greens (such as spinach, Swiss chard, radicchio, or mustard, beet, or collard greens)
1 small red sweet pepper, cut into thin strips
1 medium orange, peeled and sectioned
   Orange peel strips (optional)

Thaw fish, if frozen. For dressing, in a small bowl combine orange juice concentrate, water, soy sauce, honey, cooking oil, toasted sesame oil, and ginger.

Rinse fish; pat dry with paper towels. Place the fish on the greased unheated rack of a broiler pan. Broil 4 inches from the heat for 3 minutes. Using a wide spatula, carefully turn fish. Brush with 1 tablespoon of the dressing. Broil for 3 to 6 minutes more or until fish flakes easily with a fork.

(Or, grill fish on the greased rack of an uncovered grill directly over medium coals for 3 minutes. Carefully turn fish. Brush with 1 tablespoon of the dressing. Grill for 3 to 6 minutes more.)

Remove fish. Cover and keep warm. Place the greens in a large salad bowl. In a large skillet bring the remaining dressing to boiling. Add red pepper strips. Remove from heat. Pour over greens, tossing to coat.

To serve, divide greens mixture among dinner plates. Arrange the orange sections and fish on top of greens. If desired, garnish with orange peel strips. Serve immediately. Makes 4 servings.

Nutrition information per serving: 255 cal., 9 g total fat (2 g sat. fat), 31 mg chol., 406 mg sodium, 15 g carbo., 27 g pro.

Zesty Jalapeño Fish Fillets

Low in fat and full of flavor, this quick-to-fix recipe couldn't be easier.

1   pound fresh or frozen skinless red snapper, flounder, sole, haddock, or orange roughy fillets, ½ to 1 inch thick

3   medium carrots, cut into thin bite-size strips (1½ cups)

1   medium zucchini, cut into thin bite-size strips (1½ cups)

1½ cups water

½   teaspoon instant chicken bouillon granules

1   cup quick-cooking couscous

⅓   cup jalapeño pepper jelly

1   tablespoon white wine vinegar or vinegar

1   tablespoon snipped fresh cilantro or parsley

Fresh cilantro or parsley sprigs (optional)

Thaw fish, if frozen. Rinse fish; pat dry with paper towels. Cut fish into 4 serving-size portions. In a covered medium saucepan cook carrots in a small amount of boiling water for 2 minutes. Add zucchini and cook about 2 minutes more or until vegetables are crisp-tender; drain. Cover and keep warm.

Place fish on the greased unheated rack of a broiler pan. Sprinkle with salt and black pepper. Broil about 4 inches from the heat until fish flakes easily with a fork (allow 4 to 6 minutes per ½-inch thickness of fish). Turn 1-inch-thick fillets over halfway through broiling.

Meanwhile, in a small saucepan combine water and bouillon granules. Bring to boiling. Stir in couscous; remove from heat. Cover and let stand about 5 minutes or until liquid is absorbed.

In another small saucepan stir together jelly and vinegar. Heat and stir over low heat until jelly is melted.

To serve, fluff the couscous with a fork; stir in the snipped cilantro or parsley. Spoon the couscous onto dinner plates. Top with the fish and vegetables. Drizzle with the warm jelly mixture. If desired, garnish with cilantro or parsley sprigs. Makes 4 servings.

Nutrition information per serving: 320 cal., 2 g total fat (0 g sat. fat), 42 mg chol., 201 mg sodium, 44 g carbo., 30 g pro.

Sweet Pepper Salsa Fish

A garnish of fresh oregano complements the refreshing combination of sautéed vegetables and salsa topping.

1 pound fresh or frozen skinless fish
   fillets, about ¾ inch thick
2 tablespoons cooking oil
1½ cups fresh mushrooms, quartered
1 cup coarsely chopped green and/or
   yellow sweet pepper
1 small onion, halved lengthwise
   and sliced
1 cup bottled salsa
   Fresh oregano sprigs (optional)

Thaw fish, if frozen. Rinse fish; pat dry with paper towels. Cut fish into 4 serving-size portions; set aside.

In a large skillet heat 1 tablespoon of the oil over medium-high heat. Cook mushrooms, sweet pepper, and onion in the hot oil about 5 minutes or just until vegetables are tender. Remove vegetables with a slotted spoon; set aside.

Add the remaining 1 tablespoon cooking oil to skillet. Add fish. Cook over medium heat for 6 to 9 minutes or until fish flakes easily with a fork, turning once.

Spoon the cooked vegetables over fish. Top with salsa. Cover and cook over low heat about 2 minutes more or until heated through. If desired, garnish with fresh oregano. Makes 4 servings.

Nutrition information per serving: 190 cal., 10 g total fat (1 g sat. fat), 53 mg chol., 306 mg sodium, 8 g carbo., 21 g pro.

Storing Fish

Sooner is better when it comes to cooking fish. If you're not going to cook it right away, wrap fresh fish loosely in plastic wrap, store it in the coldest part of the refrigerator, and use within 2 days. If you purchase frozen fish, keep it in a freezer set at 0° or lower for up to 3 months. If you cut your own fillets or steaks, put them in self-sealing freezer bags or wrap in moistureproof and vaporproof wrap before freezing.

Fish à la Diable

If the fillets are small, overlap two or three to make one 4-ounce serving. If they're too large, cut them into serving-size portions.

4 4-ounce fresh or frozen croaker, mullet, flounder, whiting, turbot, or pollack fillets
2 medium carrots
1 cup sliced fresh mushrooms
⅓ cup sliced celery
½ cup plain yogurt
1 to 2 tablespoons Dijon-style mustard
½ of a medium red sweet pepper, cut into thin strips (½ cup)
½ of a medium green sweet pepper, cut into thin strips (½ cup)
1 tablespoon margarine or butter, melted
1 teaspoon all-purpose flour
3 tablespoons milk
   Fresh dill (optional)
   Lemon wedges (optional)

Thaw fish, if frozen. Rinse fish; pat dry with paper towels. Set aside.

Cut each carrot into 4 long strips (8 strips total). In a medium saucepan cook carrots, mushrooms, and celery in a small amount of boiling water about 5 minutes or until tender; drain. Separate carrots from mushrooms and celery; set vegetables aside.

In a small bowl combine the yogurt and mustard; set aside ⅓ cup of the mustard mixture. Brush the remaining mustard mixture over one side of each fillet. Place one-fourth of the red and green pepper strips and two carrot strips crosswise on mustard side of each fillet. Starting from a short end, roll up fish around vegetables.

Arrange fish rolls, seam sides down, in a 9×9×2-inch baking pan. Brush with melted margarine or butter. Bake in a 400° oven for 15 to 20 minutes or until fish flakes easily with a fork.

Meanwhile, for sauce, in a small saucepan stir flour into the reserved ⅓ cup mustard mixture; stir in milk. Add cooked mushrooms and celery. Cook and stir over medium heat until thickened and bubbly. Cook and stir for 1 minute more.

Transfer fish rolls to dinner plates. Spoon the sauce over fish. If desired, garnish with fresh dill and lemon wedges. Makes 4 servings.

Nutrition information per serving: 361 cal., 20 g total fat (5 g sat. fat), 107 mg chol., 630 mg sodium, 19 g carbo., 26 g pro.

Poached Orange Roughy with Lemon Sauce

Despite its speed, poaching is an inherently gentle way to cook. It's also one of the lightest and most healthful. Here, poaching in lemon-and-pepper-infused broth preserves the delicate flavor and texture of one of the most popular kinds of white fish.

1	pound fresh or frozen orange roughy or red snapper fillets, about ½ inch thick
1	pound asparagus
1	14½-ounce can reduced-sodium chicken broth
2	teaspoons finely shredded lemon peel
⅛	teaspoon black pepper
1	medium yellow sweet pepper, cut into bite-size strips
4	teaspoons cornstarch
2	tablespoons snipped fresh chives
2	cups hot cooked couscous or rice

Thaw fish, if frozen. Rinse fish. Cut the fish into 4 serving-size portions; set aside. Snap off and discard woody bases from asparagus. Cut asparagus in half.

In a large skillet combine 1 cup of the broth, the lemon peel, and black pepper. Bring to boiling; reduce heat. Carefully add the fish and asparagus. Cover and cook over medium-low heat for 4 minutes. Add yellow pepper. Cover and cook about 2 minutes more or until fish flakes easily with a fork. Using a slotted spatula, remove fish and vegetables; reserve liquid in skillet. Keep fish and vegetables warm.

For sauce, stir together the remaining broth and cornstarch. Stir into liquid in skillet. Cook and stir until thickened and bubbly. Cook and stir for 2 minutes more. Stir in chives. Arrange fish and vegetables on hot couscous or rice; top with sauce. Makes 4 servings.

Nutrition information per serving: 249 cal., 2 g total fat (0 g sat. fat), 60 mg chol., 390 mg sodium, 29 g carbo., 28 g pro.

Thawing Fish

To thaw fish, place the unopened package in a container in the refrigerator and allow overnight thawing for a 1-pound package. If necessary, you can place the wrapped package of fish under cold running water for 1 to 2 minutes to hasten thawing. Thawing fish at room temperature or in warm water isn't recommended, since the fish won't thaw evenly and may spoil. Do not refreeze fish.

Sesame Orange Roughy

To make onion brushes, slice roots from the end of each green onion and remove most of the upper, green portion. Slash the remaining green portion to make a fringe. Then place in ice water for a few minutes to curl the ends.

1 pound fresh or frozen orange roughy or other fish fillets, about ¾ inch thick
2 tablespoons lime or lemon juice
1 tablespoon margarine or butter
2 tablespoons water
4 teaspoons soy sauce
2 teaspoons honey
1 clove garlic, minced
½ teaspoon grated fresh ginger or ⅛ teaspoon ground ginger
½ teaspoon toasted sesame oil
½ teaspoon lime or lemon juice
¼ teaspoon pepper
1 green onion, sliced
2 teaspoons sesame seeds, toasted

Thaw fish, if frozen. Rinse fish; pat dry with paper towels. Cut fish into 4 serving-size portions. Brush both sides of fish with the 2 tablespoons lime or lemon juice.

In a large skillet cook fish in hot margarine or butter over medium heat for 6 to 9 minutes or until fish flakes easily with a fork, turning once. Transfer fish to dinner plates; cover and keep warm.

Meanwhile, in a small bowl combine water, soy sauce, honey, garlic, ginger, sesame oil, the ½ teaspoon juice, and the pepper. Carefully pour into skillet. Cook until heated through, scraping up any browned bits on bottom. Pour over fish. Sprinkle with green onion and sesame seeds. Makes 4 servings.

Nutrition information per serving: 269 cal., 5 g total fat (1 g sat. fat), 23 mg chol., 453 mg sodium, 33 g carbo., 21 g pro.

THAWING FISH

Your best bet for safety and quality is to thaw fish and shellfish slowly in the refrigerator. Place the unopened package of fish or shellfish in a container in the refrigerator and allow overnight thawing for a 1-pound package. If necessary, you can place the wrapped package under cold running water for 1 to 2 minutes to hasten thawing. Don't thaw fish or shellfish in warm water or at room temperature and do not refreeze fish; doing so is unsafe.

Fish Creole

For a refreshingly light entrée, stir-fry fish with the classic flavors of New Orleans—green pepper, celery, onion, and tomatoes.

1 pound fresh or frozen swordfish, sea bass, tuna, or tilefish steaks, cut 1 inch thick
1 14½-ounce can tomatoes, cut up
½ teaspoon sugar
½ teaspoon salt
⅛ to ¼ teaspoon ground red pepper
1 tablespoon cooking oil
1 medium onion, chopped
1 stalk celery, thinly sliced
1 medium green sweet pepper, cut into 2-inch strips
2 tablespoons snipped parsley
2 cups hot cooked rice

Thaw fish, if frozen. Rinse fish; pat dry with paper towels. Cut into 1-inch cubes. Discard any skin and bones. Set aside.

In a small bowl stir together undrained tomatoes, sugar, salt, and ground red pepper. Set aside.

Add cooking oil to a wok or large skillet. Preheat over medium-high heat (add more oil if necessary during cooking). Stir-fry onion and celery in hot oil for 2 minutes. Add sweet pepper strips; stir-fry about 2 minutes more or until vegetables are crisp-tender. Remove the vegetables from wok.

Add half of the fish cubes to wok. Stir-fry for 3 to 5 minutes or until fish flakes easily with a fork, being careful not to break up pieces. Remove from wok. Repeat with the remaining fish cubes. Remove all of the fish from wok.

Add the tomato mixture to wok. Return the cooked vegetables to wok. Stir all ingredients together to coat. Cook and stir about 3 minutes or until slightly thickened. Add parsley. Gently stir in fish. Cook for 1 to 2 minutes more or until heated through. Serve immediately in bowls over hot rice. Makes 4 servings.

Nutrition information per serving: 311 cal., 9 g total fat (2 g sat. fat), 45 mg chol., 569 mg sodium, 31 g carbo., 26 g pro.

Nutty Parmesan Fish

A light and crispy coating that features cracker crumbs, pine nuts, and Parmesan cheese makes a flavor-packed breading for these oven-fried fish sticks.

1 pound fresh or frozen orange
  roughy or haddock fillets
1 beaten egg
2 tablespoons milk
¼ cup finely crushed rich round
  crackers
2 tablespoons grated Parmesan cheese
2 tablespoons ground pine nuts or
  almonds
½ teaspoon dried basil, crushed
⅛ teaspoon pepper
2 tablespoons margarine or butter,
  melted
  Tartar Sauce (optional)

Thaw fish, if frozen. Rinse fish; pat dry with paper towels. Cut fish into 1-inch-wide strips. Set aside.

In a shallow dish combine egg and milk. In another shallow dish combine cracker crumbs, Parmesan cheese, ground nuts, basil, and pepper. Dip fish pieces into egg mixture and then roll in crumb mixture. Place coated fish in a greased shallow baking pan. Drizzle melted margarine or butter over fish.

Bake in a 500° oven until coating is golden and fish flakes easily with a fork (allow 4 to 6 minutes per ½-inch thickness). If desired, serve with Tartar Sauce. Makes 4 servings.

Tartar Sauce: In a small bowl stir together 1 cup *mayonnaise* or *salad dressing,* ¼ cup finely chopped *dill pickle* or *sweet pickle relish,* 1 tablespoon sliced *green onion,* 1 tablespoon snipped *parsley,* 1 tablespoon diced *pimiento,* and 1 teaspoon *lemon juice.* Cover and chill until serving time. Makes about 1 cup.

Nutrition information per serving: 221 cal., 13 g total fat (3 g sat. fat), 80 mg chol., 267 mg sodium, 5 g carbo., 22 g pro.

SHOPPING FOR FISH FILLETS

Trust your eyes and nose when buying fish fillets. Look for firm, moist, clean-cut fillets. Avoid those that have a strong or fishy odor and ragged edges.

Deep-Dish Tuna Pie

A convenient, off-the-shelf piecrust mix makes a flaky top that looks and tastes like you made it from scratch.

½ of an 11-ounce package piecrust mix
    (1⅓ cups)
1 large onion, chopped (1 cup)
1 medium potato, peeled and chopped
    (about 1 cup)
1 10¾-ounce can condensed cream
    of mushroom soup
⅓ cup grated Parmesan cheese
⅓ cup milk
1 tablespoon lemon juice
¾ teaspoon dried dillweed
¼ teaspoon pepper
1 16-ounce package frozen mixed
    vegetables
1 9¼-ounce can tuna, drained and
    broken into chunks
1 beaten egg

Prepare piecrust mix according to package directions, except do not roll out. Cover dough; set aside.

In a covered large skillet cook onion and potato in a small amount of boiling water about 7 minutes or until tender. Drain. Stir in soup, Parmesan cheese, milk, lemon juice, dillweed, and pepper. Cook and stir until mixture is bubbly. Gently stir in the frozen mixed vegetables and tuna. Spoon mixture into an ungreased 2-quart round casserole.

On a lightly floured surface, roll pastry into a circle 2 inches larger than the diameter of the top of the casserole and about ⅛ inch thick. Make 1-inch slits near the center of the pastry. Center pastry over top of casserole, allowing ends to hang over edge. Trim pastry ½ inch beyond edge of casserole. Turn pastry under; flute to the casserole edge, pressing gently. Brush pastry with beaten egg.

Bake in a 400° oven for 40 to 45 minutes or until crust is golden brown. Serve immediately. Makes 6 servings.

Nutrition information per serving: 386 cal., 18 g total fat (5 g sat. fat), 49 mg chol., 893 mg sodium, 35 g carbo., 21 g pro.

CHOPPED ONIONS THE EASY WAY

To chop onions quickly, first cut the onion in half. Use the cut side as a base to stabilize the piece. Slice the onion half in one direction; holding the slices together with one hand, slice in the other direction. The job is easier if you use a chef's knife because it's designed to let you grasp the handle without your fingers touching the cutting surface.

Seafood Enchiladas

Imitation seafood is made commercially by processing and re-forming minced fish to look like shellfish. It's less expensive than crab or lobster and, as an added bonus, is lower in cholesterol.

8   6-inch corn tortillas
1   medium red onion, finely chopped
       (½ cup)
2   cloves garlic, minced
1   teaspoon ground coriander
¼   teaspoon black pepper
2   tablespoons margarine or butter
3   tablespoons all-purpose flour
1   8-ounce carton dairy sour cream
1   14½-ounce can chicken broth
1   or 2 canned jalapeño peppers,
       rinsed, seeded, and chopped, or
       one 4-ounce can diced green chile
       peppers, drained
1   cup shredded Monterey Jack cheese
       (4 ounces)
12 ounces flake-style imitation
       crabmeat
    Chopped tomatoes (optional)
    Cilantro sprigs (optional)

Wrap corn tortillas in foil. Heat in a 350° oven for 10 to 15 minutes or until softened.

Meanwhile, for sauce, in a medium saucepan cook the onion, garlic, coriander, and black pepper in margarine or butter over medium heat until onion is tender. In a medium bowl stir flour into sour cream; stir in broth. Add the sour cream mixture to onion mixture. Stir in jalapeño or green chile peppers. Cook and stir until mixture is slightly thickened and bubbly. Remove from heat. Add half of the cheese, stirring until melted.

For filling, stir ½ cup of the sauce into crabmeat. Place about ¼ cup of the filling on each tortilla; roll up. Arrange tortilla rolls, seam sides down, in a lightly greased 2-quart rectangular baking dish. Top with the remaining sauce. Bake, covered, in a 350° oven for 30 to 35 minutes or until heated through.

Sprinkle with the remaining cheese. Bake, uncovered, about 5 minutes more or until cheese is melted. Let stand for 10 minutes before serving. If desired, garnish with tomatoes, cilantro, and additional finely chopped red onion. Makes 4 servings.

Nutrition information per serving: 550 cal., 30 g total fat (15 g sat. fat), 68 mg chol., 1,461 mg sodium, 44 g carbo., 26 g pro.

Fish Kabobs with Coriander Rice

Instead of broiling, you can grill these spicy kabobs. Cook them on the greased rack of an uncovered grill directly over medium coals for 8 to 12 minutes and turn occasionally.

1½ pounds fresh or frozen halibut or
     sea bass steaks, cut 1 inch thick
¼ cup water
¼ cup lime juice
3 tablespoons snipped fresh parsley or
     1 teaspoon dried parsley flakes
2 tablespoons olive oil or cooking oil
1 clove garlic, minced
1 teaspoon ground cumin
     Dash black pepper
3 small zucchini and/or yellow
     summer squash, cut into
     ¾-inch slices (3 cups)
1 large red sweet pepper, cut into
     ¾-inch pieces
2 cups water
2 cloves garlic, minced
2 teaspoons ground coriander
1 teaspoon ground cumin
½ teaspoon salt
⅛ teaspoon crushed red pepper
1 cup uncooked long grain rice
⅓ cup sliced pitted ripe olives
3 tablespoons sliced green onions
     Lime slices, halved (optional)
     Thin red sweet pepper strips
     (optional)

Thaw fish, if frozen. Rinse fish; pat dry with paper towels. Cut fish into 1-inch cubes. Place fish in a plastic bag set in a shallow dish.

For marinade, in a small bowl combine the ¼ cup water, the lime juice, parsley, oil, the 1 clove garlic, 1 teaspoon cumin, and black pepper. Pour over fish; seal bag. Marinate at room temperature for 30 minutes, turning bag occasionally.

Meanwhile, in a medium saucepan cook zucchini and/or yellow squash and sweet pepper pieces in a small amount of boiling water for 2 to 3 minutes or just until crisp-tender. Drain.

For coriander rice, in another medium saucepan combine the 2 cups water, the 2 cloves garlic, the coriander, 1 teaspoon cumin, salt, and crushed red pepper. Bring to boiling. Stir in rice; reduce heat. Cover and simmer for 15 minutes. Remove from heat. Let stand, covered, about 5 minutes more or until liquid is absorbed. Stir in olives and green onions.

While rice is cooking, drain fish, reserving marinade. Alternately thread fish, zucchini and/or yellow squash, and sweet pepper pieces onto 12 metal skewers. Brush with the reserved marinade.

Place kabobs on the greased unheated rack of a broiler pan. Broil about 4 inches from the heat for 8 to 12 minutes or until fish flakes easily with a fork, turning once. Serve the kabobs with rice. If desired, garnish with lime slices and sweet pepper strips. Makes 6 servings.

Nutrition information per serving: 311 cal., 9 g total fat (1 g sat. fat), 36 mg chol., 285 mg sodium, 31 g carbo., 27 g pro.

Easy Salmon Pasta

To save time, cook the pasta and vegetables together in the same pan.

2	cups loose-pack frozen mixed vegetables or one 10-ounce package frozen mixed vegetables
1½	cups dried corkscrew pasta
2	green onions, sliced (¼ cup)
1	10¾-ounce can condensed cheddar cheese soup
½	cup milk
½	teaspoon dried dill
¼	teaspoon dry mustard
⅛	teaspoon pepper
2	6-ounce cans skinless, boneless salmon or tuna, drained
	Fresh dill sprigs (optional)

In a large saucepan cook frozen mixed vegetables, corkscrew pasta, and green onions in boiling water for 10 to 12 minutes or just until pasta is tender. Drain well.

Stir soup, milk, dried dill, mustard, and pepper into pasta mixture. Gently fold in salmon or tuna. Cook over low heat until heated through. If desired, garnish with fresh dill. Makes 5 servings.

Nutrition information per serving: 347 cal., 9 g total fat (4 g sat. fat), 56 mg chol., 827 mg sodium, 41 g carbo., 22 g pro.

Hot Tuna Hoagies

This may be a sandwich, but you'll need a knife and fork to eat it.

1½	cups packaged shredded cabbage with carrot (coleslaw mix)
1	9¼-ounce can chunk white tuna (water pack), drained and broken into smaller chunks
2	tablespoons mayonnaise or salad dressing
2	tablespoons bottled buttermilk ranch, creamy cucumber, or creamy Parmesan salad dressing
2	hoagie buns, split and toasted
2	ounces cheddar or Swiss cheese, thinly sliced

In a medium bowl combine shredded cabbage with carrot and tuna. In a small bowl stir together mayonnaise or salad dressing and ranch, cucumber, or Parmesan salad dressing. Pour the mayonnaise mixture over tuna mixture; toss gently to coat.

Spread the tuna mixture on the hoagie bun halves. Place on the unheated rack of a broiler pan. Broil 4 to 5 inches from the heat for 2 to 3 minutes or until heated through. Top with cheese. Broil for 30 to 60 seconds more or until cheese is melted. Makes 4 servings.

Nutrition information per serving: 417 cal., 16 g total fat (5 g sat. fat), 40 mg chol., 788 mg sodium, 41 g carbo., 27 g pro.

Easy Salmon Pasta

Fish Sandwich with Basil Mayonnaise

Baking these fillets at 500° results in a crumb coating that's nice and crispy. For crumb-topped fish (opposite), toss the crumb mixture with the margarine. Brush the fillets with milk and sprinkle the crumb mixture over the top of fillets before baking. Serve with or without the buns.

Basil Mayonnaise
1 pound fresh or frozen skinless fish fillets, about ½ inch thick
¼ cup milk
½ cup fine dry bread crumbs
¼ teaspoon paprika
⅛ teaspoon salt
⅛ teaspoon pepper
2 tablespoons margarine or butter, melted
4 hamburger buns or kaiser rolls, split and toasted
Shredded lettuce

Prepare Basil Mayonnaise. Cover and chill until serving time. Thaw fish, if frozen. Rinse fish; pat dry with paper towels. Cut the fish into 4 serving-size portions; set aside. Grease a shallow baking pan; set aside.

Pour milk into a shallow dish. In another shallow dish combine bread crumbs, paprika, salt, and pepper. Dip fish in milk and roll in crumb mixture to coat. Place fish in the prepared baking pan, tucking under any thin edges. Drizzle with melted margarine or butter.

Bake in a 500° oven for 4 to 6 minutes or until fish flakes easily with a fork and coating is golden brown. Serve fish in buns or rolls with lettuce and Basil Mayonnaise. Makes 4 servings.

Basil Mayonnaise: In a small bowl stir together 3 tablespoons *mayonnaise* or *salad dressing*; 2 tablespoons *dairy sour cream*; 2 tablespoons snipped *fresh basil* or ½ teaspoon *dried basil*, crushed; and ½ teaspoon finely shredded *lemon peel*.

Nutrition information per serving: 399 cal., 22 g total fat (5 g sat. fat), 30 mg chol., 529 mg sodium, 29 g carbo., 21 g pro.

Shrimp Piccata

Lemon, garlic, and white wine characterize this exceptionally easy, yet oh-so-elegant, entrée. Accompany the meal with crisp-tender stalks of steamed asparagus and garnish with scored lemon slices.

1 pound fresh or frozen, peeled and deveined large shrimp
2 tablespoons all-purpose flour
⅓ cup dry white wine
2 tablespoons lemon juice
1 tablespoon drained capers
¼ teaspoon salt
⅛ teaspoon pepper
1 tablespoon margarine or butter
2 cloves garlic, minced
2 cups hot cooked brown rice and/or wild rice
    Lemon slices, halved (optional)

Thaw shrimp, if frozen. Rinse shrimp; pat dry with paper towels. In a medium bowl toss shrimp with flour until coated. Set aside.

For sauce, in a small bowl stir together wine, lemon juice, capers, salt, and pepper. Set aside.

Place margarine or butter in a wok or large skillet. Preheat over medium-high heat until margarine is melted (add more margarine if necessary during cooking). Stir-fry garlic in hot margarine for 15 seconds.

Add half of the shrimp to wok. Stir-fry for 2 to 3 minutes or until shrimp turn opaque. Remove from wok. Repeat with the remaining shrimp. Remove all shrimp from wok.

Add sauce to wok. Cook and stir until sauce is bubbly and slightly reduced. Return shrimp to wok. Cook and stir about 1 minute more or until heated through.

Serve immediately over hot cooked brown and/or wild rice. If desired, garnish with lemon slices. Makes 4 servings.

Nutrition information per serving: 247 cal., 4 g total fat (1 g sat. fat), 174 mg chol., 405 mg sodium, 27 g carbo., 21 g pro.

Lemony Scampi Kabobs

To peel and devein the shrimp, use your fingers to open and remove the shell from the body to the base of the tail. Using a sharp knife, make a shallow slit along the center of the shrimp's back from the head end to the base of the tail. With the knife, remove the black sand vein.

1	pound fresh or frozen large shrimp in shells
2	small zucchini, cut into ¾-inch slices (2 cups)
1	large red sweet pepper, cut into 1-inch pieces (about 1½ cups)
1	clove garlic, minced
2	tablespoons margarine or butter
1	teaspoon finely shredded lemon peel
2	tablespoons lemon juice
¼	teaspoon ground red pepper
⅛	teaspoon salt
	Lemon wedges (optional)

Thaw shrimp, if frozen. Peel shrimp, leaving tails intact. Devein shrimp; rinse and pat dry with paper towels. Set aside.

In a small saucepan cook zucchini in a small amount of boiling, lightly salted water for 2 minutes; drain. Alternately thread shrimp, zucchini, and sweet pepper onto 8 metal skewers.

In a small saucepan cook garlic in hot margarine or butter until golden brown. Stir in lemon peel, lemon juice, ground red pepper, and salt. Set aside.

Place shrimp kabobs on the rack of an uncovered grill directly over medium coals. Grill for 8 to 10 minutes or until shrimp turn opaque, turning once and brushing occasionally with lemon mixture during the last half of grilling. If desired, serve the kabobs with lemon wedges. Makes 4 servings.

Nutrition information per serving: 134 cal., 7 g total fat (1 g sat. fat), 131 mg chol., 285 mg sodium, 4 g carbo., 15 g pro.

Stir-Fried Shrimp and Broccoli

This pleasing mixture of broccoli, carrots, and seasonings tastes equally delicious with shrimp or scallops. If you prefer, leave the tails on the shrimp for a striking presentation.

- 1 pound fresh or frozen medium shrimp in shells or 12 ounces fresh or frozen scallops
- 3 tablespoons red wine vinegar
- 3 tablespoons soy sauce
- 3 tablespoons water
- 1 tablespoon cornstarch
- 1½ teaspoons sugar
- 1 tablespoon cooking oil
- 2 cloves garlic, minced
- 2 cups broccoli florets
- 1 cup thinly bias-sliced carrots
- 1 small onion, halved lengthwise and sliced
- 1 cup sliced fresh mushrooms
- 2 cups hot cooked vermicelli, fusilli pasta, or rice

Thaw shrimp or scallops, if frozen. Peel and devein shrimp or cut any large scallops in half. Rinse the shrimp or scallops; pat dry with paper towels. Set aside.

For sauce, in a small bowl combine vinegar, soy sauce, water, cornstarch, and sugar; set aside.

Add oil to a wok or large skillet. Preheat over medium-high heat (add more oil if necessary during cooking). Stir-fry garlic in hot oil for 15 seconds. Add broccoli, carrots, and onion. Stir-fry for 3 minutes. Add mushrooms; stir-fry for 1 to 2 minutes more or until vegetables are crisp-tender. Remove vegetables from wok.

Stir sauce; add to wok. Bring to boiling. Add shrimp or scallops and cook for 2 to 3 minutes or until shrimp or scallops turn opaque. Return cooked vegetables to wok. Stir all ingredients together to coat. Heat through. Serve immediately with hot cooked pasta or rice. Makes 4 servings.

Nutrition information per serving: 395 cal., 6 g total fat (1 g sat. fat), 131 mg chol., 968 mg sodium, 62 g carbo., 26 g pro.

Spicy Shrimp on Skewers

For a tangy accompaniment to the peppery shrimp, add fresh pineapple wedges to the grill alongside the shrimp during the last 5 minutes of grilling.

1½   pounds fresh or frozen large shrimp
     in shells
½   cup frozen pineapple juice
     concentrate, thawed
1   to 2 tablespoons finely chopped
     jalapeño peppers
1   teaspoon grated gingerroot or
     ⅛ teaspoon ground ginger
1   clove garlic, minced
¼   teaspoon crushed red pepper
     Hot cooked rice pilaf (optional)

Thaw shrimp, if frozen. Peel and devein shrimp. Rinse shrimp; pat dry with paper towels. Place shrimp in a plastic bag and set the bag into a shallow dish.

For marinade, in a small mixing bowl combine the pineapple juice concentrate, jalapeño peppers, ginger, garlic, and crushed red pepper. Pour over shrimp; seal bag. Marinate in the refrigerator for 1 to 2 hours, turning bag once.

Drain the shrimp, reserving marinade. Thread shrimp onto 5 long metal skewers.

Grill kabobs on an uncovered grill directly over medium coals for 6 to 8 minutes or until shrimp turn pink, turning and brushing once with marinade halfway through grilling.

(Or, in a covered grill arrange medium-hot coals around a drip pan. Test for medium heat above the pan. Place kabobs on grill rack over drip pan. Cover and grill for 8 to 10 minutes, brushing occasionally with marinade during the first half of grilling.)

If desired, serve the shrimp kabobs over hot cooked rice pilaf. Makes 5 servings.

Nutrition information per serving: 133 cal., 1 g total fat (0 g sat. fat), 157 mg chol., 181 mg sodium, 13 g carbo., 17 g pro.

Fettuccine with Herbed Shrimp

A white wine and herb sauce dresses the shrimp and pasta in this elegant entrée.

12 ounces fresh or frozen, peeled, deveined shrimp
6 ounces packaged dried plain and/or spinach fettuccine
2 cups sliced fresh mushrooms
1 large onion, chopped (1 cup)
2 cloves garlic, minced
1 tablespoon olive oil or cooking oil
¼ cup dry white wine
1 tablespoon instant chicken bouillon granules
1 tablespoon snipped fresh basil or 1 teaspoon dried basil, crushed
1½ teaspoons snipped fresh oregano or ½ teaspoon dried oregano, crushed
1 teaspoon cornstarch
⅛ teaspoon pepper
2 medium tomatoes, peeled, seeded, and chopped
¼ cup grated Parmesan cheese
¼ cup snipped parsley

Thaw shrimp, if frozen. Rinse shrimp; pat dry with paper towels. Cut shrimp in half lengthwise; set aside.

Cook pasta according to package directions. Drain; keep warm.

Meanwhile, in a large saucepan cook mushrooms, onion, and garlic in hot oil until onion is tender.

In a small mixing bowl stir together wine, bouillon granules, basil, oregano, cornstarch, and pepper. Add to mushroom mixture. Cook and stir until thickened and bubbly.

Add shrimp to mushroom mixture. Cover and simmer about 2 minutes or until shrimp turn pink. Stir in tomatoes; heat through.

Spoon the shrimp mixture over pasta. Sprinkle with Parmesan cheese and parsley. Toss to coat. Makes 4 servings.

Nutrition information per serving: 351cal., 7 g total fat (2 g sat. fat), 136 mg chol., 926 mg sodium, 44 g carbo., 25 g pro.

SELECTING SHRIMP

At fish markets or supermarket fish counters, shrimp is usually sold by the pound. The price per pound is determined by size—the bigger the shrimp, the higher the price and the fewer per pound. Select fresh shrimp that are moist and firm, have translucent flesh, and smell fresh. Signs of poor quality are an unpleasant ammonia odor and blackened edges or spots on the shells.

Easy Everyday Cooking • FISH & SEAFOOD 253

Florida Crab Cakes

Confused about whether the crabmeat you purchased is cooked? Relax, all crabmeat is sold cooked.

1 slightly beaten egg
½ cup fine dry bread crumbs
2 tablespoons finely chopped green onion
2 tablespoons mayonnaise or salad dressing
1 tablespoon snipped parsley
2 teaspoons snipped fresh thyme or ½ teaspoon dried thyme, crushed
2 teaspoons Dijon-style or Creole mustard
½ teaspoon white wine Worcestershire sauce
⅛ teaspoon salt
1½ cups flaked, cooked crabmeat or one 6-ounce can crabmeat, drained, flaked, and cartilage removed
¼ cup cornmeal
2 tablespoons cooking oil
    Mixed salad greens (optional)
    Tartar Sauce (see recipe, page 169) (optional)
    Lemon wedges (optional)

In a medium bowl combine egg, ¼ cup of the bread crumbs, green onion, mayonnaise or salad dressing, parsley, thyme, mustard, Worcestershire sauce, and salt. Add crabmeat; mix well. Shape mixture into four ¾-inch-thick patties.

In a small bowl combine the remaining bread crumbs and cornmeal. Coat patties with cornmeal mixture.

In a large skillet cook crab cakes in hot oil over medium heat about 6 minutes or until crab cakes are golden and heated through, turning once (add additional oil if necessary during cooking).

If desired, serve crab cakes on a bed of mixed greens, top with Tartar Sauce, and garnish with lemon wedges. Makes 4 servings.

Nutrition information per serving: 259 cal., 15 g total fat (2 g sat. fat), 100 mg chol., 401 mg sodium, 17 g carbo., 13 g pro.

Mustard Magic

The flavor of Florida Crab Cakes (above) takes on new dimensions depending on the mustard you use. Dijon-style mustard, made with mustard seeds, white wine, and a blend of spices, adds a clean, sharp note that complements the crab. Creole mustard, made with mustard seeds, vinegar, and horseradish, adds a hot, spicy accent.

Pan-Seared Scallops

This is a flash in the pan! Sweet scallops are given a Cajun-flavored crust, then tossed with balsamic vinegar-dressed spinach and crisp bacon. Serve with corn bread and cold beer and you have a meal that's both homey and elegant in no time flat.

1 pound fresh or frozen sea scallops
2 tablespoons all-purpose flour
1 to 2 teaspoons blackened steak seasoning or Cajun seasoning
1 tablespoon cooking oil
1 10-ounce package prewashed spinach
1 tablespoon water
2 tablespoons balsamic vinegar
¼ cup cooked bacon pieces

Thaw scallops, if frozen. Rinse scallops; pat dry with paper towels. In a plastic or paper bag combine the flour and blackened steak or Cajun seasoning. Add scallops; toss to coat.

In a 12-inch skillet cook the coated scallops in hot oil over medium heat about 6 minutes or until browned and opaque, turning once. Remove the scallops.

Add spinach to skillet; sprinkle with water. Cover and cook over medium-high heat about 2 minutes or just until spinach is wilted. Drizzle with vinegar; toss to coat evenly. Return scallops to skillet; heat through. Sprinkle with bacon. Makes 4 servings.

Nutrition information per serving: 158 cal., 6 g total fat (1 g sat. fat), 37 mg chol., 323 mg sodium, 9 g carbo., 18 g pro.

Sea Shell Scallops

If you don't have plate-size coquille shells, use four individual au gratin dishes and alter the cooking method as follows: Bake the scallops in a 450° oven for 10 to 12 minutes or until opaque. Top the scallops with the sauce and sprinkle with the crumb mixture. Bake about 3 minutes more or until crumbs are golden brown.

1 pound fresh or frozen scallops
1 10-ounce package frozen chopped
    spinach
¼ cup shredded carrot
2 tablespoons thinly sliced green
    onion
2 tablespoons margarine or butter
3 tablespoons all-purpose flour
¼ teaspoon dried tarragon, crushed
    Dash pepper
1 cup chicken or vegetable broth
⅓ cup half-and-half, light cream, or
    milk
¼ cup fine dry bread crumbs
2 tablespoons grated Parmesan cheese
2 tablespoons margarine or butter,
    melted
    Shredded carrot (optional)

Thaw scallops, if frozen, and spinach. Cut any large scallops in half. Rinse scallops; pat dry with paper towels. Drain spinach well; divide evenly among 4 coquille shells. Arrange scallops in a single layer on spinach. Broil about 4 inches from the heat for 6 to 7 minutes or until scallops turn opaque.

Meanwhile, for sauce, in a small saucepan cook the ¼ cup shredded carrot and the green onion in the 2 tablespoons margarine or butter for 1 minute. Stir in flour, tarragon, and pepper. Add broth and half-and-half, light cream, or milk all at once. Cook and stir until thickened and bubbly. Cook and stir for 1 minute more. Spoon the sauce over scallops.

In a small bowl combine bread crumbs, Parmesan cheese, and the 2 tablespoons melted margarine or butter. Sprinkle over scallops and sauce. Broil about 2 minutes more or until crumbs are golden brown. If desired, sprinkle with additional shredded carrot. Makes 4 servings.

Nutrition information per serving: 286 cal., 16 g total fat (4 g sat. fat), 44 mg chol., 656 mg sodium, 15 g carbo., 21 g pro.

Pasta with Scallops and Fresh Vegetables

When sugar snap peas are out of season, substitute fresh Chinese pea pods that have been cut in half crosswise.

1   pound fresh or frozen sea scallops
8   ounces dried fettuccine or linguine
1   tablespoon margarine or butter
1   tablespoon cooking oil
2   or 3 cloves garlic, minced
2   large carrots, thinly bias-sliced
    (about 1½ cups)
2   cups fresh sugar snap peas, strings
    and tips removed
3   green onions, thinly sliced
½   cup dry white wine or chicken broth
⅓   cup water
1   tablespoon snipped fresh dill or
    2 teaspoons snipped fresh
    tarragon
1   teaspoon instant chicken bouillon
    granules
¼   teaspoon crushed red pepper
2   tablespoons cornstarch
2   tablespoons cold water
    Cracked black pepper
¼   cup grated Parmesan cheese

Thaw scallops, if frozen. Cut any large scallops in half. Rinse scallops; pat dry with paper towels. Set aside.

In a Dutch oven cook the pasta according to package directions; drain. Return pasta to Dutch oven; toss with margarine or butter. Cover and keep warm.

Meanwhile, add oil to a wok or large skillet. Preheat over medium-high heat (add more oil if necessary during cooking). Stir-fry garlic in hot oil for 15 seconds. Add carrots; stir-fry for 4 minutes. Add sugar snap peas and green onions; stir-fry for 2 to 3 minutes more or until vegetables are crisp-tender. Remove vegetables from wok. Cool wok for 1 minute.

Carefully add wine or chicken broth, the ⅓ cup water, the dill or tarragon, chicken bouillon granules, and crushed red pepper to wok. Bring to boiling. Add scallops; reduce heat. Simmer, uncovered, for 1 to 2 minutes or until scallops turn opaque, stirring occasionally.

Stir together cornstarch and the 2 tablespoons cold water; stir into scallop mixture. Cook and stir until thickened and bubbly. Return cooked vegetables to wok; add cooked pasta. Stir all ingredients together to coat. Heat through. Serve immediately. Sprinkle each serving with the cracked black pepper. Pass the Parmesan cheese. Makes 4 servings.

Nutrition information per serving: 462 cal., 10 g total fat (2 g sat. fat), 39 mg chol., 577 mg sodium, 60 g carbo., 27 g pro.

Clam and Bacon Bundles

Brush the bundles with milk before you bake them; you'll be rewarded with a crispy, irresistibly golden brown crust.

2 slices bacon, cut up
¾ cup finely chopped broccoli
    (4 to 5 ounces)
1 medium carrot, shredded (½ cup)
1 small yellow summer squash,
    chopped (1 cup)
2 6½-ounce cans chopped clams,
    drained
⅓ of an 8-ounce tub (⅓ cup) cream
    cheese with chives and onion
2 tablespoons bottled creamy
    cucumber salad dressing
1 10-ounce package refrigerated
    pizza dough
1 tablespoon milk
1 tablespoon sesame seeds

In a large skillet cook bacon over medium heat until crisp. Drain bacon, reserving 1 tablespoon drippings in skillet. Set bacon aside.

For filling, add broccoli and carrot to the reserved drippings in skillet. Cook and stir for 2 minutes. Add squash; cook and stir for 1 minute more. Remove from heat. Stir in clams, cream cheese, cucumber salad dressing, and bacon.

Grease a baking sheet; set aside. On a lightly floured surface, roll pizza dough into a 12-inch square. Cut dough into four 6-inch squares. Place ½ cup of the filling on one corner of each square. Moisten edges and fold opposite corner over filling. Press edges with tines of a fork to seal. Brush bundles with milk. Sprinkle with sesame seeds.

Place bundles on the prepared baking sheet. Bake in a 400° oven about 20 minutes or until golden brown. Cool on a wire rack for 5 minutes. Serve warm. Makes 4 servings.

Nutrition information per serving: 390 cal., 18 g total fat (5 g sat. fat), 57 mg chol., 494 mg sodium, 35 g carbo., 23 g pro.

Meatless
DISHES

Contents

RISOTTO WITH VEGETABLES
(recipe, page 276)

Mexican Black Bean Pizza

Hearty black beans flavored with cilantro top this meat-free pizza. Serve it with a crisp green salad.

1 10-ounce package refrigerated
   pizza dough
1 15-ounce can black beans, rinsed
   and drained
2 tablespoons snipped fresh cilantro or
   parsley
2 tablespoons bottled salsa
2 cloves garlic, quartered
1 teaspoon ground cumin
¼ teaspoon bottled hot pepper sauce
1½ cups shredded Colby-Monterey Jack
   cheese blend or cheddar cheese
   (6 ounces)
½ cup chopped red sweet pepper
¼ cup sliced green onions
½ cup dairy sour cream
2 tablespoons bottled salsa

Lightly grease an 11- to 13-inch pizza pan. Unroll the pizza dough and transfer to the prepared pan, pressing dough out with your hands. Build up the edges slightly. Prick generously with a fork. Bake in a 425° oven for 7 to 10 minutes or until light brown.

Meanwhile, in a blender container or food processor bowl combine black beans, cilantro or parsley, 2 tablespoons salsa, garlic, cumin, and hot pepper sauce. Cover and blend or process until smooth, stopping to scrape down sides, if necessary.

Spread bean mixture over hot crust. Sprinkle with cheese, sweet pepper, and green onions. Bake about 10 minutes more or until cheese is melted and pizza is heated through.

In a small bowl combine sour cream and 2 tablespoons salsa. Serve the pizza with sour cream mixture. Makes 4 servings.

Nutrition information per serving: 468 cal., 20 g total fat (11 g sat. fat), 50 mg chol., 917 mg sodium, 51 g carbo., 24 g pro.

*P*IZZA DOUGH PRIMER

If you don't have refrigerated pizza dough on hand, or it's not available at your supermarket, you can prepare your own pizza dough for Mexican Black Bean Pizza (above). Use a favorite recipe or a store-bought mix. You'll need enough dough to fit an 11- to 13-inch pizza pan.

Four Bean Enchiladas

We chose kidney, garbanzo, pinto, and navy or Great Northern beans to make this tasty crowd-size recipe, but you can use any combination of beans that you like.

16 6-inch corn tortillas
 1 15-ounce can red kidney beans, rinsed and drained
 1 15-ounce can garbanzo beans, rinsed and drained
 1 15-ounce can pinto beans, rinsed and drained
 1 15-ounce can navy or Great Northern beans, rinsed and drained
 1 11-ounce can condensed cheddar cheese or nacho cheese soup
 1 10-ounce can enchilada sauce
 1 8-ounce can tomato sauce
1½ cups shredded Monterey Jack or cheddar cheese (6 ounces)
    Sliced pitted ripe olives (optional)
    Green sweet pepper strips (optional)

Wrap corn tortillas in foil and bake in a 350° oven about 10 minutes or until tortillas are warm.

For filling, in a large mixing bowl combine beans and cheese soup. Spoon about ⅓ cup filling onto one end of each tortilla. Starting from the end with the filling, roll up each tortilla.

Arrange tortillas, seam sides down, in 2 ungreased 2-quart rectangular baking dishes or 8 individual au gratin dishes.

In a medium mixing bowl stir together the enchilada sauce and tomato sauce. Pour over tortillas.

Cover and bake in the 350° oven about 30 minutes for baking dishes (about 20 minutes for au gratin dishes) or until heated through. Sprinkle with shredded cheese.

Bake, uncovered, about 5 minutes more or until cheese is melted. If desired, sprinkle the enchiladas with ripe olives and green pepper strips. Makes 8 servings.

Nutrition information per serving: 491 cal., 14 g total fat (7 g sat. fat), 29 mg chol., 1,599 mg sodium, 71 g carbo., 25 g pro.

Spicy Black Beans and Rice

Instead of rice, spoon the warm black bean mixture over squares of freshly baked corn bread.

1 medium onion, chopped (½ cup)
4 cloves garlic, minced
2 tablespoons olive oil or cooking oil
1 15-ounce can black beans, rinsed
    and drained
1 14½-ounce can Mexican-style
    stewed tomatoes
⅛ to ¼ teaspoon ground red pepper
2 cups hot cooked brown or long
    grain rice
¼ cup chopped onion (optional)

In a medium saucepan cook ½ cup onion and garlic in hot oil until onion is tender. Carefully stir in the drained beans, undrained tomatoes, and red pepper. Bring to boiling; reduce heat. Simmer, uncovered, for 15 minutes.

To serve, mound rice on dinner plates; make a well in the centers. Spoon black bean mixture into centers. If desired, sprinkle with ¼ cup onion. Makes 4 servings.

Nutrition information per serving: 279 cal., 8 g total fat (1 g sat. fat), 0 mg chol., 631 mg sodium, 47 g carbo., 11 g pro.

Warm Beans with Herbed Tomatoes and Goat Cheese

Get extra mileage out of this recipe by chilling any leftovers and serving them as salad with warm tortillas.

3 medium ripe tomatoes, seeded and
    chopped (2 cups)
¼ cup snipped fresh basil
¼ cup snipped fresh oregano
2 green onions, sliced
1 clove garlic, minced
½ teaspoon salt
¼ teaspoon pepper
1 15-ounce can small red beans or
    kidney beans
1 15-ounce can Great Northern beans
    or navy beans
4 ounces semisoft goat (chèvre) cheese
    or feta cheese, crumbled (1 cup)

In a medium bowl combine chopped tomatoes, basil, oregano, green onions, garlic, salt, and pepper. Let stand at room temperature for 30 minutes to 2 hours.

In a medium saucepan combine undrained red or kidney beans and undrained Great Northern or navy beans. Bring to boiling; reduce heat. Cover and simmer about 2 minutes or until mixture is heated through. Drain.

To serve, toss warm beans with tomato mixture. Sprinkle with cheese. Serve warm. Makes 4 servings.

Nutrition information per serving: 304 cal., 7 g total fat (4 g sat. fat), 13 mg chol., 558 mg sodium, 45 g carbo., 22 g pro.

Spicy Black Beans and Rice

Cheese Tortellini with Cannellini Bean Sauce

You can make this low-fat pasta dish in a snap thanks to refrigerated tortellini and canned beans. Try it for a busy weeknight dinner with crusty sourdough bread and fresh fruit.

1	9-ounce package refrigerated cheese-stuffed tortellini
1	15-ounce can white kidney (cannellini) beans, rinsed and drained
⅔	cup milk
⅔	cup thin slivers of red, yellow, and/or green sweet pepper
¼	cup grated Parmesan cheese
1	tablespoon snipped fresh oregano or 1 teaspoon dried oregano, crushed
¼	teaspoon salt
¼	teaspoon ground nutmeg
⅛	teaspoon black pepper
	Finely shredded Parmesan cheese (optional)
	Fresh oregano sprigs (optional)

Cook the pasta according to package directions. Drain; keep warm.

Meanwhile, for sauce, in a food processor bowl or blender container combine the beans and milk. Cover and process or blend until smooth. Transfer the bean mixture to a large skillet.

Stir in sweet pepper slivers, grated Parmesan cheese, snipped fresh or dried oregano, salt, nutmeg, and black pepper. Cook and stir until mixture is heated through.

Arrange the cooked pasta on dinner plates or a large platter. Spoon the sauce over pasta.

If desired, sprinkle each serving with finely shredded Parmesan cheese and garnish with fresh oregano sprigs. Makes 4 servings.

Nutrition information per serving: 304 cal., 6 g total fat (2 g sat. fat), 43 mg chol., 730 mg sodium, 48 g carbo., 21 g pro.

BEYOND RED KIDNEY BEANS

When you think of kidney beans, the red ones probably come to mind. But their Italian cousins, the cannellini beans, also are a versatile and delicious choice. These white, mild-tasting beans are ideal for making casseroles, soups, stews, and other one-dish meals, such as Cheese Tortellini with Cannellini Bean Sauce (above). Cannellini come in both canned and dried forms. Look for them with the other canned or dried beans in your supermarket or at Italian food specialty stores.

Couscous with Beans and Carrots

Although couscous looks like a grain, it is actually tiny pasta. In Morocco, where couscous originated, it is prepared with a variety of vegetables and meats and is served in some form at almost every meal.

1 cup water
2 medium carrots, bias-sliced (1 cup)
1 medium onion, chopped (½ cup)
½ of a vegetable bouillon cube (enough for 1 cup broth)
1½ cups fresh pea pods, halved crosswise
1 15½-ounce can reduced-sodium garbanzo beans, rinsed and drained
1 cup quick-cooking couscous
½ cup fat-free milk
1 tablespoon snipped fresh savory or 1 teaspoon dried savory, crushed
¼ teaspoon garlic powder
⅛ teaspoon pepper
½ cup shredded reduced-fat Monterey Jack cheese (2 ounces)

In a medium saucepan combine the water, carrots, onion, and vegetable bouillon cube. Bring to boiling; reduce heat. Cover and simmer for 6 minutes. Stir in the pea pods. Cover and simmer about 3 minutes more or until vegetables are crisp-tender.

Stir the garbanzo beans, couscous, milk, savory, garlic powder, and pepper into vegetable mixture. Bring just to boiling. Remove from heat. Cover and let stand for 5 minutes. Fluff with a fork. Sprinkle each serving with Monterey Jack cheese. Makes 4 servings.

Nutrition information per serving: 351 cal., 5 g total fat (2 g sat. fat), 11 mg chol., 468 mg sodium, 59 g carbo., 18 g pro.

Triple Mushroom and Rice Fajitas

This earthy three-mushroom filling paired with traditional fajita toppers makes a satisfying meatless meal. Substitute button mushrooms if you can't find the three suggested varieties in your supermarket.

½ cup uncooked regular brown rice
¼ cup water
2 tablespoons lime juice
1 tablespoon olive oil or cooking oil
2 large cloves garlic, minced
½ teaspoon ground cumin
½ teaspoon dried oregano, crushed
¼ teaspoon salt
3 ounces fresh portobello mushrooms, stemmed and thinly sliced
3 ounces fresh chanterelle or oyster mushrooms, thinly sliced
3 ounces fresh shiitake mushrooms, stemmed and thinly sliced
1 medium green and/or red sweet pepper, cut into thin strips
4 green onions, cut into 1½-inch pieces
8 7- to 8-inch flour tortillas
¼ cup slivered almonds, toasted
Green onion tops (optional)
Fresh cilantro (optional)

Cook brown rice according to package directions, except omit any salt.

Meanwhile, for marinade, in a large plastic bag set in a deep bowl combine the water, lime juice, oil, garlic, cumin, oregano, and salt. Add sliced mushrooms, sweet pepper strips, and green onion pieces; seal bag. Marinate at room temperature for 15 to 30 minutes, turning bag occasionally.

Stack tortillas; wrap in foil. Bake in a 350° oven about 10 minutes or until warm. (Or just before serving, microwave tortillas, covered with a paper towel, on 100% power [high] about 1 minute.)

For filling, in a large nonstick skillet cook undrained mushroom mixture over medium-high heat for 6 to 8 minutes or until pepper strips are tender and all but about 2 tablespoons of the liquid is evaporated, stirring occasionally. Stir in cooked brown rice and almonds; heat through.

To serve, spoon the mushroom mixture onto tortillas; roll up. If desired, tie a green onion top around each tortilla roll and garnish with cilantro. Makes 4 servings.

Nutrition information per serving: 331 cal., 9 g total fat (2 g sat. fat), 0 mg chol., 380 mg sodium, 55 g carbo., 9 g pro.

Risotto with Vegetables

Risotto (rih-ZOT-oh) is a classic Italian dish in which Arborio rice is first browned, then simmered in broth and constantly stirred so it absorbs the liquid. The finished product has a creamy consistency and a tender, but slightly firm, texture.

2 cups sliced fresh mushrooms
½ cup chopped onion (1 medium)
2 cloves garlic, minced
2 tablespoons olive oil or cooking oil
1 cup uncooked Arborio rice
3 cups vegetable or chicken broth
¾ cup asparagus or broccoli cut into bite-size pieces
¾ cup seeded and chopped tomato
¼ cup shredded carrot (1 small)
1 cup shredded fontina or Muenster cheese (4 ounces)
¼ cup grated Parmesan cheese
3 tablespoons snipped fresh basil or parsley
Tomato slices (optional)

In a large saucepan cook mushrooms, onion, and garlic in hot oil until onion is tender. Add uncooked rice. Cook and stir over medium heat about 5 minutes or until rice is golden brown.

Meanwhile, in a medium saucepan bring broth to boiling; reduce heat and simmer. Slowly add 1 cup of the broth to the rice mixture, stirring constantly. Continue to cook and stir over medium heat until liquid is absorbed. Add another ½ cup of the broth and the asparagus or broccoli to rice mixture, stirring constantly. Continue to cook and stir until liquid is absorbed. Add another 1 cup broth, ½ cup at a time, stirring constantly until broth is absorbed. (This should take about 15 minutes total.)

Stir in the remaining ½ cup broth, the chopped tomato, and carrot. Cook and stir until rice is slightly creamy and just tender. Stir in fontina or Muenster cheese, Parmesan cheese, and basil or parsley. If desired, garnish with tomato slices. Makes 4 servings.

Nutrition information per serving: 406 cal., 19 g total fat (8 g sat. fat), 38 mg chol., 1,050 mg sodium, 48 g carbo., 16 g pro.

Zesty Vegetable Enchiladas

With melted cheese and tomato on top, these lentils and fresh vegetables wrapped in tortillas make a meal in themselves.

1⅓ cups water
½ cup dry lentils, rinsed and drained
8 6- or 7-inch flour tortillas
Nonstick cooking spray
2 medium carrots, thinly sliced
(1 cup)
1 medium zucchini or yellow summer
squash, quartered lengthwise and
sliced (2 cups)
2 teaspoons chili powder or
1 teaspoon ground cumin
1 14½-ounce can chunky Mexican-
style tomatoes
1 cup shredded reduced-fat Monterey
Jack cheese (4 ounces)
¼ teaspoon salt
Dash bottled hot pepper sauce
(optional)

In a medium saucepan combine water and lentils. Bring to boiling; reduce heat. Cover and simmer for 15 to 20 minutes or until tender. Drain lentils; set aside.

Meanwhile, stack tortillas; wrap in foil. Bake in a 350° oven about 10 minutes or until warm. (Or just before filling, microwave tortillas, covered with a paper towel, on 100% power [high] about 1 minute.) Coat a 2-quart rectangular baking dish with cooking spray; set aside.

Lightly coat a large skillet with cooking spray. Preheat over medium heat. Stir-fry carrots in hot skillet for 2 minutes. Add zucchini or yellow squash and chili powder or cumin. Stir-fry for 2 to 3 minutes or until vegetables are crisp-tender. Remove from heat. Stir in lentils, about half of the undrained tomatoes, ¾ cup of the cheese, the salt, and, if desired, hot pepper sauce.

Divide the vegetable mixture among warm tortillas; roll up tortillas. Place tortillas, seam sides down, in the prepared baking dish. Lightly coat tops of tortillas with cooking spray.

Bake in a 350° oven for 12 to 15 minutes or until enchiladas are heated through and tortillas are crisp.

Meanwhile, in a small saucepan heat the remaining undrained tomatoes. Spoon the tomatoes over enchiladas. Top with the remaining cheese. Makes 4 servings.

Nutrition information per serving: 401 cal., 10 g total fat (4 g sat. fat), 20 mg chol., 889 mg sodium, 58 g carbo., 21 g pro.

Savory Shepherd's Pie

To speed preparation, substitute packaged instant mashed potatoes (enough for 4 servings) for the 3 small potatoes and stir the garlic mixture into the prepared instant potatoes.

3 small potatoes (12 ounces)
2 cloves garlic, minced
½ teaspoon dried basil, crushed
2 tablespoons margarine or butter
¼ teaspoon salt
2 to 4 tablespoons milk
1 medium onion, chopped
1 medium carrot, sliced
1 tablespoon cooking oil
1 15-ounce can kidney beans, rinsed and drained
1 14½-ounce can tomatoes, drained and cut up
1 10-ounce package frozen mixed vegetables or whole kernel corn
1 8-ounce can tomato sauce
1 teaspoon Worcestershire sauce
½ teaspoon sugar
1 cup shredded cheddar cheese
  Paprika (optional)

Peel and quarter potatoes. In a covered large saucepan cook potatoes in a small amount of boiling, lightly salted water for 20 to 25 minutes or until tender. Drain.

Mash with a potato masher or beat with an electric mixer on low speed. In a small saucepan cook garlic and basil in margarine or butter for 15 seconds. Add to mashed potatoes along with salt. Gradually beat in enough of the milk to make light and fluffy. Set aside.

For filling, in a medium saucepan cook onion and carrot in hot oil until onion is tender. Stir in beans, tomatoes, frozen vegetables, tomato sauce, Worcestershire sauce, and sugar. Heat until mixture is bubbly.

Transfer filling to an ungreased 8×8×2-inch baking pan. Drop mashed potatoes in 4 mounds over filling. Sprinkle with cheddar cheese and, if desired, paprika. Bake in a 375° oven for 25 to 30 minutes or until heated through and cheese starts to brown. Makes 4 servings.

Nutrition information per serving: 456 cal., 19 g total fat (8 g sat. fat), 31 mg chol., 1,130 mg sodium, 60 g carbo., 20 g pro.

Herbed Pasta Primavera

For the best flavor, use fresh parsley, fresh basil, and freshly shredded Parmesan cheese.

6	ounces packaged dried linguine, spaghetti, or fettuccine
1	cup water
2	teaspoons cornstarch
2	teaspoons instant vegetable or chicken bouillon granules
1	tablespoon olive oil
2	cloves garlic, minced
8	ounces asparagus, cut into 1-inch pieces
2	medium carrots, thinly bias-sliced
1	medium onion, chopped
1	6-ounce package frozen pea pods, thawed and well drained
⅔	cup sliced almonds
¼	cup snipped parsley
1½	teaspoons dried basil, crushed
¼	teaspoon pepper
⅓	cup finely shredded Parmesan cheese

Cook pasta according to package directions. Drain; keep warm. Meanwhile, for sauce, in a small bowl stir together the water, cornstarch, and vegetable or chicken bouillon granules. Set aside.

Add olive oil to a wok or large skillet. Preheat over medium-high heat. Stir-fry garlic in hot oil for 15 seconds. Add asparagus, carrots, and onion; stir fry for 2 minutes. Add pea pods, nuts, parsley, basil, and pepper. Stir-fry about 1 minute more or until vegetables are crisp-tender. Remove vegetable mixture from wok.

Stir sauce; add to wok. Cook and stir until thickened and bubbly. Cook and stir for 1 minute more. Return vegetable mixture to wok. Cook and stir until heated through. Serve immediately over pasta. Sprinkle with Parmesan cheese. Makes 4 servings.

Nutrition information per serving: 432 cal., 19 g total fat (3 g sat. fat), 7 mg chol., 642 mg sodium, 52 g carbo., 17 g pro.

Lemony Alfredo-Style Fettuccine

Do you avoid pasta Alfredo because it's so high in fat? This luscious Alfredo-like sauce is made with reduced-fat cream cheese and evaporated fat-free milk to help keep the fat in check so you can indulge any time you like.

2   cups loose-pack frozen mixed
      vegetables
8   ounces dried spinach fettuccine or
      plain fettuccine
2   ounces reduced-fat cream cheese
      (Neufchâtel), cut up
½   cup evaporated fat-free milk
¼   cup grated Parmesan cheese
½   teaspoon finely shredded lemon peel
¼   teaspoon freshly ground pepper
      Dash ground nutmeg

Cook mixed vegetables according to package directions, except omit any salt; drain. Cover and keep warm.

Cook fettuccine according to package directions until tender but still firm, except omit any oil or salt; drain. Return fettuccine to saucepan.

Add cooked mixed vegetables, cream cheese, evaporated milk, Parmesan cheese, lemon peel, pepper, and nutmeg to cooked fettuccine. Heat through, tossing gently until cream cheese is melted and fettuccine is well coated. Serve immediately. Makes 4 servings.

Nutrition information per serving: 339 cal., 6 g total fat (4 g sat. fat), 17 mg chol., 256 mg sodium, 55 g carbo., 16 g pro.

COOKING WITH REDUCED-FAT CHEESES

Reduced-fat cheeses need a little extra care when it comes to cooking. Follow these tips for best results:
• Avoid boiling sauces and soups that use reduced-fat cheese; boiling causes the cheese to toughen.
• Shredding or cutting up reduced-fat cheese before adding it to heated mixtures induces melting more easily.
• When broiling or toasting cheese-topped dishes, remove them just as the cheese begins to melt.

Vegetable Lasagna

In a hurry? Substitute 2 cups of prepared spaghetti sauce for the Red Pepper Sauce in this recipe.

6 no-boil lasagna noodles or regular lasagna noodles
8 ounces zucchini and/or yellow summer squash, halved lengthwise and sliced
2 cups sliced fresh mushrooms
⅓ cup chopped onion
2 teaspoons olive oil
1 cup fat-free or low-fat ricotta cheese
¼ cup finely shredded Parmesan cheese
¼ teaspoon black pepper
   Red Pepper Sauce
1 cup shredded part-skim mozzarella cheese (4 ounces)
1 medium tomato, seeded and chopped
   Fresh oregano sprigs (optional)

Soak the no-boil lasagna noodles in warm water for 10 minutes. (Or, cook regular noodles according to package directions, except omit salt.) Drain.

Meanwhile, in a large skillet cook zucchini and/or yellow squash, mushrooms, and onion in hot olive oil about 6 minutes or until squash is tender, stirring occasionally. Drain well.

In a small bowl stir together ricotta cheese, Parmesan cheese, and black pepper. To assemble, place 3 lasagna noodles in a 2-quart square baking dish, trimming to fit as necessary. Top with ricotta mixture, half of the vegetable mixture, half of the Red Pepper Sauce, and half of the mozzarella cheese. Layer with the remaining lasagna noodles, vegetable mixture, and sauce.

Bake in a 375° oven for 30 minutes. Sprinkle with remaining mozzarella cheese and the tomato. Bake about 5 minutes more or until heated through. Let stand for 10 minutes before serving. If desired, garnish with oregano sprigs. Makes 6 servings.

Red Pepper Sauce: In a large skillet cook 3 cups chopped *red sweet pepper* and 4 whole cloves *garlic* in 1 tablespoon *olive oil* or *cooking oil* over medium heat for 20 minutes, stirring occasionally. (Or, use one 12-ounce jar *roasted red sweet peppers,* drained. Omit cooking step.) Place mixture in a blender container. Cover and blend until nearly smooth. Add ½ cup *water,* ¼ cup *tomato paste,* 2 tablespoons *red wine vinegar,* and 1 tablespoon snipped *fresh oregano* or ½ teaspoon *dried oregano,* crushed. Cover and blend just until nearly smooth. Return to skillet; heat through. Makes 2 cups.

Nutrition information per serving: 249 cal., 9 g total fat (3 g sat. fat), 18 mg chol., 292 mg sodium, 28 g carbo., 17 g pro.

Tofu and Cheese-Stuffed Shells

No one will ever know that these giant pasta shells contain tofu—unless you tell.

12 packaged dried jumbo pasta shells
¼ cup shredded carrot
1 green onion, sliced
8 ounces tofu (fresh bean curd), drained
½ cup ricotta cheese
½ cup shredded cheddar cheese
½ cup shredded mozzarella cheese
1 egg white
¼ teaspoon salt
¼ teaspoon pepper
1 14½-ounce can tomatoes, cut up
½ of a 6-ounce can (⅓ cup) tomato paste
1 teaspoon dried basil, crushed
1 teaspoon dried oregano, crushed
½ teaspoon sugar
¼ teaspoon garlic powder
¼ teaspoon fennel seed, crushed (optional)
    Grated Parmesan cheese (optional)

Cook pasta according to package directions. Drain pasta; rinse with cold water. Drain again.

Meanwhile, in a small saucepan cook carrot and green onion in a small amount of water until tender. Drain.

For filling, in a medium mixing bowl mash tofu with a fork. Stir in carrot mixture, ricotta cheese, cheddar cheese, ¼ cup of the mozzarella cheese, egg white, salt, and pepper. Set aside.

For sauce, in a medium saucepan combine the undrained cut-up tomatoes, tomato paste, basil, oregano, sugar, garlic powder, and, if desired, fennel seed. Bring to boiling; reduce heat. Simmer, uncovered, for 10 minutes.

To assemble, stuff each pasta shell with about 1 rounded tablespoon filling. Place in an ungreased 2-quart square baking dish. Pour the sauce over stuffed pasta shells.

Cover and bake in a 350° oven about 25 minutes or until heated through. Sprinkle with the remaining mozzarella cheese. If desired, serve with Parmesan cheese. Makes 4 servings.

Nutrition information per serving: 318 cal., 13 g total fat (6 g sat. fat), 32 mg chol., 558 mg sodium, 32 g carbo., 21 g pro.

Nutty Orzo and Vegetables

Check the pasta aisle carefully—tiny, rice-shaped orzo may be labeled rosamarina.

½ cup dried orzo pasta (rosamarina)

2 cups loose-pack frozen mixed vegetables

1 15-ounce can garbanzo beans, rinsed and drained

1 14½-ounce can low-sodium stewed tomatoes

1¼ cups bottled light spaghetti sauce

1 tablespoon snipped fresh thyme

¼ cup chopped cashews or slivered almonds, toasted

¼ cup shredded reduced-fat mozzarella cheese (1 ounce)

Fresh thyme sprigs (optional)

In a large saucepan cook orzo according to package directions, except omit any salt. Add frozen mixed vegetables after 5 minutes of cooking. Drain. Return orzo mixture to saucepan.

Stir garbanzo beans, undrained tomatoes, spaghetti sauce, and the snipped thyme into cooked orzo mixture. Bring to boiling; reduce heat. Cover and simmer for 5 minutes.

Before serving, stir in toasted cashews or almonds. Spoon orzo mixture onto dinner plates or into serving bowls. Sprinkle each serving with mozzarella cheese. If desired, garnish with fresh thyme sprigs. Makes 4 servings.

Nutrition information per serving: 313 cal., 7 g total fat (2 g sat. fat), 4 mg chol., 364 mg sodium, 53 g carbo., 13 g pro.

*B*EAN WISDOM

Canned beans can save you time, but they also contribute sodium to your diet. A way to resolve this problem is to rinse the beans in a colander under running water and let them drain. You'll get great-tasting beans without the salty liquid that comes with them.

Pasta with Garden Vegetables

Two kinds of Italian cheese, Romano and provolone, combine with corkscrew pasta and an array of fresh vegetables to create a family favorite.

1 tablespoon cooking oil
1 clove garlic, minced
2 small zucchini, sliced ¼ inch thick (2 cups)
1 small yellow summer squash, sliced ¼ inch thick (1 cup)
2 cups sliced fresh mushrooms
⅓ cup sliced green onions
1 large tomato, chopped (1½ cups)
½ teaspoon dried oregano, crushed
⅛ teaspoon freshly ground pepper
8 ounces dried corkscrew pasta, cooked and drained
¼ cup finely shredded Romano or Parmesan cheese
1 cup shredded provolone or mozzarella cheese (4 ounces)

Add cooking oil to a wok or large skillet. Preheat over medium-high heat (add more oil if necessary during cooking). Stir-fry garlic in hot oil for 15 seconds.

Add zucchini and yellow squash; stir-fry for 3 minutes. Add mushrooms and green onions; stir-fry about 1 minute or until vegetables are crisp-tender. Add tomato, oregano, and pepper; stir-fry for 2 minutes more. Remove from heat.

Add the hot cooked pasta and the Romano or Parmesan cheese to vegetable mixture; toss to combine. Serve immediately. Sprinkle each serving with provolone or mozzarella cheese and additional pepper. Makes 4 servings.

Nutrition information per serving: 412 cal., 14 g total fat (7 g sat. fat), 27 mg chol., 340 mg sodium, 53 g carbo., 19 g pro.

Egg Ragout

This simple supper is the perfect conclusion to any weekend recreation, from a hike in the woods to a snooze on the couch. It's a scrumptious, creamy egg and vegetable mélange that makes the most of pantry staples.

1½ cups fresh sugar snap peas, strings and tips removed
1 cup baby sunburst squash, cut into quarters
4 green onions, thinly bias-sliced
4 teaspoons margarine or butter
2 tablespoons all-purpose flour
1¼ cups milk
2 tablespoons grated Parmesan cheese
1 teaspoon sweet-hot mustard or Dijon-style mustard
4 hard-cooked eggs,* coarsely chopped
4 bagels, split and toasted, or 4 slices whole wheat bread, toasted

In a covered medium saucepan cook sugar snap peas and sunburst squash in a small amount of boiling salted water for 2 to 4 minutes or until crisp-tender; drain.

In a large saucepan cook green onions in hot margarine or butter over medium heat until tender. Stir in flour. Add milk all at once. Cook and stir until thickened and bubbly. Stir in Parmesan cheese and mustard; add cooked vegetables. Cook and stir about 1 minute more or until heated through.

Gently stir eggs into vegetable mixture. Serve the egg mixture over toasted bagels or bread. Makes 4 servings.

*Note: To cook the eggs, place them in a medium saucepan. Add enough cold water to come 1 inch above the eggs. Bring to boiling; reduce heat. Cover and simmer for 15 minutes; drain. Run cold water over eggs or place eggs in ice water until cool enough to handle; drain. If desired, cover and chill up to 1 week. Peel eggs.

Nutrition information per serving: 392 cal., 13 g total fat (4 g sat. fat), 221 mg chol., 600 mg sodium, 49 g carbo., 19 g pro.

Vegetable Frittata

When you need a spur-of-the-moment meal, this egg dish saves the day. Serve it with sliced cucumbers, tossed in a light vinaigrette, and hearty bread.

1   cup water
1   cup broccoli florets
½   cup finely chopped carrot
    Nonstick cooking spray
¼   cup sliced green onions
¾   cup shredded reduced-fat cheddar
        or Swiss cheese (3 ounces)
2   8-ounce cartons refrigerated or
        frozen egg product, thawed
1   tablespoon snipped fresh basil or
        1 teaspoon dried basil, crushed
1   tablespoon Dijon-style mustard
¼   teaspoon pepper
    Tomato slices (optional)
    Fresh tarragon sprigs (optional)

In a medium saucepan combine the water, broccoli, and carrot. Bring to boiling; reduce heat. Cover and simmer for 6 to 8 minutes or until vegetables are crisp-tender. Drain well.

Coat a large nonstick skillet with cooking spray. Spread the cooked vegetables and green onions in bottom of skillet. Sprinkle with half of the cheese. In a medium bowl stir together the egg product, basil, mustard, and pepper. Pour over vegetables and cheese.

Cook over medium heat. As mixture sets, run a spatula around edge of skillet, lifting egg mixture so the uncooked portion flows underneath. Continue cooking and lifting the edge until egg mixture is nearly set (the surface will be moist). Remove from heat. Cover and let stand for 3 to 4 minutes or until top is set.

To serve, cut the frittata into wedges. Sprinkle with the remaining cheese. If desired, garnish with tomato slices and tarragon sprigs. Makes 8 servings.

Nutrition information per serving: 101 cal., 3 g total fat (1 g sat. fat), 6 mg chol., 287 mg sodium, 6 g carbo., 11 g pro.

Mu Shu Vegetable Roll-Ups

Instead of wrapping up our Mu Shu vegetables in the traditional Peking pancakes, we went Mexican and used ready-made flour tortillas. For easier handling, be sure to warm the tortillas before filling.

2   tablespoons water
2   tablespoons soy sauce
½   teaspoon sugar
½   teaspoon cornstarch
8   to 10 8-inch flour tortillas
1   tablespoon cooking oil
1   teaspoon grated gingerroot
2   cloves garlic, minced
2   medium carrots, cut into julienne
       strips
½   of a small head cabbage, shredded
       (3 cups)
1   medium zucchini, cut into julienne
       strips (1¼ cups)
4   cups sliced fresh mushrooms
2   cups fresh bean sprouts
½   of a medium jicama, peeled and cut
       into julienne strips (1 cup)
8   ounces firm tofu (bean curd), well
       drained and cut into ¾-inch cubes
8   green onions, sliced (1 cup)
¼   cup hoisin sauce
     Cherry tomato flowers (optional)
     Green onion brushes (optional)

For sauce, in a small bowl stir together water, soy sauce, sugar, and cornstarch. Set aside.

Wrap tortillas in foil and bake in a 350° oven about 10 minutes or until warm. [Or, just before serving, microwave tortillas, covered, on 100% power (high) about 1 minute or until warm.]

Meanwhile, pour cooking oil into a wok or large skillet. Preheat over medium-high heat (add more oil if necessary during cooking). Stir-fry gingerroot and garlic in hot oil for 15 seconds. Add carrot strips; stir-fry for 1 minute. Add cabbage and zucchini; stir-fry for 1 minute. Add mushrooms, bean sprouts, and jicama strips. Stir-fry for 1 to 2 minutes more or until vegetables are crisp-tender. Push vegetables from center of wok.

Stir sauce; add to center of wok. Cook and stir until thickened and bubbly. Add tofu and sliced green onions. Gently stir all ingredients together to coat. Cover and cook about 2 minutes more or until mixture is heated through.

Spread warm tortillas with hoisin sauce. Spoon the vegetable mixture onto each tortilla. Fold over one side of tortilla to cover some of the filling. Then fold the two adjacent sides of tortilla over filling. Secure with toothpicks, if necessary. If desired, garnish with tomato flowers and green onion brushes. Serve immediately. Makes 4 or 5 servings.

Nutrition information per serving: 399 cal., 12 g total fat (2 g sat. fat), 0 mg chol., 1,811 mg sodium, 57 g carbo., 20 g pro.

Mandarin Tofu Stir-Fry

Tofu takes on whatever flavors you mix with it. In this case a sweet-and-sour sauce does the trick.

½ cup bottled sweet-and-sour sauce
⅛ teaspoon ground red pepper
1 tablespoon cooking oil
6 green onions, bias-sliced into 1-inch pieces (1 cup)
½ of a medium red or green sweet pepper, cut into thin strips
2 cups fresh pea pods or one 6-ounce package frozen pea pods, thawed
1 16-ounce package extra-firm tofu (fresh bean curd), well drained and cut into ¾-inch cubes
1 11-ounce can mandarin orange sections, drained, or 3 medium oranges, peeled and sectioned
2 cups hot cooked rice
2 tablespoons unsalted dry roasted peanuts

For sauce, in a small bowl stir together sweet-and-sour sauce and ground red pepper. Set aside.

Add cooking oil to a wok or large skillet. Preheat over medium-high heat (add more oil if necessary during cooking). Stir-fry green onions and sweet pepper in hot oil for 1 minute. If using fresh pea pods, add to wok. Stir-fry for 1 to 2 minutes more or until vegetables are crisp-tender. Push vegetables from center of wok.

Add sauce to center of wok. Cook and stir until bubbly. Add tofu, orange sections, and, if using, thawed frozen pea pods. Gently stir all ingredients together to coat. Cover and cook for 1 to 2 minutes more or until heated through.

Serve immediately with hot cooked rice. Sprinkle with peanuts. Makes 4 servings.

Nutrition information per serving: 360 cal., 12 g total fat (2 g sat. fat), 0 mg chol., 117 mg sodium, 53 g carbo., 15 g pro.

TOFU TIPS

A process similar to the one used for making cheese transforms soybean milk into soybean curd, also called tofu. Tofu is sold in blocks or cakes and comes in soft, firm, and extra-firm varieties. Extra-firm tofu is recommended for stir-fried dishes because it holds its shape well. Look for it in the refrigerated area of your supermarket produce section.

Southwest Skillet

This stove-top main course is built on classic Southwestern favorites you can find in most supermarkets.

2   tablespoons sliced almonds
1   yellow sweet pepper, cut into thin
      bite-size strips
1   fresh jalapeño pepper, seeded and
      chopped
1   tablespoon olive oil or cooking oil
4   medium tomatoes (about
      1¼ pounds), peeled and chopped
1½ to 2 teaspoons purchased Mexican
      seasoning or Homemade Mexican
      Seasoning
¼   teaspoon salt
4   eggs
1   ripe medium avocado, seeded,
      peeled, and sliced (optional)
    Fresh chile peppers (optional)

In a large skillet cook almonds over medium heat for 4 to 5 minutes or until light brown, stirring occasionally. Remove from skillet; set aside. In the same skillet cook sweet pepper and jalapeño pepper in hot oil about 2 minutes or until peppers are tender. Stir in tomatoes, Mexican seasoning, and salt. Bring to boiling; reduce heat. Cover and simmer for 5 minutes.

Break one of the eggs into a measuring cup. Carefully slide the egg into the simmering tomato mixture. Repeat with remaining eggs. Sprinkle the eggs lightly with salt and black pepper.

Cover and cook eggs over medium-low heat for 3 to 5 minutes or until the whites are completely set and the yolks begin to thicken but are not firm.

To serve, transfer eggs to dinner plates with a slotted spoon. Stir tomato mixture; then spoon it around eggs on plates. Sprinkle with the toasted almonds. If desired, serve with avocado slices and garnish with chile peppers. Makes 4 servings.

Homemade Mexican Seasoning: In a small bowl stir together 1 to 1½ teaspoons *chili powder* and ½ teaspoon *ground cumin.*

Nutrition information per serving: 392 cal., 13 g total fat (4 g sat. fat), 221 mg chol., 600 mg sodium, 49 g carbo., 19 g pro.

South-of-the-Border Pie

Kidney beans, brown rice, eggs, and cheddar cheese provide the protein while chili powder and cumin provide the kick. Serve this Mexican-style dish with a simple tossed salad.

1 medium onion, chopped
2 cloves garlic, minced
1 tablespoon olive oil or cooking oil
1 to 2 teaspoons chili powder
1 teaspoon ground cumin
¼ teaspoon salt
1 15-ounce can red kidney beans,
    rinsed and drained
1½ cups cooked brown rice
1 cup shredded cheddar cheese
    (4 ounces)
¾ cup milk
2 slightly beaten eggs
    Green sweet pepper strips (optional)
    Salsa (optional)

Lightly grease a 10-inch quiche dish or pie plate. Set aside. In a large saucepan cook onion and garlic in hot oil until tender. Stir in chili powder, cumin, and salt. Cook and stir for 1 minute more. Cool. Stir in beans, cooked brown rice, cheese, milk, and eggs.

Spoon the bean mixture into the prepared baking dish. Bake in a 350° oven about 25 minutes or until the center is set. Let stand for 10 minutes. If desired, sprinkle the pie with green pepper strips and serve with salsa. Makes 6 servings.

Nutrition information per serving: 254 cal., 12 g total fat (5 g sat. fat), 93 mg chol., 366 mg sodium, 26 g carbo., 14 g pro.

Southern Grits Casserole with Red Pepper Relish

To make a roasted pepper relish, substitute one 12-ounce jar roasted red sweet peppers for the fresh sweet peppers. Drain and chop the roasted peppers and stir into the cooked onion mixture.

4 cups water
1 cup quick-cooking grits
4 slightly beaten eggs
2 cups shredded cheddar cheese
   (8 ounces)
½ cup milk
¼ cup sliced green onions
1 to 2 jalapeño peppers, seeded
   (if desired) and chopped
½ teaspoon garlic salt
¼ teaspoon white pepper
   Sliced green onions (optional)
2 medium red sweet peppers, chopped
   (2 cups)
1 small red onion, chopped (½ cup)
2 cloves garlic, minced
1 tablespoon margarine or butter
⅓ cup snipped parsley
1 tablespoon white wine vinegar

In a large saucepan bring water to boiling. Slowly stir in grits. Gradually stir about 1 cup of the hot mixture into the eggs. Return to saucepan. Remove from heat.

Stir the shredded cheese, milk, ¼ cup green onions, jalapeño peppers, garlic salt, and white pepper into the grits mixture.

Spoon the grits mixture into an ungreased 2-quart casserole. Bake in a 350° oven for 45 to 50 minutes or until a knife inserted near center comes out clean If desired, sprinkle with additional green onions.

Meanwhile, for relish, in a medium saucepan cook the red sweet peppers, red onion, and garlic in margarine or butter just until peppers are tender. Remove from heat. Stir in parsley and vinegar.

Let relish stand at room temperature at least 30 minutes. Serve the relish with grits. Makes 4 servings.

Nutrition information per serving: 403 cal., 27 g total fat (14 g sat. fat), 275 mg chol., 731 mg sodium, 16 g carbo., 23 g pro.

Tofu Pitas with Mango Salsa

Although the ingredients for Jamaican jerk seasoning differ from brand to brand, this Caribbean blend typically includes chile peppers, thyme, and spices. Look for it in the seasoning aisle of your supermarket.

2 tablespoons lime juice or lemon
  juice
1 teaspoon cooking oil
½ teaspoon purchased Jamaican
  jerk seasoning or Homemade
  Jamaican Jerk Seasoning
  (recipe, page 129)
1 10½-ounce package extra-firm light
  tofu (fresh bean curd)
  Nonstick cooking spray
⅓ cup quick-cooking couscous
  Mango Salsa
3 large pita bread rounds, halved
  crosswise
  Spinach leaves or torn lettuce leaves
  Lime slices (optional)
  Fresh thyme or marjoram sprigs
  (optional)

For marinade, in a shallow dish or pie plate combine the lime or lemon juice, oil, and Jamaican jerk seasoning. Cut tofu into ½-inch slices. Add tofu slices to marinade and brush marinade over slices. Cover and marinate at room temperature for 30 minutes, turning slices once and brushing with marinade. (Or cover and marinate in the refrigerator up to 6 hours, turning and brushing slices occasionally with marinade.)

Coat a grill basket with cooking spray. Place tofu slices in prepared grill basket. Discard marinade. Place basket with tofu slices on the rack of an uncovered grill directly over medium-hot coals. Grill about 10 minutes or until heated through, turning once. (Or coat the unheated rack of a broiler pan with cooking spray. Place tofu on prepared rack. Broil 5 to 6 inches from the heat about 8 minutes, turning once.) Cut the tofu slices into cubes.

Meanwhile, cook couscous according to package directions, except omit any butter or salt.

To serve, add tofu cubes and cooked couscous to Mango Salsa; toss gently to combine. Line pita halves with spinach or lettuce leaves. Spoon the tofu mixture into pita halves. If desired, garnish with lime slices and fresh thyme or marjoram. Makes 6 servings.

Mango Salsa: In a medium bowl combine 1 cup peeled and chopped *mango*; 1 small *tomato*, seeded and chopped; ½ of a medium *cucumber*, seeded and chopped; 1 thinly sliced *green onion*; 2 tablespoons snipped *fresh cilantro*; 1 *fresh jalapeño pepper*, seeded and chopped; and 1 tablespoon *lime or lemon juice*. Cover and chill until serving time. Makes about 2 cups.

Nutrition information per serving: 179 cal., 2 g total fat (0 g sat. fat), 0 mg chol., 251 mg sodium, 32 g carbo., 9 g pro.

Roasted Vegetable Medley with Rice

Roasting the potatoes, carrots, and fennel in a marjoram, vinegar, and oil dressing gives them a robust oven-browned flavor.

Nonstick cooking spray
12 ounces tiny new potatoes, quartered
4 medium carrots, thinly bias-sliced
1 small fennel bulb, halved lengthwise
    and thinly sliced
⅓ cup vinegar
1 tablespoon water
1 tablespoon olive oil or cooking oil
2 teaspoons snipped fresh marjoram
    or ½ teaspoon dried marjoram,
    crushed
1½ teaspoons sugar
½ teaspoon celery seeds
⅛ teaspoon garlic powder
1 15½-ounce can reduced-sodium
    garbanzo beans, rinsed and
    drained
2 cups water
1 vegetable bouillon cube (enough
    for 2 cups broth)
1 cup uncooked jasmine rice or long
    grain rice
Leafy fennel tops (optional)

Coat a 15×10×1-inch baking pan with cooking spray. In the prepared baking pan combine the potatoes, carrots, and fennel. In a small bowl combine vinegar, the 1 tablespoon water, the oil, marjoram, sugar, celery seeds, and garlic powder. Pour over vegetables; toss to coat.

Roast in a 450° oven for 35 minutes, stirring once. Add garbanzo beans, tossing to combine. Roast about 5 minutes more or until vegetables are tender and beans are heated through.

Meanwhile, in a small saucepan combine the 2 cups water and the bouillon cube. Bring to boiling. Stir in uncooked rice; reduce heat. Cover and cook for 15 to 20 minutes or until rice is tender and liquid is absorbed.

To serve, fluff cooked rice with a fork. Serve the roasted vegetables with the hot cooked rice. If desired, garnish with leafy fennel tops. Makes 4 servings.

Nutrition information per serving: 411 cal., 6 g total fat (1 g sat. fat), 0 mg chol., 499 mg sodium, 81 g carbo., 11 g pro.

Vegetarian Fried Rice

Transform fried rice from a side dish into a sumptuous meal by adding extra eggs and lots of vegetables.

5	slightly beaten eggs
1	tablespoon soy sauce
2	tablespoons cooking oil
1	small onion, chopped (⅓ cup)
1	clove garlic, minced
2	stalks celery, thinly bias-sliced (1 cup)
1½	cups sliced fresh mushrooms
1	medium green sweet pepper, chopped (¾ cup)
4	cups cold cooked rice
1	8-ounce can bamboo shoots, drained
2	medium carrots, shredded (1 cup)
¾	cup frozen peas, thawed
3	tablespoons soy sauce
3	green onions, sliced (⅓ cup)
	Crinkle-cut carrot slices (optional)

In a small bowl combine eggs and 1 tablespoon soy sauce. Set aside.

Add 1 tablespoon of the cooking oil to a wok or large skillet. Preheat over medium heat. Stir-fry chopped onion and garlic in hot oil about 2 minutes or until crisp-tender.

Add the egg mixture to wok and stir gently to scramble. When eggs are set, remove from wok. Cut up any large pieces of egg mixture. Let wok cool slightly.

Add remaining oil to cooled wok. Preheat over medium-high heat (add more oil if necessary during cooking). Stir-fry celery in hot oil for 1 minute. Add the mushrooms and green pepper; stir-fry for 1 to 2 minutes more or until vegetables are crisp-tender.

Add cooked rice, bamboo shoots, shredded carrots, and peas. Sprinkle with 3 tablespoons soy sauce. Cook and stir for 4 to 6 minutes or until heated through. Add the cooked egg mixture and green onions. Cook and stir about 1 minute more or until heated through.

If desired, garnish fried rice with carrot slices. Serve immediately. Makes 4 or 5 servings.

Nutrition information per serving: 438 cal., 14 g total fat (3 g sat. fat), 266 mg chol., 1,177 mg sodium, 61 g carbo., 17 g pro.

Curried Vegetable Stir-Fry

This flavorful vegetable entrée fuses Asian stir-frying with curry and European Brussels sprouts.

2 cups water
1¼ cups quick-cooking pearl barley
1 cup fresh Brussels sprouts, halved,
    or frozen Brussels sprouts, thawed
    and halved
1 cup cold water
4 teaspoons cornstarch
1 to 2 teaspoons curry powder
1 teaspoon instant vegetable bouillon
    granules
  Nonstick spray coating
2 medium red, yellow, and/or green
    sweet peppers, cut into bite-size
    strips (1½ cups)
2 tablespoons thinly sliced green
    onion
1 cup bias-sliced carrots
¼ cup peanuts

Bring 2 cups water to boiling. Stir in barley. Return to boiling; reduce heat. Simmer, covered, for 10 to 12 minutes or until tender. If necessary, drain. Cook Brussels sprouts in a small amount of boiling water for 3 minutes. Drain. For sauce, stir together 1 cup water, cornstarch, curry powder, and bouillon granules.

Spray an unheated wok or large skillet with nonstick coating. Preheat over medium-high heat. Stir-fry the peppers and green onion in hot wok for 1 minute. Add the Brussels sprouts and carrots; stir-fry for 3 minutes. Push from center of wok. Stir sauce; add to center of wok. Cook and stir until thickened and bubbly. Stir all ingredients together to coat. Cook and stir for 2 minutes more. Serve immediately over barley. Sprinkle with peanuts. Makes 4 servings.

Nutrition information per serving: 320 cal., 6 g total fat (a g sat. fat), 0 mg chol., 333 mg sodium, 59 g carbo., 10 g pro.

BIAS-SLICING

To bias-slice vegetables, such as carrots or green onions, or meats, hold a sharp knife at a 45-degree angle to the vegetable or meat and cut into thin diagonal slices. Partially freezing the meat before bias-slicing makes it easier to cut thin slices.

Spaghetti Squash Italiano

Spaghetti squash is a tasty, low-calorie, high-vitamin substitute for spaghetti.

2 small spaghetti squash (1¼ to 1½ pounds each)
4 ounces mozzarella cheese, cut into small cubes (1 cup)
3 medium tomatoes, seeded and chopped (2 cups)
4 green onions, sliced
½ cup pine nuts or coarsely chopped walnuts, toasted
¼ cup snipped fresh basil or parsley
1 tablespoon olive oil or cooking oil
2 cloves garlic, minced
2 tablespoons grated Parmesan cheese

Halve the squash lengthwise and remove the seeds. Prick skin all over with a sharp knife. Place halves, cut sides down, in a 3-quart rectangular baking dish. Cover and bake in a 350° oven for 60 to 70 minutes or until squash is tender.

Using a fork, carefully rake the squash pulp to separate it into strands, leaving the strands in the shells. Sprinkle one-fourth of the mozzarella cheese over each shell; toss lightly. Push the squash mixture up the sides of the shells.

Meanwhile, for filling, in a medium mixing bowl combine tomatoes, green onions, nuts, basil or parsley, oil, and garlic. Spoon the filling into squash shells. Sprinkle with Parmesan cheese.

Return to baking dish. Bake about 20 minutes more or until filling is heated through. Makes 4 servings.

Nutrition information per serving: 304 cal., 20 g total fat (6 g sat. fat), 18 mg chol., 237 mg sodium, 23 g carbo., 15 g pro.

QUICK-COOKING SPAGHETTI SQUASH

Save time by cooking spaghetti squash in your microwave oven. Prick whole squash with a sharp knife. Place squash in a microwave-safe baking dish. Micro-cook, uncovered, on 100% power (high) for 15 to 20 minutes or until tender. Let stand for 5 minutes. Halve squash lengthwise and remove seeds.

Eggplant Parmigiana

In this healthful version of eggplant parmigiana, the fat content is minimized by parboiling the eggplant and zucchini instead of frying them and by using reduced-fat cheeses.

1 medium eggplant (about 1 pound)
2 cups zucchini bias-sliced about
   ¼ inch thick
¼ teaspoon salt
1 cup light ricotta cheese or low-fat
   cottage cheese, drained
1 15-ounce container refrigerated
   fat-free vegetable marinara sauce
   or 2 cups bottled light spaghetti
   sauce
1 small tomato, thinly sliced
½ cup shredded reduced-fat mozzarella
   cheese (2 ounces)
2 tablespoons grated Parmesan cheese

If desired, peel eggplant. Cut eggplant into ½-inch slices; halve each slice. In a large saucepan cook the eggplant, zucchini, and salt in a small amount of boiling water for 4 minutes. Drain vegetables; pat dry with paper towels.

Divide the eggplant and zucchini among 4 individual au gratin dishes or casseroles. Top with the ricotta or cottage cheese. Spoon the marinara sauce or spaghetti sauce over cheese and top with sliced tomato. Sprinkle with the mozzarella cheese and Parmesan cheese.

Bake in a 350° oven for 20 to 25 minutes or until heated through. Makes 4 servings.

Nutrition information per serving: 212 cal., 6 g total fat (3 g sat. fat), 21 mg chol., 560 mg sodium, 27 g carbo., 15 g pro.

ℰGGPLANT—A PERENNIAL FAVORITE

Popular dishes such as Eggplant Parmigiana (above) rely on the dark purple, pear-shape eggplant. There are several types of eggplant available, including western, white, Japanese, and small (baby) eggplant. When selecting one, look for a plump, glossy, heavy fruit. Don't buy one that's scarred, bruised, or has dull skin. Its green stem cap should be fresh looking and free of mold. You can refrigerate an eggplant up to 2 days before using.

Garden Veggie Burgers

Two toppings—sharp red onion and a tangy spinach-feta combination—add zest to these grilled meatless burgers.

2 medium red onions
¼ cup bottled vinaigrette salad
    dressing (room temperature)
4 refrigerated or frozen meatless
    burger patties
4 cups spinach leaves
1 clove garlic, minced
1 tablespoon olive oil
½ cup crumbled feta cheese (2 ounces)
4 hamburger buns

For onion topping, cut onions into ½-inch slices. Place onions on the rack of an uncovered grill directly over medium coals. Grill for 15 to 20 minutes or until tender, turning once and brushing occasionally with salad dressing. Add the meatless patties to grill alongside onions; grill for 8 to 10 minutes or until heated through, turning once.

For spinach topping, in a large skillet cook and stir the spinach and garlic in hot olive oil over medium-high heat about 30 seconds or just until spinach is wilted. Remove from heat. Stir in the feta cheese.

To serve, place onion slices on bottoms of buns. Top with the grilled burgers, spinach topping, and bun tops. Makes 4 servings.

Nutrition information per serving: 350 cal., 14 g total fat (4 g sat. fat), 17 mg chol., 920 mg sodium, 37 g carbo., 21 g pro.

Sautéed Onion & Tomato Sandwiches

When laps double as the dining table, the best TV dinner is something easy and out-of-hand. This hearty whole-grain sandwich serves perfectly. Pass around beer, brownies, and your biggest napkins.

2   medium onions, sliced
1   teaspoon olive oil
8   slices hearty whole grain bread
       (toasted, if desired)
     Honey mustard
4   lettuce leaves, shredded
3   small red and/or yellow tomatoes,
       thinly sliced
     Small fresh basil leaves
4   ounces spreadable Brie cheese or
       ½ of an 8-ounce tub cream cheese

In a large skillet cook the onion slices in hot olive oil over medium-high heat for 5 to 7 minutes or until tender and just starting to brown. Remove from heat. Cool onions slightly.

To assemble, lightly spread half of the bread slices with honey mustard. Top with shredded lettuce, cooked onion slices, and tomato slices. Sprinkle with basil leaves.

Spread the remaining bread slices with Brie or cream cheese. Place on top of sandwiches. Makes 4 servings.

Nutrition information per serving: 287 cal., 12 g total fat (6 g sat. fat), 28 mg chol., 490 mg sodium, 35 g carbo., 12 g pro.

Cheese and Veggie Sandwiches

If you're watching your sodium intake, you can reduce the salt in the cottage cheese by placing it in a colander and rinsing under cold water.

1½ cups cottage cheese, drained
¼   cup shredded carrot
¼   cup chopped celery or green sweet
       pepper
½   teaspoon finely snipped fresh chives
¼   cup plain low-fat yogurt
8   small slices whole grain bread
2   tablespoons horseradish mustard
     Spinach or lettuce leaves
4   tomato slices

In a medium bowl combine the cottage cheese, carrot, celery or green pepper, and chives. Stir in the yogurt.

Spread the whole grain bread slices with horseradish mustard. Place the spinach or lettuce leaves on half of the bread slices. Top with the cottage cheese mixture, tomato slices, and the remaining bread slices. Makes 4 servings.

Nutrition information per serving: 232 cal., 7 g total fat (3 g sat. fat), 13 mg chol., 722 mg sodium, 29 g carbo., 16 g pro.

Sautéed Onion & Tomato Sandwiches

Cookies
& CAKES

Contents

CITRUS-HAZELNUT BARS
(recipe, page 331)

Triple-Chocolate Chunk Cookies

For the true chocoholic, there is no such thing as too much chocolate. These chunky, oversize treats contain a trio of chocolates.

1 cup butter
¾ cup granulated sugar
¾ cup packed brown sugar
1 teaspoon baking soda
2 eggs
1 teaspoon vanilla
3 ounces unsweetened chocolate, melted and cooled
2 cups all-purpose flour
8 ounces semisweet chocolate, cut into ½-inch pieces, or 1⅓ cups large semisweet chocolate pieces
6 ounces white baking bar, cut into ½-inch pieces, or 1 cup white baking pieces
1 cup chopped black walnuts or pecans (optional)

Lightly grease a cookie sheet; set aside. In a large mixing bowl beat the butter with an electric mixer on medium to high speed for 30 seconds.

Add the granulated sugar, brown sugar, and baking soda; beat until combined. Beat in eggs and vanilla until combined. Stir in melted chocolate. Beat in as much of the flour as you can with the mixer. Stir in any remaining flour with a wooden spoon. Stir in the chocolate and white baking pieces and, if desired, nuts.

Drop dough by a ¼-cup dry measure or a scoop about 4 inches apart onto the prepared cookie sheet.

Bake in a 350° oven for 12 to 14 minutes or until edges are firm. Cool on cookie sheet for 1 minute. Transfer the cookies to a wire rack; cool. Makes about 22 cookies.

Nutrition information per cookie: 280 cal., 17 g total fat (10 g sat. fat), 44 mg chol., 158 mg sodium, 33 g carbo., 3 g pro.

DROP COOKIE HINTS

For attractive standard-size drop cookies, use a spoon from your flatware set—not a measuring spoon—to drop them, keeping the mounds the same size and spacing them evenly on the cookie sheet. Don't crowd the mounds. When a recipe calls for a greased cookie sheet, use only a light coating of shortening. A heavy coating will cause the cookies to spread too much. Also, don't drop the dough onto a hot cookie sheet. The heat will cause the cookies to flatten. Instead, use two sheets or cool one sheet between batches.

Oatmeal Jumbos

Make these cookies large or small. Both sizes are big in peanut butter and chocolate taste.

1	cup peanut butter
½	cup butter
1½	cups packed brown sugar
½	cup granulated sugar
1½	teaspoons baking powder
½	teaspoon baking soda
3	eggs
2	teaspoons vanilla
4	cups rolled oats
1½	cups candy-coated milk chocolate pieces
¾	cup chopped peanuts, walnuts, or pecans

In a large mixing bowl beat peanut butter and butter with an electric mixer on medium to high speed for 30 seconds. Add the brown sugar, granulated sugar, baking powder, and soda; beat until combined.

Beat in the eggs and vanilla until combined. Stir in the rolled oats. Stir in the candy-coated milk chocolate pieces and nuts.

Drop dough by a ¼-cup dry measure or a scoop about 4 inches apart onto an ungreased cookie sheet. Bake in a 350° oven about 15 minutes or until edges are lightly browned.

(Or, for small cookies, drop dough by a rounded teaspoon about 2 inches apart onto an ungreased cookie sheet. Bake in a 350° oven about 10 minutes.)

Cool for 1 minute on the cookie sheet. Transfer the cookies to a wire rack; cool. Makes about 26 large or about 60 small cookies.

Nutrition information per large cookie: 272 cal., 14 g total fat (4 g sat. fat), 34 mg chol., 173 mg sodium, 32 g carbo., 7 g pro.

Browned Butter Cookies

The French term for browned butter is "beurre noisette," referring to butter that's cooked to a light hazelnut color. Coincidentally, browned butter has a nutty flavor too.

½ cup butter
1½ cups packed brown sugar
1 teaspoon baking soda
½ teaspoon baking powder
¼ teaspoon salt
2 eggs
1 teaspoon vanilla
2½ cups all-purpose flour
1 8-ounce carton dairy sour cream
1 cup coarsely chopped walnuts
Browned Butter Icing

Grease a cookie sheet; set aside. In a large mixing bowl beat butter with an electric mixer on medium to high speed for 30 seconds. Add brown sugar, baking soda, baking powder, and salt; beat until combined. Beat in eggs and vanilla until fluffy.

Beat in as much of the flour as you can with the mixer. Stir in any remaining flour and the sour cream with a wooden spoon. Stir in coarsely chopped walnuts.

Drop dough by a rounded teaspoon about 2 inches apart onto the prepared cookie sheet.

Bake in a 350° oven about 10 minutes or until set. Transfer cookies to a wire rack; cool. Frost cookies with Browned Butter Icing. Makes about 56 cookies.

Browned Butter Icing: In a medium saucepan heat ¼ cup *butter* over medium heat until butter turns the color of light brown sugar. Remove from heat. Stir in 2 cups sifted *powdered sugar* and enough boiling *water* (1 to 2 tablespoons) to make an icing of spreading consistency. Frost cooled cookies immediately after preparing frosting. If the frosting becomes grainy, soften with a few drops of hot water.

Nutrition information per cookie: 97 cal., 5 g total fat (2 g sat. fat), 16 mg chol., 66 mg sodium, 13 g carbo., 1 g pro.

Pecan Drops

Select the nicest pecan halves for the cookie tops and chop the rest before stirring them into the dough.

½   cup butter
2   cups sifted powdered sugar
1¾ cups all-purpose flour
⅓   cup milk
1   egg
1   teaspoon baking powder
1   teaspoon vanilla
1   cup coarsely chopped pecans
    Granulated sugar
    Pecan halves (optional)

Lightly grease a cookie sheet; set aside. In a large mixing bowl beat the butter with an electric mixer on medium to high speed for 30 seconds.

Add powdered sugar, about half of the flour, half of the milk, the egg, baking powder, and vanilla. Beat until combined. Beat or stir in the remaining flour and the remaining milk. Stir in chopped pecans.

Drop dough by a rounded teaspoon about 2 inches apart onto the prepared cookie sheet. Sprinkle with granulated sugar. If desired, lightly press a pecan half in the center of each cookie.

Bake in a 375° oven for 8 to 10 minutes or until edges are light brown. Transfer the cookies to a wire rack; cool. Makes about 36 cookies.

Nutrition information per cookie: 90 cal., 5 g total fat (1 g sat. fat), 9 mg chol., 36 mg sodium, 11 g carbo., 1 g pro.

Fudge Ecstasies

You'll think you broke the chocolate bank when you bite into one of these chewy, double-chocolate, nut-filled wonders.

1 12-ounce package (2 cups)
    semisweet chocolate pieces
2 ounces unsweetened chocolate,
    chopped
2 tablespoons butter
2 eggs
⅔ cup sugar
¼ cup all-purpose flour
1 teaspoon vanilla
¼ teaspoon baking powder
1 cup chopped nuts

Grease a cookie sheet; set aside. In a heavy medium saucepan combine 1 cup of the chocolate pieces, the unsweetened chocolate, and butter. Cook and stir over medium-low heat until melted. Remove from heat.

Add the eggs, sugar, flour, vanilla, and baking powder. Beat until combined, scraping sides of pan occasionally. Stir in the remaining chocolate pieces and the nuts.

Drop dough by a rounded teaspoon about 2 inches apart onto the prepared cookie sheet.

Bake in a 350° oven for 8 to 10 minutes or until edges are firm and surfaces are dull and slightly cracked. Transfer cookies to a wire rack; cool. Makes about 36 cookies.

Nutrition information per cookie: 101 cal., 6 g total fat (1 g sat. fat), 14 mg chol., 13 mg sodium, 12 g carbo., 2 g pro.

Best-Ever Bourbon Brownies

The unusual addition of bourbon gives ever-popular brownies a distinctive flavor. If you prefer to cook without alcohol, simply omit the first drizzling step.

½   cup granulated sugar
⅓   cup butter
2   tablespoons water
1   cup semisweet chocolate pieces
2   eggs
1   teaspoon vanilla
¾   cup all-purpose flour
¼   teaspoon baking soda
¼   teaspoon salt
½   cup chopped pecans
2   to 3 tablespoons bourbon
     Butter Frosting
1   ounce semisweet chocolate, melted

Grease an 8×8×2-inch baking pan; set aside. In a medium saucepan combine granulated sugar, butter, and water. Cook and stir over medium heat just until mixture boils. Remove from heat. Add chocolate pieces, stirring until melted. Add eggs and vanilla, beating with a wooden spoon just until combined.

Combine flour, baking soda, and salt. Stir flour mixture and pecans into chocolate mixture. Spread batter in the prepared pan.

Bake in a 350° oven about 20 minutes or until edges are set and begin to pull away from sides of pan.

Using a fork, prick the warm brownies several times. Drizzle bourbon evenly over brownies. Cool in pan on a wire rack.

Spread Butter Frosting over brownies; drizzle with melted chocolate. Cut into bars. Makes 16 to 20 brownies.

Butter Frosting: In a small mixing bowl beat 3 tablespoons *butter* with an electric mixer on medium to high speed for 30 seconds. Gradually add 1½ cups sifted *powdered sugar*, beating well. Slowly beat in 2 teaspoons *milk* and ¼ teaspoon *vanilla*. If necessary, beat in enough additional milk to make a frosting of spreading consistency.

Nutrition information per brownie: 235 cal., 13 g total fat (6 g sat. fat), 44 mg chol., 129 mg sodium, 24 g carbo., 2 g pro.

Top-of-the-World Brownies

You can't possibly resist these chewy fudge-nut brownies. Each wears a billowing thunderhead of crisp chocolate meringue.

¾ cup butter
3 ounces unsweetened chocolate,
    coarsely chopped
1⅓ cups sugar
2 teaspoons vanilla
3 eggs
1 cup all-purpose flour
2 tablespoons unsweetened cocoa
    powder
½ cup coarsely chopped hazelnuts
    (filberts) or pecans
2 egg whites
⅔ cup sugar
1 tablespoon unsweetened cocoa
    powder

Line the bottom and sides of an 8×8×2-inch baking pan with heavy foil; grease the foil. Set pan aside.

In a medium saucepan cook and stir the ¾ cup butter and the unsweetened chocolate over low heat just until melted. Remove from heat. Using a wooden spoon, stir in the 1⅓ cups sugar and the vanilla. Cool about 5 minutes.

Add eggs, one at a time, beating just until combined after each addition. Stir in flour and the 2 tablespoons cocoa powder. Spread batter evenly in prepared pan. Sprinkle with nuts; set aside.

For meringue, in a small mixing bowl beat the egg whites with an electric mixer on medium to high speed about 1 minute or until soft peaks form (tips curl). Gradually add the ⅔ cup sugar, beating on high speed until stiff peaks form (tips stand straight) and sugar is almost dissolved. Reduce speed to low; beat in the 1 tablespoon cocoa powder. Using a tablespoon, carefully spoon the meringue in 16 even mounds on top of the brownie batter, keeping about ½ inch of space between each mound.

Bake in a 350° oven about 1 hour or until a wooden toothpick inserted near the center of the brownie portion comes out clean. Cool in pan on a wire rack at least 1 hour. Using foil, lift whole brownie from pan. Cut into 16 squares. Makes 16 brownies.

Nutrition information per brownie: 269 cal., 15 g total fat (7 g sat. fat), 63 mg chol., 107 mg sodium, 34 g carbo., 4 g pro.

Triple Peanut Bars

A drizzle of Peanut Butter Icing dresses up these bars for special occasions, but they taste every bit as scrumptious without it.

Nonstick cooking spray
1 18-ounce roll refrigerated peanut butter cookie dough
1 12-ounce package (2 cups) semisweet chocolate pieces
1 14-ounce can (1¼ cups) sweetened condensed milk
1½ cups dry-roasted peanuts
1 10-ounce package peanut butter-flavored pieces
   Peanut Butter Icing (optional)

Lightly coat a 15×10×1-inch baking pan with cooking spray; set aside. Using floured hands, press cookie dough onto bottom of prepared pan.

Sprinkle chocolate pieces evenly over dough. Drizzle with sweetened condensed milk. Sprinkle with the peanuts and peanut butter pieces; press firmly.

Bake in a 350° oven about 25 minutes or until edges are firm. Cool in pan on a wire rack. If desired, drizzle with Peanut Butter Icing. Cut into bars. Store, covered, in the refrigerator. Makes about 72 bars.

Peanut Butter Icing: In a small bowl beat together 1 cup sifted *powdered sugar*, ¼ cup *peanut butter*, and 1 tablespoon *milk*. Beat in enough additional milk, 1 teaspoon at a time, to make an icing of drizzling consistency.

Nutrition information per bar: 111 cal., 6 g total fat (2 g sat. fat), 4 mg chol., 70 mg sodium, 11 g carbo., 2 g pro.

Cranberry-Macadamia Bars

Bake up a batch of these bars during the holiday/cranberry season. Like tiny slices of tart, they add a unique shape and bold color to your holiday cookie tray.

1¼   cups all-purpose flour
¾   cup sugar
½   cup butter
½   cup finely chopped macadamia nuts, hazelnuts (filberts), or pecans
2   beaten eggs
1¼   cups sugar
2   tablespoons milk
1   teaspoon finely shredded orange peel
1   teaspoon vanilla
1   cup finely chopped cranberries
½   cup finely chopped macadamia nuts, hazelnuts (filberts), or pecans
½   cup coconut

For crust, in a medium bowl stir together flour and the ¾ cup sugar. Using a pastry blender, cut in butter until mixture resembles coarse crumbs. Stir in ½ cup nuts. Press the mixture into the bottom of an ungreased 13×9×2-inch baking pan. Bake in a 350° oven for 10 to 15 minutes or until crust is light brown around edges.

Meanwhile, in a small bowl combine eggs, the 1¼ cups sugar, the milk, orange peel, and vanilla. Beat until combined. Pour over the hot crust. Sprinkle with cranberries, ½ cup nuts, and the coconut.

Bake about 30 minutes or until golden brown. Cool slightly in pan on a wire rack. While warm, cut into 24 bars; cut bars in half diagonally. Cool in pan. Makes 48 bars.

Nutrition information per bar: 88 cal., 4 g total fat (2 g sat. fat), 14 mg chol., 23 mg sodium, 12 g carbo., 1 g pro.

Ultimate Bar Cookies

Crush any leftover bars and sprinkle over ice cream as a topping.

2 cups all-purpose flour
½ cup packed brown sugar
½ cup butter, softened
1 cup coarsely chopped walnuts
1 3½-ounce jar macadamia nuts,
    coarsely chopped (1 cup)
1 6-ounce package white baking bars,
    coarsely chopped (1 cup)
1 cup milk chocolate pieces
¾ cup butter
½ cup packed brown sugar

In a medium bowl beat flour, ½ cup brown sugar, and ½ cup butter with an electric mixer on medium speed until mixture forms fine crumbs. Press into the bottom of an ungreased 13×9×2-inch baking pan. Bake in a 350° oven about 15 minutes or until lightly browned.

Transfer pan to a wire rack. Sprinkle nuts, baking bars, and milk chocolate pieces over hot crust. Cook and stir ¾ cup butter and ½ cup brown sugar until bubbly. Cook and stir for 1 minute more. Pour over nuts and chocolate in pan. Bake about 15 minutes more or just until bubbly around edges. Cool in pan on a wire rack. Cut into desired shapes. Makes 36 bars.

Nutrition information per bar: 188 cal., 13 g total fat (6 g sat. fat), 18 mg chol., 12 mg sodium, 16 g carbo., 2 g pro.

Mocha Brownies

These buttery mocha brownies boast plenty of semisweet chocolate and a delightful hint of tangerine.

⅔ cup butter
⅓ cup unsweetened cocoa powder
1 teaspoon instant coffee crystals
1 cup granulated sugar
2 eggs
1 teaspoon vanilla
¾ cup all-purpose flour
½ cup semisweet chocolate pieces or
    chopped semisweet chocolate
1 teaspoon finely shredded tangerine
    or orange peel
    Powdered sugar (optional)

Grease an 8x8x2-inch baking pan. Set aside. In a medium sauce-pan melt butter. Stir in cocoa powder and coffee crystals. Remove from heat. Stir in the granulated sugar. Stir in eggs, one at a time, and vanilla. Beat lightly by hand just until combined. Stir in flour. Stir in chocolate pieces and shredded peel.

Spread into prepared pan. Bake in a 350° oven for 30 minutes. Cool in pan on a wire rack. If desired, sift powdered sugar over top. Cut into bars. Makes 24 brownies.

Nutrition information per brownie: 123 cal., 7 g total fat (2 g sat. fat), 24 mg chol., 52 mg sodium, 13 g carbo., 1 g pro.

Citrus-Hazelnut Bars

Definitely a bar cookie with lots of appeal—these double citrus and nutty delights are not overly sweet and make a great accompaniment to an afternoon tea break.

⅓ cup butter
¼ cup granulated sugar
1 cup all-purpose flour
⅓ cup finely chopped hazelnuts
     (filberts) or chopped almonds,
     toasted
2 eggs
¾ cup granulated sugar
2 tablespoons all-purpose flour
1 teaspoon finely shredded orange
     peel
2 tablespoons orange juice
1 teaspoon finely shredded lemon peel
1 tablespoon lemon juice
½ teaspoon baking powder
     Powdered sugar (optional)

For crust, in a medium mixing bowl beat the butter with an electric mixer on medium to high speed for 30 seconds. Add the ¼ cup granulated sugar. Beat until thoroughly combined. Beat in the 1 cup flour and about half of the nuts until mixture is crumbly.

Press mixture onto bottom of an ungreased 8×8×2-inch baking pan. Bake in a 350° oven about 10 minutes or until lightly browned.

Meanwhile, in a medium mixing bowl combine eggs, the ¾ cup granulated sugar, the 2 tablespoons flour, orange peel, orange juice, lemon peel, lemon juice, and baking powder. Beat on medium speed about 2 minutes or until combined. Pour over hot crust. Sprinkle with the remaining nuts.

Bake about 20 minutes more or until light brown around the edges and center is set. Cool in pan on a wire rack. If desired, sift powdered sugar over top. Cut into bars. Store bars, covered, in the refrigerator. Makes 20 bars.

Nutrition information per bar: 111 cal., 5 g total fat (1 g sat. fat), 25 mg chol., 43 mg sodium, 16 g carbo., 2 g pro.

Fairy Drops

These cookies literally sparkle when spread with Almond Frosting and sprinkled with crushed candies. Or top them with a simple sprinkling of plain or colored sugar.

1 cup butter
1 cup sifted powdered sugar
1 cup granulated sugar
1 teaspoon baking soda
1 teaspoon cream of tartar
1 teaspoon salt
1 cup cooking oil
2 eggs
2 teaspoons almond extract
4½ cups all-purpose flour
   Plain or colored granulated sugar
      or Almond Frosting
   Crushed hard candies (optional)

In a large mixing bowl beat butter with an electric mixer on medium to high speed for 30 seconds. Add powdered sugar, the 1 cup granulated sugar, the baking soda, cream of tartar, and salt; beat until fluffy. Beat in oil, eggs, and almond extract just until combined.

Beat in as much of the flour as you can with the mixer. Stir in any remaining flour with a wooden spoon. Cover and chill the dough for 30 minutes.

Working with one-fourth of the dough at a time, shape dough into 1¼-inch balls. (The dough will be soft; keep it chilled as you work with a portion.) Arrange balls about 2 inches apart on an ungreased cookie sheet. With the palm of your hand or, if desired, the bottom of a glass or a patterned cookie stamp dipped in granulated sugar, gently flatten balls to about ¼-inch thickness. Sprinkle with plain or colored granulated sugar (unless flattened with sugared glass or stamp) or leave plain for frosting.

Bake in a 350° oven for 10 to 12 minutes or until edges just begin to brown. Transfer cookies to a wire rack; cool. If desired, frost the cookies with Almond Frosting and sprinkle with crushed candies. Makes about 84 cookies.

Almond Frosting: In a medium mixing bowl beat ½ cup *butter* with an electric mixer on medium to high speed until fluffy. Beat in ½ teaspoon *almond extract* and ½ teaspoon *vanilla*. Alternately add 2½ to 3½ cups sifted *powdered sugar* and 3 tablespoons *half-and-half, light cream,* or *milk*, beating until the frosting is smooth and of spreading consistency. If desired, stir in a few drops *food coloring* to tint frosting.

Nutrition information per cookie: 77 cal., 5 g total fat (2 g sat. fat), 10 mg chol., 61 mg sodium, 8 g carbo., 1 g pro.

Spiral Cookies

Make the dough for these whimsical pink-and-white spirals and chill it overnight. When company comes, just slice and bake them while you're making tea. You'll have pretty cookies to serve warm from the oven.

1 cup butter
1½ cups sugar
1½ teaspoons baking powder
½ teaspoon salt
1 egg
1 teaspoon vanilla
½ teaspoon peppermint extract
   (optional)
2½ cups all-purpose flour
   Red paste food coloring

In a large mixing bowl beat butter with an electric mixer on medium to high speed for 30 seconds. Add sugar, baking powder, and salt; beat until combined. Beat in the egg, vanilla, and, if desired, peppermint extract until combined. Beat in as much of the flour as you can with the mixer. Stir in any remaining flour with a wooden spoon.

Divide dough in half. Tint one portion of the dough with paste food coloring. Knead coloring into dough until well mixed. If dough is too sticky to handle, wrap each half in waxed paper or plastic wrap and chill about 1 hour or until easy to handle.

On a lightly floured surface, roll each half of dough into a 12×8-inch rectangle. Using a large spatula and your hands, place one rectangle on top of the other. Press down gently with your hands to seal. Starting from a long side, tightly roll up into a spiral. Wrap in waxed paper or plastic wrap and chill at least 2 hours or until firm.

Using a sharp knife, cut roll into ¼-inch slices. Place slices about 1 inch apart on an ungreased cookie sheet. Bake in a 375° oven for 8 to 10 minutes or until edges are firm and light brown.

Cool on cookie sheet for 1 minute. Transfer cookies to a wire rack; cool. Makes about 48 cookies.

Nutrition information per cookie: 81 cal., 4 g total fat (2 g sat. fat), 15 mg chol., 63 mg sodium, 11 g carbo., 1 g pro.

Caraway Cookies

Popular in New England bakeries about a century ago, these crisp treats inspired homemakers to duplicate them at home. You'll be delightfully surprised by the burst of caraway in every sweet bite.

2 cups all-purpose flour
1 tablespoon caraway seeds
1 teaspoon baking powder
¼ teaspoon baking soda
¼ teaspoon salt
½ cup butter
1 cup sugar
2 eggs

In a medium bowl stir together flour, caraway seeds, baking powder, baking soda, and salt; set aside.

In a large mixing bowl beat butter with an electric mixer on medium to high speed for 30 seconds. Add sugar; beat until combined. Beat in eggs, one at a time, beating well after each addition. Beat in as much of the flour mixture as you can with the mixer. Stir in any remaining flour mixture with a wooden spoon. Divide dough in half. Cover and chill about 3 hours or until easy to handle.

Lightly grease a cookie sheet; set aside. On a lightly floured surface, roll each half of the dough to ⅛-inch thickness. Using 2½-inch cookie cutters, cut dough into desired shapes. Place cookies about 2 inches apart on the prepared cookie sheet.

Bake in a 375° oven for 7 to 8 minutes or until edges are light brown. Transfer the cookies to a wire rack; cool. Makes about 54 cookies.

Nutrition information per cookie: 48 cal., 2 g total fat (1 g sat. fat), 13 mg chol., 45 mg sodium, 7 g carbo., 1 g pro.

Jam Thumbprints

Have these cookies baked, cooled, and on hand for drop-in company. Fill them right before serving.

⅔ cup butter
½ cup sugar
2 egg yolks
1 teaspoon vanilla
1½ cups all-purpose flour
2 slightly beaten egg whites
1 cup finely chopped walnuts
⅓ to ½ cup apricot, strawberry, or
    cherry jam or preserves

Grease a cookie sheet. Set aside. In a large mixing bowl beat butter with an electric mixer on medium to high speed for 30 seconds. Add sugar; beat until combined, scraping side of bowl occasionally.

Beat in egg yolks and vanilla until combined. Beat in as much of the flour as you can with the mixer. Stir in the remaining flour. Cover and chill about 1 hour or until easy to handle.

Shape dough into 1-inch balls. Roll balls in egg whites, then coat with walnuts. Place about 1 inch apart on the prepared cookie sheet. Press your thumb into the center of each ball.

Bake in a 375° oven for 10 to 12 minutes or until edges are lightly browned. Transfer to a wire rack; cool. Before serving, fill centers of cookies with jam or preserves. Makes about 42 cookies.

Nutrition information per cookie: 79 cal., 5g total fat (2 g sat. fat), 18 mg chol., 33 mg sodium, 8 g carbo., 1 g pro.

ᴍARGARINE IN BAKING

The recipes in this chapter call for butter, not margarine, because it ensures the best results. Although baked goods made with some margarines can be satisfactory, choosing the right margarine is tricky. Many margarines contain more water than oil, which will yield undesirable results. If you choose to use margarine, select a stick margarine that lists at least 80 percent vegetable oil or 100 calories per tablespoon on the package. Diet, whipped, liquid, and soft spreads or margarines are for table use—not baking. Their high water content can make baked goods wet and tough.

Upside-Down Pineapple-Orange Cake

For a twist on pineapple upside-down cake, we added mandarin oranges, using half a can of pineapple slices and half a can of orange sections. If you prefer to make the cake with just one fruit, use a whole can.

⅔ cup packed brown sugar
6 tablespoons butter
1½ teaspoons finely shredded orange peel
1 11-ounce can mandarin orange sections
1 8-ounce can pineapple slices
1⅓ cups all-purpose flour
1¼ teaspoons baking powder
½ teaspoon salt
6 tablespoons butter
1 cup granulated sugar
¼ teaspoon almond extract
2 eggs
⅔ cup dairy sour cream
Sweetened Whipped Cream (optional)

In a saucepan combine brown sugar, 6 tablespoons butter, and orange peel. Cook and stir over medium heat until mixture is bubbly. Pour into an ungreased 9×9×2-inch baking pan.

Drain the oranges and pineapple. Cut half of the pineapple slices in half. Arrange the half slices of pineapple and half of the orange sections in pan. (Reserve remaining oranges and pineapple for another use.) Combine flour, baking powder, and salt.

In a large mixing bowl beat 6 tablespoons butter with an electric mixer on medium to high speed for 30 seconds. Add granulated sugar and almond extract; beat until combined. Add eggs, one at a time, beating well after each. Alternately add flour mixture and sour cream, beating on low to medium speed after each addition just until combined. Spoon over fruit.

Bake in a 350° oven for 35 to 40 minutes or until a wooden toothpick inserted near the center comes out clean. Cool in pan on a wire rack for 5 minutes. Invert onto a serving plate. Serve warm. If desired, top with Sweetened Whipped Cream. Makes 8 servings.

Sweetened Whipped Cream: In a chilled medium mixing bowl combine 1 cup *whipping cream,* 2 tablespoons *granulated sugar,* and ½ teaspoon *vanilla.* Beat with an electric mixer on medium to high speed until soft peaks form (tips curl).

Nutrition information per serving: 455 cal., 21 g total fat (12 g sat. fat), 107 mg chol., 371 mg sodium, 64 g carbo., 4 g pro.

Banana Cake with Penuche Frosting

For a combination that's hard to beat, frost this easy-to-make cake right in the pan with the creamy brown sugar frosting.

2½   cups all-purpose flour
1½   cups granulated sugar
1½   teaspoons baking powder
 1   teaspoon baking soda
 ½   teaspoon salt
 1   cup mashed ripe bananas (about
        3 bananas)
 ⅔   cup buttermilk or sour milk*
 ½   cup shortening
 1   teaspoon vanilla
 2   eggs
        Penuche Frosting
        Chopped nuts (optional)

Grease a 13×9×2-inch baking pan. Set aside. In a large mixing bowl combine flour, 1½ cups sugar, baking powder, baking soda, and salt. Add the bananas, buttermilk or sour milk, shortening, and vanilla.

Beat with an electric mixer on low speed until combined. Add eggs. Beat on medium speed for 2 minutes. Pour into the prepared pan.

Bake in a 350° oven about 35 minutes or until a wooden toothpick inserted near the center comes out clean. Cool completely in pan on a wire rack.

Frost with Penuche Frosting. If desired, immediately sprinkle with chopped nuts. Makes 12 to 16 servings.

*Note: To make ⅔ cup sour milk, place 2 teaspoons *lemon juice* or *vinegar* in a glass measuring cup. Add enough *milk* to make ⅔ cup total liquid; stir. Let stand for 5 minutes before using.

Penuche Frosting: In a medium saucepan melt ⅓ cup *butter* over medium heat. Stir in ⅔ cup packed *brown sugar*. Cook and stir until bubbly. Remove from heat. Add 3 tablespoons *milk*, beating vigorously until smooth. By hand, beat in enough sifted *powdered sugar* (about 2½ cups) to make a frosting of spreading consistency. Frost cake immediately.

Nutrition information per serving: 470 cal., 15 g total fat (6 g sat. fat), 50 mg chol., 274 mg sodium, 82 g carbo., 4 g pro.

Busy-Day Cake

No time to bake? Stir up this one-bowl cake in only minutes with easy-to-keep-on-hand ingredients. Another time, skip the topping and serve it with fresh fruit and whipped cream.

1⅓ cups all-purpose flour
⅔ cup granulated sugar
2 teaspoons baking powder
⅔ cup milk
¼ cup butter, softened
1 egg
1 teaspoon vanilla
    Broiled Coconut Topping

Grease and flour an 8×1½-inch round baking pan. Set aside. In a large mixing bowl combine the flour, ⅔ cup sugar, and baking powder. Add the milk, butter, egg, and vanilla.

Beat with an electric mixer on low speed for 30 seconds. Beat on medium speed for 1 minute. Pour the batter into the prepared pan.

Bake in a 350° oven for 25 to 30 minutes or until a wooden toothpick inserted near the center comes out clean. Remove from heat.

Spread the Broiled Coconut Topping over the warm cake. Broil about 4 inches from the heat for 3 to 4 minutes or until topping is golden brown. Cool cake slightly in pan on a wire rack. Serve warm. Makes 8 servings.

Broiled Coconut Topping: In a medium mixing bowl stir together ¼ cup packed *brown sugar* and 2 tablespoons softened *butter.* Stir in 1 tablespoon *milk.* Stir in ½ cup flaked *coconut,* and, if desired, ¼ cup chopped *nuts.*

Nutrition information per serving: 281 cal., 11 g total fat (6 g sat. fat), 51 mg chol., 128 mg sodium, 42 g carbo., 4 g pro.

Cream Cheese-Poppy Seed Pound Cake

Cream cheese and butter team up to ensure a moist texture and rich flavor in this melt-in-your-mouth cake.

1 cup butter
1 8-ounce package cream cheese
6 eggs
3 cups all-purpose flour
1 teaspoon baking powder
¼ teaspoon salt
2¼ cups granulated sugar
¼ cup poppy seed
2 teaspoons vanilla
　 Lemon Icing

Bring the butter, cream cheese, and eggs to room temperature. Meanwhile, grease and lightly flour a 10-inch tube pan; set aside.

Combine flour, baking powder, and salt. Set aside. In a large mixing bowl beat butter and cream cheese with an electric mixer on medium to high speed about 30 seconds or until softened. Gradually add granulated sugar, 2 tablespoons at a time, beating on medium speed about 5 minutes or until very light and fluffy.

Add poppy seed and vanilla. Add eggs, one at a time, beating on low to medium speed for 1 minute after each addition and scraping bowl frequently. Gradually add flour mixture, beating on low speed just until combined. Pour batter into prepared pan.

Bake in a 325° oven about 1¼ hours or until a wooden toothpick inserted near center comes out clean. Cool in pan on a wire rack for 15 minutes. Remove from pan. Cool completely on wire rack. Drizzle with Lemon Icing. Makes 16 to 20 servings.

Lemon Icing: In a small bowl combine 1½ cups sifted *powdered sugar* and ½ teaspoon finely shredded *lemon peel*. Stir in enough *lemon juice* (1 to 2 tablespoons) to make an icing of drizzling consistency.

Nutrition information per serving: 415 cal., 19 g total fat (11 g sat. fat), 126 mg chol., 239 mg sodium, 55 g carbo., 6 g pro.

Nutmeg Cake with Lemon Sauce

This light spice cake fills the role of lunch-box treat or after-school snack.

2 cups all-purpose flour
1 teaspoon baking powder
1 teaspoon baking soda
1 teaspoon ground nutmeg
¼ teaspoon salt
¼ cup butter
¼ cup shortening
1½ cups sugar
½ teaspoon vanilla
3 eggs
1 cup buttermilk or sour milk*
Lemon Sauce
Lemon slices, halved (optional)

Grease a 13×9×2-inch baking pan; set aside. Combine flour, baking powder, baking soda, nutmeg, and salt; set aside.

In a large mixing bowl beat butter and shortening with an electric mixer on medium to high speed for 30 seconds. Add sugar and vanilla; beat until combined. Add eggs, one at a time, beating well after each addition. Alternately add flour mixture and buttermilk or sour milk, beating on low speed after each addition just until combined. Pour batter into prepared pan.

Bake in a 350° oven for 30 to 35 minutes or until a wooden toothpick inserted near center comes out clean. Cool cake slightly in pan on a wire rack. Serve the warm cake with Lemon Sauce. If desired, garnish with lemon slices. Makes 12 servings.

Lemon Sauce: In a small saucepan stir together ¾ cup *sugar*, 5 teaspoons *cornstarch*, and dash *salt*. Stir in 1 cup *water*. Cook and stir over medium heat until thickened and bubbly. Cook and stir for 2 minutes more. Remove from heat. Stir in 1 teaspoon finely shredded *lemon peel*, 3 tablespoons *lemon juice*, 2 tablespoons *butter*, and, if desired, 1 drop *yellow food coloring*.

*Note: To make sour milk, place 1 tablespoon *lemon juice* or *vinegar* in a glass measuring cup. Add enough *milk* to make 1 cup total liquid; stir. Let stand for 5 minutes before using.

Nutrition information per serving: 338 cal., 12 g total fat (5 g sat. fat), 69 mg chol., 297 mg sodium, 55 g carbo., 4 g pro.

Granny Cake

Also known as the "hummingbird cake," this homey, church-social-style recipe has been shared over backyard fences for years.

3 cups all-purpose flour
2 cups granulated sugar
1 teaspoon baking soda
1 teaspoon ground nutmeg
½ teaspoon salt
½ teaspoon ground cloves
¾ cup butter
2 cups mashed ripe bananas
1 8-ounce can crushed pineapple
3 eggs
2 teaspoons vanilla
1 cup finely chopped pecans
Powdered sugar (optional)

Grease and flour a 10-inch fluted tube pan; set aside. In a medium bowl stir together flour, granulated sugar, baking soda, nutmeg, salt, and cloves; set aside.

In a large mixing bowl beat butter with an electric mixer on medium to high speed for 30 seconds. Add bananas, undrained pineapple, eggs, and vanilla; beat until combined. Add flour mixture. Beat on low speed until combined. Beat on medium speed for 1 minute. Fold in pecans. Spread batter in the prepared pan.

Bake in a 325° oven for 70 to 75 minutes or until a wooden toothpick inserted near center comes out clean. Cool in pan on a wire rack for 10 minutes. Remove from pan. Cool completely on wire rack.

If desired, decorate cake with a powdered-sugar design. Place a paper doily on top of cake. Sift powdered sugar over doily to fill cutout designs. Carefully remove doily. Makes 12 servings.

Nutrition information per serving: 481 cal., 19 g total fat (8 g sat. fat), 84 mg chol., 328 mg sodium, 74 g carbo., 6 g pro.

Upside-Down Chip Cake

Carefully spoon the cake batter over the coconut and pecans so, when the cake is inverted, the topping stays evenly distributed.

3 tablespoons butter
½ cup packed brown sugar
4 teaspoons water
½ cup coconut
½ cup coarsely chopped pecans
1 cup all-purpose flour
⅔ cup granulated sugar
½ cup unsweetened cocoa powder
¼ cup packed brown sugar
2 teaspoons baking powder
½ cup milk
¼ cup butter, softened
2 eggs
1 teaspoon vanilla
¾ cup miniature semisweet
    chocolate pieces

Place the 3 tablespoons butter in a 9×1½-inch round baking pan. Heat in a 350° oven until butter is melted. Stir in the ½ cup brown sugar and the water. Sprinkle with coconut and pecans. Set aside.

In a medium mixing bowl stir together flour, granulated sugar, cocoa powder, the ¼ cup brown sugar, and the baking powder. Add milk, the ¼ cup butter, the eggs, and vanilla.

Beat with an electric mixer on low speed until combined. Beat on medium speed for 1 minute. By hand, stir in ½ cup of the chocolate pieces. Spoon batter into the prepared pan.

Bake for 40 to 45 minutes or until cake feels firm in center when lightly touched. Cool in pan on a wire rack for 5 minutes. Loosen edge of cake from pan; invert onto a serving plate.

Immediately sprinkle remaining chocolate pieces over topping. Let stand about 30 minutes before slicing. Serve warm. Makes 8 servings.

Nutrition information per serving: 456 cal., 24 g total fat (11 g sat. fat), 83 mg chol., 239 mg sodium, 52 g carbo., 6 g pro.

Tiramisu

This recipe simplifies classic tiramisu (tee-rah-MEE-su) by using a purchased angel cake. Most important, it's as light as a feather.

1 8-ounce package reduced-fat cream cheese (Neufchâtel), softened
½ cup sifted powdered sugar
3 tablespoons coffee liqueur
1 8-ounce container frozen light whipped dessert topping, thawed
¼ cup fat-free dairy sour cream
2 tablespoons coffee liqueur
1 8- to 10-inch round angel food cake
¼ cup strong black coffee
2 tablespoons coffee liqueur
   Mocha Fudge Sauce (optional)
   Edible flowers (optional)

For filling, in a large mixing bowl combine the cream cheese, powdered sugar, and the 3 tablespoons coffee liqueur. Beat with an electric mixer on medium speed until blended and smooth. Stir in ½ cup of the whipped dessert topping. Set aside.

For frosting, in a medium bowl combine remaining whipped dessert topping, the sour cream, and 2 tablespoons coffee liqueur. Set aside.

Using a serrated knife, cut the angel food cake horizontally into three layers. Place one layer on a serving platter and two layers on large dinner plates. Using a long-tined fork or a skewer, poke holes in tops of all three layers. In a small bowl combine the coffee and 2 tablespoons coffee liqueur; drizzle over all layers. Spread the first layer with half of the filling. Add a second layer and spread with the remaining filling. Add top layer of cake. Frost cake with the frosting. (If desired, cover and chill up to 4 hours.)

If desired, just before serving, drizzle top and sides with some of the Mocha Fudge Sauce. If using, drizzle dessert plates with the remaining sauce; cut cake into wedges and place wedges on top of sauce. If desired, garnish with flowers. Makes 16 servings.

Mocha Fudge Sauce: In a small bowl dissolve 1 teaspoon *instant coffee crystals* in 1 teaspoon hot *water*. Stir in ¼ cup *chocolate-flavored syrup*.

Nutrition information per serving: 155 cal., 5 g total fat (4 g sat. fat), 11 mg chol., 203 mg sodium, 21 g carbo., 3 g pro.

Carrot Cake with Lemony Icing

This show-off makes its mark with sweet spring carrots and buttermilk cake batter. As if that's not enough, it's topped off with chunky walnuts and thick lemon icing.

  2 cups all-purpose flour
  1 teaspoon baking powder
  ½ teaspoon baking soda
  ⅛ teaspoon salt
  ½ cup shortening
1¾ cups sugar
  1 teaspoon vanilla
  4 egg whites
  1 cup buttermilk or sour milk (see note, page 344)
2½ cups shredded carrots
     Lemony Icing
  1 cup chopped walnuts
     Walnut halves (optional)
     Carrot curls (optional)

Grease and lightly flour two 8×1½-inch or 9×1½-inch round baking pans; set aside. Stir together flour, baking powder, baking soda, and salt; set aside.

In a large mixing bowl beat shortening with an electric mixer on medium to high speed for 30 seconds. Add sugar and vanilla; beat until combined. Add egg whites, one at a time, beating well after each addition. Alternately add flour mixture and buttermilk or sour milk, beating on low speed after each addition just until combined. Using a wooden spoon, stir in shredded carrots. Divide batter between the prepared pans.

Bake in a 350° oven for 35 to 40 minutes for 8-inch pans (30 to 35 minutes for 9-inch pans) or until a wooden toothpick inserted near centers comes out clean. Cool in pans on wire racks for 10 minutes. Remove from pans. Cool completely on wire racks. Prepare the Lemony Icing.

To assemble cake, place one cake layer on a serving plate. Spoon about ⅔ cup icing over top of layer. Sprinkle with half of the chopped walnuts. Place the second cake layer, top side up, on first layer. Spoon the remaining icing over top of cake. Sprinkle with the remaining chopped walnuts. If desired, garnish with walnut halves and carrot curls. Makes 12 servings.

Lemony Icing: In a medium bowl stir together 3 cups sifted *powdered sugar* and enough *lemon juice* (about 3 tablespoons) to make an icing of glazing consistency.

Nutrition information per serving: 444 cal., 15 g total fat (3 g sat. fat), 1 mg chol., 160 mg sodium, 73 g carbo., 6 g pro.

Deep Chocolate Cake with Malt Topping

It's hip to be square, but this stunning cake can be round too. Use 9×1½-inch round baking pans instead of 8-inch square pans.

½ cup unsweetened cocoa powder
2 cups all-purpose flour
1 teaspoon baking powder
½ teaspoon baking soda
⅔ cup butter
1¾ cups sugar
3 eggs
4 ounces unsweetened chocolate, melted and cooled
2 teaspoons vanilla
1½ cups milk
    Chocolate Malt Frosting
2 cups malted milk balls or miniature malted milk balls

Grease three 8×8×2-inch baking pans; lightly dust each pan with 1 teaspoon of the cocoa powder. Set aside. In a medium bowl stir together flour, baking powder, baking soda, and the remaining cocoa powder. Set aside.

In a large mixing bowl beat butter with an electric mixer on medium to high speed for 30 seconds. Add sugar; beat until combined. Add eggs, one at a time, beating well after each addition. Beat in chocolate and vanilla. Alternately add flour mixture and milk, beating on low speed after each addition until combined. Divide among prepared pans.

Bake in a 350° oven for 17 to 20 minutes or until a wooden toothpick inserted near the centers comes out clean. Cool in pans on wire racks for 10 minutes. Remove from pans. Cool completely on wire racks. Prepare the Chocolate Malt Frosting.

To assemble cake, spread ¾ cup of the frosting on the tops of 2 of the cake layers; stack layers. Add top layer; frost the top and sides of the cake, reserving some frosting for piping. Place the remaining frosting in a decorating bag fitted with a medium round tip. Starting from the bottom, pipe a zigzag pattern on sides and top edge of cake. If desired, coarsely chop or halve some of the malted milk balls. Decorate the cake with milk balls. Store, covered, in the refrigerator. Makes 20 servings.

Chocolate Malt Frosting: In a large saucepan bring 2 cups *whipping cream* just to boiling over medium-high heat. Remove from heat. Stir in ⅓ cup *malt powder*. Add two 11½-ounce packages *milk chocolate pieces* (do not stir). Cover and let stand for 5 minutes. Stir until smooth. Transfer to a large mixing bowl (mixture will be thin). Cover and chill for 3 hours. Set bowl of frosting in a larger bowl of ice water. Beat frosting with an electric mixer on medium speed about 3 minutes or until fluffy and of spreading consistency.

Nutrition information per serving: 540 cal., 32 g total fat (17 g sat. fat), 83 mg chol., 263 mg sodium, 61 g carbo., 8 g pro.

Daffodil Cake

Celebrate the rites of spring with this classic angel food cake marbled with lemon-yellow sponge cake. It's only fitting that your table feature a simple centerpiece with daffodils from your garden.

1½ cups egg whites (11 or 12 large)
1 cup sifted cake flour or sifted
    all-purpose flour
¾ cup granulated sugar
2 teaspoons vanilla
1½ teaspoons cream of tartar
¼ teaspoon salt
¾ cup granulated sugar
6 egg yolks
1½ teaspoons finely shredded
    lemon peel
    Tangy Lemon Frosting
    Finely shredded lemon peel
    (optional)

In a very large mixing bowl allow egg whites to stand at room temperature for 30 minutes. Meanwhile, sift together flour and ¾ cup granulated sugar three times. Set aside. Add vanilla, cream of tartar, and salt to egg whites. Beat with an electric mixer on medium to high speed until soft peaks form (tips curl). Gradually add ¾ cup granulated sugar, about 2 tablespoons at a time, beating until stiff peaks form (tips stand straight). Sift one-fourth of the flour mixture over egg white mixture; fold in gently. (If too full, transfer to a larger bowl.) Repeat with the remaining flour mixture, using one-fourth of the mixture each time. Transfer half of the batter to another bowl.

In a small mixing bowl beat egg yolks on high speed about 6 minutes or until thick and lemon colored. Fold in the 1½ teaspoons lemon peel. Gently fold yolk mixture into half of the batter. Alternately spoon yellow batter and white batter into an ungreased 10-inch tube pan. Swirl a metal spatula through batters to marble.

Bake on the lowest rack in a 350° oven for 40 to 45 minutes or until top springs back when lightly touched. Immediately invert cake in pan; cool completely. Remove from pan. Place upside down on a serving plate. Frost with Tangy Lemon Frosting. If desired, sprinkle with additional lemon peel. Makes 12 servings.

Tangy Lemon Frosting: In a large mixing bowl beat ½ cup *butter* with an electric mixer on medium to high speed for 30 seconds. Gradually beat in 5½ cups sifted *powdered sugar*, ½ teaspoon finely *shredded lemon peel*, and ⅓ cup *lemon juice*. Beat in enough additional *lemon juice*, if necessary, to make a frosting of spreading consistency.

Nutrition information per serving: 424 cal., 10 g total fat (5 g sat. fat), 127 mg chol., 189 mg sodium, 79 g carbo., 5 g pro.

Desserts

Contents

CHEESECAKE SUPREME
(recipe, page 369)

Peach Cobbler with Cinnamon-Swirl Biscuits

Many cobbler recipes have a drop biscuit topping, but this one has tender biscuit slices filled with a nut-and-spice mixture.

1 cup all-purpose flour
1 tablespoon brown sugar
1½ teaspoons baking powder
¼ teaspoon salt
⅛ teaspoon baking soda
¼ cup butter
⅓ cup milk
½ cup finely chopped walnuts
3 tablespoons brown sugar
¼ teaspoon ground cinnamon
1 tablespoon butter, melted
⅔ cup packed brown sugar
4 teaspoons cornstarch
½ teaspoon finely shredded lemon peel
6 cups sliced peeled peaches or 6 cups frozen unsweetened peach slices
⅔ cup water

For biscuits, in a medium mixing bowl stir together flour, 1 tablespoon brown sugar, baking powder, salt, and baking soda.

With a pastry blender, cut in ¼ cup butter until the mixture resembles coarse crumbs. Make a well in the center. Add milk all at once. Using a fork, stir just until dough forms a ball.

On a lightly floured surface, knead dough gently for 10 to 12 strokes. Roll or pat dough into a 12×6-inch rectangle. Combine walnuts, 3 tablespoons brown sugar, and cinnamon. Brush dough with melted butter and sprinkle with nut mixture. Starting from a short side, roll up jelly-roll style. Seal edge. Cut into six 1-inch slices. Set aside.

For filling, in a large saucepan stir together ⅔ cup brown sugar, cornstarch, and lemon peel. Add peaches and water. Cook and stir until thickened and bubbly.

Pour the hot filling into an ungreased 2-quart rectangular baking dish. Arrange the biscuit slices, cut sides down, on hot filling. Bake in a 375° oven about 25 minutes or until biscuits are golden brown. Makes 6 servings.

Nutrition information per serving: 436 cal., 17 g total fat (3 g sat. fat), 13 mg chol., 315 mg sodium, 71 g carbo., 5 g pro.

Blueberries with Shortcake Drops

The tiny shortcakes make a great solo snack, and they're even yummier buried in a little bowl of blueberries and berry syrup.

1½   cups all-purpose flour
2   tablespoons sugar
1   teaspoon baking powder
¼   teaspoon baking soda
¼   teaspoon ground cardamom
        (optional)
⅓   cup cold butter
1   beaten egg
¼   cup plain low-fat yogurt
3   tablespoons milk
4   cups blueberries
        Blueberry-Cardamom Syrup

Grease a baking sheet; set aside. For shortcake drops, in a medium bowl stir together flour, the 2 tablespoons sugar, the baking powder, baking soda, and, if desired, cardamom. Using a pastry blender, cut in butter until mixture resembles coarse crumbs.

In a small bowl combine egg, yogurt, and milk. Add to flour mixture, stirring just until moistened. Drop dough by a teaspoon into 1-inch mounds onto the prepared baking sheet.

Bake in a 400° oven about 10 minutes or until golden brown. Transfer shortcake drops to a wire rack; cool slightly.

Divide shortcake drops and blueberries among dessert dishes. Drizzle with Blueberry-Cardamom Syrup. Makes 6 servings.

Blueberry-Cardamom Syrup: In a small saucepan combine 1 cup *blueberries*, ½ cup *water*, ¼ cup *sugar*, 2 teaspoons *lime juice* or *lemon juice*, and ¼ teaspoon *ground cardamom*. Bring to boiling, stirring to dissolve sugar; reduce heat. Simmer, uncovered, about 10 minutes or until slightly thickened, stirring occasionally. Remove from heat; cool slightly. Pour the syrup through a fine-mesh sieve; discard solids. Cool. Makes ¾ cup.

Nutrition information per serving: 382 cal., 12 g total fat (7 g sat. fat), 66 mg chol., 259 mg sodium, 64 g carbo., 6 g pro.

Peach and Almond Crisp

Select peaches that have a healthy golden yellow skin without tinges of green. Ripe fruit yields slightly to gentle pressure.

8 cups sliced, peeled peaches or
   nectarines or frozen unsweetened
   peach slices
⅔ cup packed brown sugar
¾ cup all-purpose flour
½ cup rolled oats
½ cup sliced almonds, toasted
3 tablespoons granulated sugar
½ cup butter
⅓ cup granulated sugar
½ teaspoon ground cinnamon
¼ teaspoon ground nutmeg
⅛ teaspoon ground ginger
¼ cup peach nectar or orange juice
   Vanilla ice cream (optional)

Thaw peaches, if frozen. Do not drain. For topping, in a medium bowl stir together brown sugar, ½ cup of the flour, the oats, almonds, and the 3 tablespoons granulated sugar. Using a pastry blender, cut in butter until mixture resembles coarse crumbs.

For filling, in a large bowl stir together the remaining flour, the ⅓ cup granulated sugar, the cinnamon, nutmeg, and ginger. Add the peach or nectarine slices with their juice and peach nectar or orange juice; toss gently to coat. Transfer filling to an ungreased 3-quart rectangular baking dish. Sprinkle with topping.

Bake in a 400° oven for 30 to 35 minutes or until fruit is tender and topping is golden brown. Serve warm or at room temperature. If desired, serve with ice cream. Makes 12 servings.

Nutrition information per serving: 258 cal., 11 g total fat (5 g sat. fat), 20 mg chol., 94 mg sodium, 40 g carbo., 3 g pro.

*P*EACH POINTERS

To ripen peaches, place them in a paper bag at room temperature for a few days or until desired ripeness. Once the peaches are ripe, store them in the refrigerator. To remove the peel from a peach, dip the peach into boiling water for 20 seconds. Then use a paring knife to remove the skin. If the skin doesn't peel easily, return the peach to the boiling water for a few more seconds.

Chocolate-Sauced Pears

Say yes to dessert. These luscious pears contain fewer than than 120 calories and only 1 gram of fat per serving.

4   small pears
2   tablespoons lemon juice
2   teaspoons vanilla
½   teaspoon ground cinnamon
2   tablespoons chocolate-flavored syrup

Core pears from bottom ends, leaving stems intact. Peel pears. If necessary, cut a thin slice from bottoms of pears to help them stand upright. Place pears in a 2-quart square baking dish. In a small bowl stir together lemon juice, vanilla, and cinnamon; brush onto pears. Pour any extra lemon juice mixture over pears.

Cover and bake in a 375° oven for 30 to 35 minutes or until pears are tender. Cool slightly.

To serve, place warm pears, stem ends up, in dessert dishes. Pour the baking liquid through a fine-mesh sieve placed over a small bowl; discard solids. Stir chocolate syrup into strained liquid; drizzle over pears. Makes 4 servings.

Nutrition information per serving: 116 cal., 1 g total fat (0 g sat. fat), 0 mg chol., 5 mg sodium, 29 g carbo., 1 g pro.

Maple-Glazed Bananas

Warm and buttery maple sauce flavors every scrumptious bite of this rich dessert.

½   cup butter or margarine
½   cup packed brown sugar
½   cup pure maple syrup or maple-
       flavored syrup
1   teaspoon finely shredded lemon peel
1   tablespoon lemon juice
¼   teaspoon ground cloves
6   firm, ripe bananas, halved
       lengthwise and cut into 1-inch
       pieces
1   quart vanilla ice cream

In a heavy large skillet melt butter or margarine over medium heat. Stir in brown sugar, maple syrup, lemon peel, lemon juice, and cloves. Bring to boiling; reduce heat. Simmer, uncovered, for 2 minutes.

Add bananas; spoon some of the syrup mixture over bananas. Cover and cook about 2 minutes more or until heated through.

Scoop ice cream into dessert dishes. Spoon the warm bananas and syrup mixture over ice cream. Makes 8 servings.

Nutrition information per serving: 403 cal., 19 g total fat (12 g sat. fat), 60 mg chol., 175 mg sodium, 60 g carbo., 3 g pro.

Chocolate-Sauced Pears

Pineapple-Orange Crepes

If you like, make the crepes up to two days before serving them. Stack them with waxed paper between the layers and store in an airtight container in the refrigerator.

½   cup all-purpose flour
⅓   cup milk
½   teaspoon finely shredded orange peel
⅓   cup orange juice
1   egg
2   teaspoons cooking oil
½   of a fresh pineapple, peeled, cored, and sliced
2   tablespoons butter or margarine
¼   cup packed brown sugar
1   tablespoon cornstarch
½   cup orange juice
2   medium oranges, peeled and sectioned
1   tablespoon rum (optional)
¼   cup chopped pecans or slivered almonds, toasted
¼   cup coconut, toasted
    Strawberries (optional)

For crepes, in a small bowl combine the flour, milk, orange peel, the ⅓ cup orange juice, the egg, and oil. Beat with a rotary beater until well mixed.

Heat a lightly greased 6-inch skillet over medium heat. Spoon 2 tablespoons of the batter into the skillet; lift and tilt the skillet to spread batter. Return to heat; brown on one side only. Invert pan over paper towels; remove crepe. Repeat with the remaining batter, greasing skillet occasionally.

Fold each crepe in half, browned side out. Fold in half again, forming a triangle. Place crepes in a single layer on a baking sheet. Keep warm in a 300° oven while making the sauce.

For sauce, cut the pineapple slices into fourths; set aside. In a medium saucepan melt butter or margarine. Stir in brown sugar and cornstarch. Add the ½ cup orange juice. Cook and stir until thickened and bubbly. Cook and stir for 1 minute more. Add the pineapple, orange sections, and, if desired, rum. Cook over low heat, stirring gently, until heated through.

Arrange folded crepes on dessert plates. Spoon the sauce over crepes. Sprinkle with toasted nuts and coconut. If desired, garnish with strawberries. Makes 4 servings.

Nutrition information per serving: 345 cal., 17 g total fat (5 g sat. fat), 70 mg chol., 102 mg sodium, 45 g carbo., 6 g pro.

Chocolate-Irish Cream Cheesecake

Impress your guests with this home-baked version of a favorite often found on dessert carts in fine restaurants.

1 cup finely crushed chocolate wafers (about 17 cookies)*
¼ cup butter or margarine, melted
½ teaspoon ground cinnamon
3 8-ounce packages cream cheese, softened
1 8-ounce carton dairy sour cream
1 8-ounce package semisweet chocolate, melted and cooled
1 cup sugar
3 eggs
½ cup Irish cream liqueur**
2 tablespoons whipping cream or milk
2 teaspoons vanilla
⅓ cup semisweet chocolate pieces, melted (optional)

For crust, in a small bowl combine crushed wafers, butter or margarine, and cinnamon. Press mixture onto the bottom of an ungreased 9- or 10-inch* springform pan. Set aside.

For filling, in a large bowl beat cream cheese, sour cream, the 8 ounces melted chocolate, and sugar with an electric mixer on medium to high speed until smooth. Add eggs all at once. Beat on low speed just until combined. Stir in liqueur, cream or milk, and vanilla.

Pour into prepared pan. Place springform pan in a shallow baking pan. Bake in a 325° oven for 50 to 60 minutes or until center appears nearly set when shaken.

Cool in springform pan on a wire rack for 15 minutes. Loosen the cheesecake from side of pan; cool for 30 minutes more. Remove side of pan; cool for 1 hour. Cover and chill for 4 to 24 hours. To serve, if desired, drizzle cheesecake with the ⅓ cup melted chocolate. Makes 12 to 16 servings.

*Note: If using a 10-inch springform pan, use 1¼ cups crushed chocolate wafers for the crust.

**Note: If you prefer to use less liqueur, substitute whipping cream or milk for some of the liqueur.

Nutrition information per serving: 525 cal., 37 g total fat (20 g sat. fat), 134 mg chol., 295 mg sodium, 34 g carbo., 7 g pro.

Cheesecake Supreme

Check for doneness by gently shaking the pan rather than inserting a knife, which will make a crack. When the cheesecake is done, a 1-inch area in the center will jiggle a little: this area will firm after cooling.

1¾ cups finely crushed graham crackers
¼ cup finely chopped walnuts
½ teaspoon ground cinnamon
½ cup butter or margarine, melted
2 8-ounce packages cream cheese, softened
1 cup sugar
2 tablespoons all-purpose flour
1 teaspoon vanilla
½ teaspoon finely shredded lemon peel (optional)
2 eggs
1 egg yolk
¼ cup milk
   Raspberries (optional)
   Raspberry Sauce (optional)

For crust, combine the graham crackers, walnuts, and cinnamon. Stir in butter or margarine. If desired, reserve ¼ cup of the crumb mixture for topping. Press the remaining crumb mixture onto the bottom and about 2 inches up the side of an 8- or 9-inch springform pan.

For filling, in a large mixing bowl beat cream cheese, sugar, flour, vanilla, and, if desired, lemon peel with an electric mixer on low speed until combined. Add eggs and egg yolk all at once. Beat on low speed just until combined. Stir in milk. Pour into the prepared pan. If desired, sprinkle with the reserved crumbs.

Place springform pan in a shallow baking pan. Bake in a 375° oven for 45 to 50 minutes for the 8-inch pan (35 to 40 minutes for the 9-inch pan) or until center appears nearly set when shaken.

Cool in pan on a wire rack for 15 minutes. Loosen crust from pan. Cool for 30 minutes more. Remove side of pan. Cool completely. Cover and chill at least 4 hours. If desired, garnish with raspberries and serve with Raspberry Sauce. Makes 12 to 16 servings.

Raspberry Sauce: In a blender container cover and blend 3 cups fresh or thawed, frozen *raspberries* (do not drain), half at a time, until smooth. Press berries through a sieve; discard seeds. In a saucepan combine ⅓ cup *sugar* and 1 teaspoon *cornstarch*. Add sieved berries. Cook and stir until thickened and bubbly. Cook and stir for 2 minutes more. Cool. Makes about 1 cup.

Nutrition information per serving: 429 cal., 32 g total fat (18 g sat. fat), 137 mg chol., 329 mg sodium, 30 g carbo., 7 g pro.

Coffee Éclairs

These sumptuous, tender shells are filled with ice cream and topped with a smooth coffee-flavored sauce.

1   cup water
½   cup butter
1   cup all-purpose flour
4   eggs
1   quart coffee or vanilla ice cream
1½ cups cold water
3   tablespoons cornstarch
1   tablespoon instant coffee crystals
1   cup light-colored corn syrup
2   tablespoons butter
1   teaspoon vanilla
½   cup chopped pecans (optional)

Grease a large baking sheet; set aside. In a medium saucepan combine the 1 cup water and the ½ cup butter. Bring to boiling. Add flour all at once, stirring vigorously. Cook and stir until mixture forms a ball that doesn't separate. Remove from heat. Cool for 10 minutes. Add eggs, one at a time, beating well after each addition until smooth.

Spoon dough into a decorating bag fitted with a large plain round tip (about ½-inch opening). Pipe 10 to 12 strips of dough, about 3 inches apart, onto the prepared baking sheet, making each strip about 4 inches long, 1 inch wide, and ¾ inch high.

Bake in a 400° oven about 40 minutes or until golden brown. Transfer to a wire rack; cool. Cut éclairs in half lengthwise and remove soft dough from centers. Fill bottom halves with ice cream; replace tops. Cover and freeze until serving time.

Meanwhile, for sauce, in a medium saucepan combine the 1½ cups cold water, the cornstarch, and coffee crystals. Stir in corn syrup. Cook and stir until thickened and bubbly. Cook and stir for 2 minutes more. Remove from heat. Add the 2 tablespoons butter and the vanilla; stir until butter is melted.

To serve, remove éclairs from freezer and let stand about 15 minutes to soften. Spoon some of the warm sauce over éclairs. If desired, sprinkle with pecans. (Cover and chill any leftover sauce up to 1 week. Reheat sauce and serve with ice cream.) Makes 10 to 12 éclairs.

Nutrition information per éclair: 385 cal., 19 g total fat (11 g sat. fat), 139 mg chol., 207 mg sodium, 49 g carbo., 6 g pro.

Fresh Pear Custard Tart

Be sure to use ripe pears for this tart. Those that are too firm or unripe make it difficult to eat. If you're really in a pinch, substitute sliced, well-drained canned pears.

Baked Tart Shell
½ cup granulated sugar
2 tablespoons cornstarch
2 cups fat-free milk
2 beaten eggs
4 teaspoons finely chopped
    crystallized ginger
1 teaspoon vanilla
⅔ cup pear nectar
1½ teaspoons cornstarch
3 ripe small pears
½ cup berries (such as raspberries,
    blackberries, and/or blueberries)
Desired garnishes (such as sifted
    powdered sugar, mint leaves, and/
    or edible flowers)

Prepare Baked Tart Shell. For vanilla cream, in a heavy medium saucepan combine granulated sugar and the 2 tablespoons cornstarch. Stir in milk. Cook and stir over medium heat until thickened and bubbly. Cook and stir for 2 minutes more. Remove from heat.

Gradually stir about 1 cup of the hot mixture into beaten eggs. Return all of the egg mixture to saucepan. Stir in ginger. Cook and stir until bubbly; reduce heat. Cook and stir for 2 minutes more. Remove from heat. Stir in vanilla. Pour the vanilla cream into tart shell. Cover and chill until ready to assemble.

Meanwhile, for glaze, in a small saucepan combine pear nectar and the 1½ teaspoons cornstarch. Cook and stir until thickened and bubbly. Cook and stir for 2 minutes more. Remove from heat. Cover and cool to room temperature.

To assemble tart, peel, core, and thinly slice pears. Arrange pear slices in a concentric pattern over the vanilla cream. Pour the cooled glaze over pears, spreading evenly. Cover and chill for 1 to 4 hours. To serve, sprinkle the tart with berries. Top with desired garnishes. Makes 10 servings.

Baked Tart Shell: In a medium bowl stir together 1¼ cups *all-purpose flour* and ¼ teaspoon *salt*. Combine ¼ cup *fat-free milk* and 3 tablespoons *cooking oil*; add all at once to flour mixture. Stir with a fork until a dough forms. Form into a ball. On a lightly floured surface, roll dough from center to edge into a 13-inch circle. Ease pastry into an 11-inch tart pan with a removable bottom, being careful not to stretch pastry. Trim pastry even with rim of tart pan. Generously prick bottom, sides, and corners of pastry with a fork. Bake in a 450° oven for 10 to 12 minutes or until golden brown. Cool on a wire rack.

Nutrition information per serving: 216 cal., 6 g total fat (1 g sat. fat), 44 mg chol., 96 mg sodium, 37 g carbo., 5 g pro.

Chocolate-Topped Fruited Phyllo Tarts

Flaky phyllo pastry meets indulgent chocolate and sweet-tart dried fruit in these irresistible bite-size tarts. To make them ahead, store, covered, in the refrigerator up to two days. Before serving, let stand at room temperature about 30 minutes.

6 ounces semisweet chocolate, cut up
¼ cup whipping cream
¼ cup snipped dried apricots
¼ cup snipped dried cherries
¼ cup brandy
½ cup finely chopped almonds
24 1¾-inch baked miniature phyllo shells

In a medium saucepan combine chocolate and whipping cream. Cook and stir over low heat until smooth. Remove from heat; cool.

In a small bowl combine apricots, cherries, and brandy. Cover and let stand about 45 minutes or until fruit is softened; drain well. Stir in ¼ cup of the almonds.

Place about 1 teaspoon of the fruit mixture in the bottom of each phyllo shell. Spoon about 1 teaspoon of the chocolate mixture into each shell. Sprinkle with the remaining almonds. Makes 24 tarts.

Nutrition information per tart: 93 cal., 6 g total fat (2 g sat. fat), 4 mg chol., 11 mg sodium, 9 g carbo., 2 g pro.

Apple-Blueberry Pastries

Take a platter of these petite pastries to your next potluck.

2 tablespoons sugar
1 tablespoon cornstarch
2 medium apples, peeled, cored,
    and chopped (about 2 cups)
½ cup fresh or frozen blueberries
1½ teaspoons water
½ teaspoon finely shredded
    orange peel
1 17¼-ounce package (2 sheets)
    frozen puff pastry
    Easy Orange Icing
    Edible flowers (optional)

Line a large baking sheet with foil; set aside. For filling, in a medium saucepan stir together the sugar and cornstarch. Add apples, blueberries, and water. Cook and stir over medium heat until thickened and bubbly. Cook and stir for 2 minutes more. Stir in orange peel. Remove from heat. Cool completely.

Let folded puff pastry thaw at room temperature for 20 minutes. On a lightly floured surface, unfold and roll each sheet of pastry into a 15×10-inch rectangle. Cut each sheet into ten 5×3-inch rectangles.

Spoon about 1 tablespoon of the filling on half of each rectangle to within ½ inch of edges. Brush edges with water. Starting from a short side, lift pastry up and over filling. Press edges with the tines of a fork to seal. Place on the prepared baking sheet.

Bake in a 375° oven for 18 to 20 minutes or until golden. Remove and cool on a wire rack. Drizzle with Easy Orange Icing. If desired, garnish with edible flowers. Makes 20 pastries.

Easy Orange Icing: In a small mixing bowl stir together 1 cup sifted *powdered sugar,* 1 tablespoon *orange juice,* and ¼ teaspoon *vanilla.* Stir in additional *orange juice,* 1 teaspoon at a time, to make an icing of drizzling consistency.

Nutrition information per serving: 142 cal., 8 g total fat (0 g sat. fat), 0 mg chol., 92 mg sodium, 18 g carbo., 1 g pro.

Apple-Cranberry Streusel Pie

A whisper of cream gives the filling of this streusel-crowned creation a touch of richness. Dried cranberries or tart cherries provide lively bursts of flavor.

Baked Pastry Shell
½ cup dried cranberries or dried
    tart cherries
6 large cooking apples, peeled, cored,
    and sliced (6 cups)
⅔ cup granulated sugar
3 tablespoons all-purpose flour
1 teaspoon apple pie spice
1 teaspoon finely shredded lemon peel
¼ teaspoon salt
⅓ cup half-and-half or light cream
⅓ cup all-purpose flour
⅓ cup packed brown sugar
⅓ cup finely chopped pecans or
    walnuts, toasted
¼ teaspoon ground nutmeg
3 tablespoons butter
    Vanilla Icing

Prepare Baked Pastry Shell. Reduce the oven temperature to 375°. In a small bowl cover dried cranberries or cherries with boiling water. Cover and let stand for 5 minutes; drain.

For filling, in a large bowl combine apples and cranberries or cherries. Spoon filling into pastry shell. In a small bowl combine granulated sugar, the 3 tablespoons flour, the apple pie spice, lemon peel, and salt. Stir in half-and-half or light cream. Pour over filling. For topping, in a medium bowl combine the ⅓ cup flour, the brown sugar, nuts, and nutmeg. Using a pastry blender, cut in butter until the pieces are pea-size. Sprinkle over filling. To prevent overbrowning, cover edges of pie with foil.

Bake in the 375° oven for 45 minutes. Remove foil. Bake for 10 to 15 minutes more or until topping is golden brown and fruit is tender. Cool on a wire rack for 45 minutes. Drizzle with Vanilla Icing. Serve warm or cool. Store, covered, in the refrigerator. Makes 8 servings.

Baked Pastry Shell: In a medium bowl stir together 1¼ cups *all-purpose flour* and ¼ teaspoon *salt*. Using a pastry blender, cut in ⅓ cup *shortening* until pieces are pea-size. Using 4 to 5 tablespoons *cold water*, sprinkle 1 tablespoon water at a time over mixture, gently tossing with a fork until all is moistened. Form into a ball. On a lightly floured surface, roll from center to edge into a 12-inch circle. Ease pastry into a 9-inch pie plate, being careful not to stretch pastry. Trim ½ inch beyond edge. Fold under extra pastry; crimp edge. Line pastry with a double thickness of foil. Bake in a 450° oven for 8 minutes. Remove foil. Bake for 5 to 6 minutes more until golden brown. Cool.

Vanilla Icing: In a small bowl combine ½ cup sifted *powdered sugar*, 1 teaspoon *milk*, and ¼ teaspoon *vanilla*. Stir in enough additional milk, 1 teaspoon at a time, to make an icing of drizzling consistency.

Nutrition information per serving: 447 cal., 18 g total fat (9 g sat. fat), 15 mg chol., 186 mg sodium, 72 g carbo., 4 g pro.

Cheddar-Rosemary-Crusted Pear Pie

The sweetness of firm, ripe pears complements the assertive flavor of fresh rosemary found in the pastry. Cheddar cheese bonds the three flavors together.

Cheddar-Rosemary Pastry
- ¾ cup sugar
- 3 tablespoons cornstarch
- 2 tablespoons pear nectar, orange juice, or apple juice
- 8 cups thinly sliced, peeled pears
  White cheddar cheese (optional)
  Fresh rosemary sprigs (optional)

Prepare Cheddar-Rosemary Pastry. On a lightly floured surface, roll half of the dough from center to edge into a 13-inch circle. Ease pastry into a 9- or 9½-inch deep-dish pie plate, being careful not to stretch the pastry.

For filling, in a large bowl stir together sugar and cornstarch. Stir in nectar or fruit juice. Add pear slices; toss gently to coat. Spoon filling into pastry-lined pie plate. Trim pastry even with rim of pie plate.

Roll remaining dough into a 12-inch circle. Cut slits to allow steam to escape. Place pastry on filling; trim ½ inch beyond edge of pie plate. Fold top pastry under bottom pastry; crimp edge. To prevent overbrowning, cover edges of pie with foil. Place pie on a baking sheet.

Bake in a 375° oven for 25 minutes. Remove foil. Bake for 25 to 35 minutes more or until top is golden brown and filling is bubbly. Cool on a wire rack.

To serve, cut pie into wedges. If desired, serve with white cheddar cheese and garnish with rosemary sprigs. Makes 8 servings.

Cheddar-Rosemary Pastry: In a large bowl stir together 2½ cups *all-purpose flour*, 1½ teaspoons snipped *fresh rosemary*, and ½ teaspoon *salt*. Using a pastry blender, cut in ⅔ cup *shortening* until pieces are pea-size. Stir in ½ cup finely shredded *white cheddar cheese* (2 ounces). Using 7 to 8 tablespoons *cold water*, sprinkle 1 tablespoon water at a time over mixture, gently tossing with a fork until all is moistened. Divide in half. Form each half into a ball.

Nutrition information per serving: 496 cal., 19 g total fat (6 g sat. fat), 7 mg chol., 191 mg sodium, 76 g carbo., 6 g pro.

Mince-Peach Pie

Although traditionally made with minced meat and suet, you can purchase today's all-fruit mincemeat in jars.

Pastry for Double-Crust Pie
1 29-ounce can peach slices, drained
      and cut up
1 27-ounce jar (2⅔ cups) mincemeat
      Milk (optional)
      Granulated sugar (optional)
      Vanilla ice cream or Hard Sauce
        (optional)

Prepare Pastry for Double-Crust Pie. On a lightly floured surface, roll half of the dough from center to edge into a 12-inch circle. Ease pastry into a 9-inch pie plate, being careful not to stretch pastry.

For filling, in a large bowl stir together peaches and mincemeat. Spoon the filling into pastry-lined pie plate. Trim the pastry even with rim of pie plate.

Roll remaining dough into a 12-inch circle. Using hors d'oeuvre cutters, make cutouts in dough to allow steam to escape. Place pastry on filling; trim ½ inch beyond edge of pie plate. Fold top pastry under bottom pastry; crimp edge. If desired, brush pastry with milk and sprinkle with granulated sugar. To prevent overbrowning, cover edges of pie with foil. Place pie on a baking sheet.

Bake in a 375° oven for 25 minutes. Remove foil. Bake for 20 to 25 minutes more or until pastry is golden brown. Cool on a wire rack. To serve, cut pie into wedges. If desired, serve with ice cream or Hard Sauce. Makes 8 servings.

Pastry for Double-Crust Pie: In a large bowl stir together 2 cups *all-purpose flour* and ½ teaspoon *salt*. Using a pastry blender, cut in ⅔ cup *shortening* until pieces are pea-size. Using 6 to 7 tablespoons *cold water*, sprinkle 1 tablespoon water at a time over mixture, gently tossing with a fork until all is moistened. Divide dough in half. Form each half into a ball.

Hard Sauce: In a small bowl beat together 1¼ cups sifted *powdered sugar* and ¾ cup softened *butter* until fluffy. Beat in 3 tablespoons *brandy, rum,* or *orange juice* and ½ teaspoon *vanilla.* Store, covered, in the refrigerator up to 2 weeks. Let stand at room temperature about 30 minutes before serving. Makes 1¼ cups.

Nutrition information per serving: 536 cal., 18 g total fat (4 g sat. fat), 0 mg chol., 422 mg sodium, 89 g carbo., 5 g pro.

Pumpkin Pecan Pie

Filled with lots of crunchy pecans, this special dessert will become a must at your Thanksgiving celebration.

3   slightly beaten eggs
1   15-ounce can pumpkin
¾   cup sugar
½   cup dark-colored corn syrup
1   teaspoon vanilla
¾   teaspoon ground cinnamon
1   unbaked 9-inch piecrust
1   cup chopped pecans
    Whipped cream (optional)
    Ground cinnamon (optional)

In a medium mixing bowl combine eggs, pumpkin, sugar, corn syrup, vanilla, and ¾ teaspoon cinnamon; mix well. Pour into piecrust. Sprinkle with pecans.

Bake in a 350° oven for 50 to 55 minutes or until a knife inserted near center comes out clean. Cool on a wire rack. Refrigerate within 2 hours; cover for longer storage. If desired, serve pie with whipped cream and sprinkle with additional cinnamon. Makes 8 servings.

Nutrition information per serving: 412 cal., 20 g total fat (4 g sat. fat), 80 mg chol., 108 mg sodium, 55 g carbo., 6 g pro.

Rice Pudding

This creamy rice pudding is a soothing conclusion to a spicy meal.

½   cup golden raisins
¼   cup rum
3   cups milk
½   cup long grain rice
3   inches stick cinnamon
¼   cup sugar
1   teaspoon vanilla
    Ground cinnamon

In a small bowl combine raisins and rum. Set aside. In a heavy medium saucepan combine milk, uncooked rice, and stick cinnamon. Bring to boiling; reduce heat. Cover and simmer about 20 minutes or until rice is tender. Remove stick cinnamon.

Drain the raisins, discarding rum. Stir the raisins, sugar, and vanilla into rice mixture. Sprinkle with ground cinnamon. Serve warm or chilled. Makes 6 servings.

Nutrition information per serving: 200 cal., 3 g total fat (2 g sat. fat), 9 mg chol., 64 mg sodium, 38 g carbo., 6 g pro.

Brownie Pudding

As this homey dessert bakes, a layer of cake magically rises to the top, leaving a chocolaty sauce underneath.

1   cup all-purpose flour
¾   cup granulated sugar
2   tablespoons unsweetened cocoa
        powder
2   teaspoons baking powder
¼   teaspoon salt
½   cup milk
2   tablespoons cooking oil
1   teaspoon vanilla
½   cup chopped walnuts
¾   cup packed brown sugar
¼   cup unsweetened cocoa powder
1½ cups boiling water

Grease an 8×8×2-inch baking pan; set aside. In a medium mixing bowl stir together the flour, granulated sugar, 2 tablespoons cocoa powder, baking powder, and salt. Stir in the milk, cooking oil, and vanilla. Stir in walnuts.

Pour into the prepared pan. In another medium bowl stir together brown sugar and ¼ cup cocoa powder. Stir in the boiling water; slowly pour over batter. Bake in a 350° oven for 40 minutes. Cool on a wire rack for 45 to 60 minutes. Serve warm. Makes 6 to 8 servings.

Nutrition information per serving: 368 cal., 12 g total fat (2 g sat. fat), 2 mg chol., 271 mg sodium, 65 g carbo., 5 g pro.

Flan

You can find this well-loved inverted caramel custard imported directly from Spain on Mexican dessert menus everywhere. Traditionally used, canned milk gives flan a rich, caramel flavor.

⅓ cup sugar
3 beaten eggs
1 12-ounce can (1½ cups)
      evaporated milk
⅓ cup sugar
1 teaspoon vanilla
    Fresh fruit (optional)
    Edible flowers (optional)

To caramelize sugar, in a heavy skillet cook ⅓ cup sugar over medium-high heat until the sugar begins to melt, shaking skillet occasionally. Do not stir. Once the sugar starts to melt, reduce heat to low and cook about 5 minutes or until all of the sugar is melted and is golden brown, stirring as needed with a wooden spoon.

Remove skillet from heat and immediately pour caramelized sugar into an 8-inch flan pan or an 8×1½-inch round baking pan (or divide caramelized sugar among six 6-ounce custard cups). Working quickly, rotate pan or cups so sugar coats the bottom as evenly as possible. Cool. In a medium bowl combine the eggs, evaporated milk, ⅓ cup sugar, and vanilla.

Place flan pan or custard cups in a 13×9×2-inch baking pan on an oven rack. Pour egg mixture into flan pan or cups. Pour the hottest tap water available into the 13-inch pan around the flan pan or cups to a depth of about ½ inch.

Bake in a 325° oven for 30 to 35 minutes for flan pan (35 to 40 minutes for custard cups) or until a knife inserted near the center comes out clean. Immediately remove flan pan or cups from hot water. Cool on a wire rack. Cover and chill for 4 to 24 hours.

To unmold flan, loosen edge with a knife, slipping end of knife down side of pan to let in air. Carefully invert a serving platter over pan (or a dessert plate over a custard cup); turn dishes over together to release flan. Spoon any caramelized sugar that remains in pan on top. If desired, serve the flan with fresh fruit and garnish with edible flowers. Makes 6 servings.

Nutrition information per serving: 202 cal., 7 g total fat (3 g sat. fat), 123 mg chol., 92 mg sodium, 28 g carbo., 7 g pro.

Ginger Custard with Plum Sauce

For a rosy red sauce, choose a variety of plums with red skin, such as Red Beaut, Ace, or Queen Ann.

4	slightly beaten eggs
2	cups milk
½	cup sugar
1	teaspoon vanilla
½	teaspoon ground ginger
6	fresh medium plums, pitted and coarsely chopped (2½ cups)
⅓	cup sugar
1	tablespoon lemon juice
1	tablespoon water
1½	teaspoons cornstarch
½	teaspoon vanilla

In a medium mixing bowl combine eggs, milk, ½ cup sugar, 1 teaspoon vanilla, and ginger. Beat until well combined but not foamy. Place six 6-ounce custard cups in a large shallow baking pan on oven rack. Pour egg mixture into custard cups. Pour hot water into pan around custard cups to reach halfway up sides of cups.

Bake in a 350° oven for 30 to 35 minutes or until a knife inserted near centers comes out clean. Remove cups from water. Cool on a wire rack at least 20 minutes.

Meanwhile, for plum sauce, in a medium saucepan combine plums, ⅓ cup sugar, and lemon juice. Bring to boiling; reduce heat. Cover and simmer about 8 minutes or until plums are tender. Stir together water and cornstarch. Stir into plum mixture. Cook and stir until thickened and bubbly. Cook and stir for 2 minutes more. Remove from heat. Stir in ½ teaspoon vanilla.

To serve, unmold the custards onto dessert plates. Spoon the plum sauce over custards. Makes 6 servings.

Nutrition information per serving: 241 cal., 5 g total fat (2 g sat. fat), 148 mg chol., 83 mg sodium, 42 g carbo., 7 g pro.

*P*ERFECTLY RIPE PLUMS

To purchase plums at their peak, look for firm, plump, well-shaped fruit with good color for its variety. Press a plum gently; it should give slightly. The bloom (light gray cast) on the skin is natural protection and doesn't affect quality. Avoid overly soft, bruised, or very hard fruit. To ripen plums at home, store at room temperature for 1 to 2 days. Then refrigerate them for up to 5 days.

Sweet Indian Pudding

A warm scoop of this cinnamon-molasses dessert brings a soothing end to your day. Be sure to spoon up every last bit of the sweet syrup you'll find at the bottom of the baking dish.

1	cup milk
⅓	cup yellow cornmeal
2	tablespoons margarine or butter, cut up
⅓	cup molasses
¼	cup granulated sugar
½	teaspoon ground ginger
½	teaspoon ground cinnamon
¼	teaspoon salt
2	beaten eggs
1½	cups milk
	Whipped cream (optional)
	Raw sugar crystals (optional)

In a medium saucepan combine the 1 cup milk, the cornmeal, and margarine or butter. Bring to boiling, stirring constantly; reduce heat. Cover and cook over low heat for 5 minutes. Remove from heat.

Stir in molasses, granulated sugar, ginger, cinnamon, and salt. Combine eggs and the 1½ cups milk; stir into cornmeal mixture. Pour into an ungreased 1-quart casserole.

Bake in a 350° oven for 1¼ hours. Cool on a wire rack for 1 to 1½ hours. Serve warm. If desired, top with whipped cream and sprinkle lightly with raw sugar crystals. Makes 6 servings.

Nutrition information per serving: 218 cal., 8 g total fat (4 g sat. fat), 89 mg chol., 217 mg sodium, 32 g carbo., 6 g pro.

FAST DESSERT IDEAS

Even if you're short on time, dessert doesn't have to be a lost prospect. Try one of these simple ideas:
- Fresh fruit sliced and tossed with a little honey and sprinkled with toasted almonds.
- A tea bar set up with several types of tea, lemon slices, milk, honey, and sugar, as well as purchased tea biscuits or assorted cookies.
- A cheese course that features a selection of cheeses and fresh fruits: ripe pears with blue cheese, berries and apples with Brie, and oranges with thin wedges of Parmesan.

Berries 'n' Brownies

Berries 'n' Brownies

Just three major ingredients—raspberries, bakery brownies, and whipped cream—result in this fancy showstopper. If you have the time, go ahead and bake your own brownies.

4 cups raspberries
4 to 5 tablespoons sugar
2 teaspoons finely shredded
   orange peel
2 cups whipping cream
¼ cup raspberry liqueur (Chambord)
   (optional)
4 3-inch squares purchased brownies
   (such as milk chocolate, blond,
   or marbled brownies), cut into
   irregular chunks

Set aside 8 to 10 of the berries. In a medium bowl combine the remaining berries, the sugar, and orange peel. Spoon the berry mixture into a 1- to 1½-quart compote dish or serving bowl.

In a chilled medium mixing bowl combine whipping cream and, if desired, raspberry liqueur. Beat with chilled beaters of an electric mixer on medium speed until soft peaks form (tips curl). Spoon the whipped cream on top of raspberry mixture. Top with the brownie chunks and the reserved raspberries. Makes 12 servings.

Nutrition information per serving: 263 cal., 19 g total fat (10 g sat. fat), 69 mg chol., 63 mg sodium, 23 g carbo., 3 g pro.

Cookies and Cream

Choose your favorite soft cookie. Any type works as long as you can cut it with a fork.

½ cup whipping cream
2 tablespoons honey
½ cup dairy sour cream
24 purchased large soft cookies
   (such as ginger or oatmeal)
   Honey

In a chilled small mixing bowl combine whipping cream and the 2 tablespoons honey. Beat with chilled beaters of an electric mixer on medium speed until soft peaks form (tips curl). Fold in sour cream. (If desired, cover and chill up to 1 hour.)

To serve, place a cookie on each dessert plate. Top with a spoonful of whipped cream mixture. Top with another cookie and another spoonful of whipped cream mixture. Top with a third cookie and the remaining whipped cream mixture. Drizzle with additional honey. Makes 8 servings.

Nutrition information per serving: 456 cal., 21 g total fat (10 g sat. fat), 43 mg chol., 310 mg sodium, 61 g carbo., 5 g pro.

Cinnamon Meringues with Fruit

For crispy meringue shells, serve them right away. However, if you like softer, marshmallowlike shells, chill them for up to 2 hours before serving.

2 egg whites
½ teaspoon ground cinnamon
½ teaspoon vanilla
¼ teaspoon cream of tartar
½ cup sugar
2 cups sliced peeled peaches or sliced nectarines
2 tablespoons sugar
1 tablespoon cornstarch
2 cups fresh fruit (such as sliced peeled peaches or kiwifruit and/or sliced nectarines or strawberries)

For meringue shells, cover a baking sheet with plain brown paper (specially made for baking). Draw six 3-inch squares or six 3½-inch circles on the paper. In a small mixing bowl beat the egg whites, cinnamon, vanilla, and cream of tartar with an electric mixer on medium speed until soft peaks form. Gradually add the ½ cup sugar, beating on high speed until stiff peaks form and sugar is almost dissolved.

Spoon meringue mixture into a decorating bag fitted with a medium plain-round or star tip (about ¼-inch opening). Pipe shells onto the prepared baking sheet. (Or, using a spoon or a spatula, spread the meringue mixture over the squares or circles on the prepared baking sheet, building up sides to form shells.)

Bake in a 300° oven for 30 minutes. Turn off the heat and let meringue shells dry in the oven with the door closed for at least 1 hour. (Do not open oven.) Peel off paper.

For sauce, place 2 cups peaches or nectarines in a blender container or food processor bowl. Cover and blend or process until nearly smooth. Pour into a saucepan. Mix 2 tablespoons sugar and cornstarch; stir into peach mixture. Cook and stir until thickened and bubbly. Cook and stir for 2 minutes more.

To serve, place meringue shells on dessert plates. Spoon the sauce into meringue shells. Top with fresh fruit. Serve immediately or cover and chill up to 2 hours. Makes 6 servings.

Nutrition information per serving: 138 cal., 0 g total fat (0 g sat. fat), 0 mg chol., 19 mg sodium, 34 g carbo., 2 g pro.

Peaches 'n' Cream Ice Cream

The slight tang of cream cheese helps balance the sweetness of peaches in this smooth ice cream.

2½   cups half-and-half or light cream
¾   cup granulated sugar
½   cup packed brown sugar
2   beaten eggs
1   8-ounce package cream cheese
     or reduced-fat cream cheese
     (Neufchâtel), softened
2   cups fresh or frozen unsweetened
     peach slices, thawed
½   teaspoon finely shredded lemon peel
1   tablespoon lemon juice
1   teaspoon vanilla
2   rolled sugar ice-cream cones
¼   cup sliced almonds, toasted
     Peach slices (optional)

In a large saucepan combine 1½ cups of the half-and-half or light cream, the granulated sugar, brown sugar, and eggs. Cook and stir over medium heat just until boiling; remove from heat. (Mixture will appear curdled.) Set aside.

In a large mixing bowl beat cream cheese with an electric mixer on medium speed until smooth. Gradually beat in the hot egg mixture. Cover and chill for 2 hours.

In a blender container or food processor bowl place half of the peach slices. Cover and blend or process until nearly smooth. Coarsely chop the remaining peach slices; set aside.

Stir pureed peaches, the remaining half-and-half or light cream, the lemon peel, lemon juice, and vanilla into chilled mixture. Freeze in a 4- or 5-quart ice cream freezer according to manufacturer's directions.

Remove dasher from freezer. Stir in chopped peaches. Ripen ice cream for 4 hours.

Meanwhile, for topping, in a plastic bag crush ice cream cones with a rolling pin, reserving bottom tips, if desired, for garnish. Combine crushed ice cream cones and almonds.

To serve, scoop ice cream into mugs or bowls and sprinkle with topping. If desired, garnish with ice-cream cone tips and additional peach slices. Makes 14 servings.

Nutrition information per serving: 241 cal., 12 g total fat (7 g sat. fat), 64 mg chol., 78 mg sodium, 29 g carbo., 4 g pro.

Frosty Chocolate-Cherry Yogurt

Yogurt swirled with cherries and chocolate makes a cool, creamy, and scrumptious alternative to ice cream.

2 16-ounce cartons (3½ cups) vanilla
   yogurt (no gelatin added)*
2½ cups fresh or frozen pitted dark
   sweet cherries
⅓ cup milk
⅓ cup light-colored corn syrup
½ cup miniature semisweet
   chocolate pieces
   Fresh dark sweet cherries (optional)

In a blender container or food processor bowl combine yogurt, 1 cup of the pitted cherries, milk, and corn syrup. Cover and blend or process until mixture is almost smooth. (If using a food processor, process half at a time.)

Freeze in a 2-quart ice-cream freezer according to manufacturer's directions until almost firm. Add the remaining pitted cherries and chocolate. Continue to freeze as directed until firm. If desired, serve with additional fresh cherries. Makes 12 servings.

*Note: Yogurt without gelatin gives this dessert a better texture. Check the ingredients on the label.

Nutrition information per serving: 299 cal., 8 g total fat (2 g sat. fat), 9 mg chol., 107 mg sodium, 55 g carbo., 8 g pro.

English Toffee Ice Cream

If you're making this frozen treat for kids, substitute milk for the coffee.

4 1.4-ounce bars chocolate-covered
   English toffee
2 cups whipping cream
1 14-ounce can sweetened
   condensed milk
½ cup strong coffee, cooled
1½ teaspoons vanilla

Crush toffee bars by placing them between two pieces of waxed paper and crushing them with a rolling pin. Set aside. Combine the whipping cream, sweetened condensed milk, coffee, and vanilla. Chill.

Beat with an electric mixer on low speed until slightly thickened. Fold in the crushed toffee. Spoon into a 2-quart square baking dish or a 9x5x3-inch loaf pan. Cover and freeze ice cream several hours or until firm. Makes 12 servings.

Nutrition information per serving: 315 cal., 21 g total fat (12 g sat. fat), 68 mg chol., 94 mg sodium, 27 g carbo., 4 g pro.

Frosty Chocolate-Cherry Yogurt

INDEX

METRIC INFORMATION

The charts on this page provide a guide for converting measurements from the U.S. customary system, which is used throughout this book, to the metric system.

PRODUCT DIFFERENCES

Most of the ingredients called for in the recipes in this book are available in most countries. However, some are known by different names. Here are some common American ingredients and their possible counterparts:

■ Sugar (white) is granulated, fine granulated, or castor sugar.

■ Powdered sugar is icing sugar.

■ All-purpose flour is enriched, bleached, or unbleached white household flour. When self-rising flour is used in place of all-purpose flour in a recipe that calls for leavening, omit the leavening agent (baking soda or baking powder) and salt.

■ Light-colored corn syrup is golden syrup.

■ Cornstarch is cornflour.

■ Baking soda is bicarbonate of soda.

■ Vanilla or vanilla extract is vanilla essence.

■ Green, red, or yellow sweet peppers are capsicums or bell peppers.

■ Golden raisins are sultanas.

VOLUME AND WEIGHT

The United States traditionally uses cup measures for liquid and solid ingredients. The chart, top right, shows the approximate imperial and metric equivalents. If you are accustomed to weighing solid ingredients, the following approximate equivalents will be helpful.

■ 1 cup butter, castor sugar, or rice = 8 ounces = ½ pound = 250 grams

■ 1 cup flour = 4 ounces = ¼ pound = 125 grams

■ 1 cup icing sugar = 5 ounces = 150 grams

Canadian and U.S. volume for a cup measure is 8 fluid ounces (237 ml), but the standard metric equivalent is 250 ml.

1 British imperial cup is 10 fluid ounces.

In Australia, 1 tablespoon equals 20 ml, and there are 4 teaspoons in the Australian tablespoon.

Spoon measures are used for smaller amounts of ingredients. Although the size of the tablespoon varies slightly in different countries, for practical purposes and for recipes in this book, a straight substitution is all that's necessary. Measurements made using cups or spoons always should be level unless stated otherwise.

COMMON WEIGHT RANGE REPLACEMENTS

Imperial / U.S.	Metric
½ ounce	15 g
1 ounce	25 g or 30 g
4 ounces (¼ pound)	115 g or 125 g
8 ounces (½ pound)	225 g or 250 g
16 ounces (1 pound)	450 g or 500 g
1¼ pounds	625 g
1½ pounds	750 g
2 pounds or 2¼ pounds	1,000 g or 1 Kg

OVEN TEMPERATURE EQUIVALENTS

Fahrenheit Setting	Celsius Setting*	Gas Setting
300°F	150°C	Gas Mark 2 (very low)
325°F	160°C	Gas Mark 3 (low)
350°F	180°C	Gas Mark 4 (moderate)
375°F	190°C	Gas Mark 5 (moderate)
400°F	200°C	Gas Mark 6 (hot)
425°F	220°C	Gas Mark 7 (hot)
450°F	230°C	Gas Mark 8 (very hot)
475°F	240°C	Gas Mark 9 (very hot)
500°F	260°C	Gas Mark 10 (extremely hot)
Broil	Broil	Grill

*Electric and gas ovens may be calibrated using celsius. However, for an electric oven, increase celsius setting 10 to 20 degrees when cooking above 160°C. For convection or forced air ovens (gas or electric) lower the temperature setting 25°F/10°C when cooking at all heat levels.

BAKING PAN SIZES

Imperial / U.S.	Metric
9×1½-inch round cake pan	22- or 23×4-cm (1.5 L)
9×1½-inch pie plate	22- or 23×4-cm (1 L)
8×8×2-inch square cake pan	20×5-cm (2 L)
9×9×2-inch square cake pan	22- or 23×4.5-cm (2.5 L)
11×7×1½-inch baking pan	28×17×4-cm (2 L)
2-quart rectangular baking pan	30×19×4.5-cm (3 L)
13×9×2-inch baking pan	34×22×4.5-cm (3.5 L)
15×10×1-inch jelly roll pan	40×25×2-cm
9×5×3-inch loaf pan	23×13×8-cm (2 L)
2-quart casserole	2 L

U.S. / STANDARD METRIC EQUIVALENTS

⅛ teaspoon = 0.5 ml	⅓ cup = 3 fluid ounces = 75 ml
¼ teaspoon = 1 ml	½ cup = 4 fluid ounces = 125 ml
½ teaspoon = 2 ml	⅔ cup = 5 fluid ounces = 150 ml
1 teaspoon = 5 ml	¾ cup = 6 fluid ounces = 175 ml
1 tablespoon = 15 ml	1 cup = 8 fluid ounces = 250 ml
2 tablespoons = 25 ml	2 cups = 1 pint = 500 ml
¼ cup = 2 fluid ounces = 50 ml	1 quart = 1 litre